Energy Risk Management

Energy Risk Management

A Non-Technical Introduction to Energy Derivatives

By

Steve Leppard

Published by Risk Books, a Division of Incisive Financial Publishing Ltd

Haymarket House
28–29 Haymarket
London SW1Y 4RX
Tel: 144 (0)20 7484 9700
Fax: 144 (0)20 7484 9800
E-mail: books@incisivemedia.com
Sites: www.riskbooks.com
www.incisivemedia.com

© 2005 the Editor and the named Authors, all rights fully reserved.

ISBN 1 904339 74 3

British Library Cataloguing in Publication Data
A catalogue record for this book is available from the British Library

Managing Editor: Laurie Donaldson
Development Editor: Steve Fairman
Designer: Rebecca Bramwell

Typeset by Mizpah Publishing Services Private Limited, Chennai, India
Printed and bound in Great Britain by Antony Rowe Ltd

Conditions of sale
All rights reserved. No part of this publication may be reproduced in any material form whether by photocopying or storing in any medium by electronic means whether or not transiently or incidentally to some other use for this publication without the prior written consent of the copyright owner except in accordance with the provisions of the Copyright, Designs and Patents Act 1988 or under the terms of a licence issued by the Copyright Licensing Agency Limited of 90, Tottenham Court Road, London W1P 0LP.

Warning: the doing of any unauthorised act in relation to this work may result in both civil and criminal liability.

Every effort has been made to ensure the accuracy of the text at the time of publication, this includes efforts to contact each author to ensure the accuracy of their details at publication is correct. However, no responsibility for loss occasioned to any person acting or refraining from acting as a result of the material contained in this publication will be accepted by the copyright owner, the editor, the authors or Incisive Media Plc.

Many of the product names contained in this publication are registered trade marks, and Risk Books has made every effort to print them with the capitalisation and punctuation used by the trademark owner. For reasons of textual clarity, it is not our house style to use symbols such as TM, ®, etc. However, the absence of such symbols should not be taken to indicate absence of trademark protection; anyone wishing to use product names in the public domain should first clear such use with the product owner.

Contents

Foreword		**xi**
Acknowledgements		**xiii**
Biography		**xv**
1	**Introduction**	**1**
	Energy risk management	1
	The risk management process	2
	Style of presentation in the report	4
	Chapter review and look ahead	5
2	**Risk in Energy Markets**	**7**
	Financial and commodity markets	7
	Understanding risk	11
	Designing a risk management programme	14
	Chapter review and look ahead	16
3	**Market Value of Physical and Financial Commitments**	**17**
	Preamble	17
	Commitments, positions and market prices	17
	Position	17
	Market prices	19
	Contracts and mark-to-market quantities	21
	Mark-to-market is valid only for an instant	24
	Chapter review and look ahead	27
	Technical appendix: Interest rates and compounding conventions	27
4	**Physical Transactions and Basic Hedging Instruments**	**31**
	Physical transactions	31
	Preamble	31
	Physical producer	31
	Physical consumer	32
	Physical transformer	34
	Risk analysis	35
	Physical futures and forwards	39
	Futures contracts	39
	Forward contracts	43

	Fixed-for-floating swaps	45
	Other types of swap	58
	Floating-for-floating swaps	59
	Quanto swaps	61
	Indexation swaps	66
	Other swap types	67
	Chapter review and look ahead	69
	Technical appendix: Futures margining	70
	Technical appendix: Pricing of OTC linear instruments	70
5	**Fundamental Option Concepts**	**73**
	The language and nature of options	73
	Why and how are options used by hedgers?	80
	"Moneyness" and option values	83
	Factors impacting option value	88
	More on volatility	94
	Moving beyond European options	98
	Asian options	98
	Integrated physical and risk management contracts	102
	American options	107
	Swaptions	109
	The cost of hedging with options	112
	Chapter review and look ahead	115
	Technical appendix: Black–Scholes option valuation	116
6	**Derivatives Packages**	**117**
	Combining derivatives into a package	117
	Relationship between put and call option values	122
	Collars and premium reduction	125
	Three-way options	128
	Buy-downs and participations	133
	Structures with volume and term flexibility	144
	Integrated physical and financial structures	150
	Chapter review and look ahead	153
7	**Further Topics in Derivatives Structuring**	**155**
	Exotic options and tailored structures	155
	Spread and basket options	156
	Digital options	163
	Quanto options	167
	Other option and structure types	171
	Real options	172
	Risk-analysis example: Hedge-based financing	179
	Currency market risk questions	182
	Commodity market questions	182
	Interest rate risk questions	182
	Technical/force majeure risk questions	183
	Proxy-risk questions	183
	Volumetric-risk questions	184
	Chapter review and look ahead	185
	Technical appendix: Getting the most out of your quants	185
	Technical appendix: Option value needn't increase with increasing volatility	187
	Technical appendix: Diagrammatic notation	188
8	**Wider Risk Management Questions**	**193**
	Market risk	193
	Market risk concepts	195
	Market VaR techniques	200
	Controlling market risk exposures	205
	Beyond market risk: Physical risk management	206

The risk matrix approach to transaction analysis	207
Introductory notes	207
The galaxy of risks	208
The risk management process	208
Philosophy of the risk matrix approach	211
What is the process?	211
Mapping responsibilities and following the approach	212
Discussion of some of the risks	212
Accounting risk	213
Market risks	213
Credit risks	213
Force majeure	213
Curve construction and data risks	214
Reputational risk	214
Rolling out the approach in your company	214
Conclusion	**217**
References	**219**
Preamble	219
General and finance	219
Energy derivatives	220
Real options	220
Risk management	221
Quantitative derivative finance	221
Index	**223**

This guide is dedicated to Dad, Mum, Rita and Russell

Foreword

In the last few years the subjects of security of energy supply and energy price stability have been raised on executives' agendas. Energy prices affect us all, and the fact that you are holding this report shows that you have an interest in understanding and controlling energy risk. This report has been written with the express purpose of introducing you to the language and concepts of this vital area.

In traded markets risk finds the home in which it is best managed; those who seek stability may transfer their exposures to those who specialise in the warehousing, management and optimisation of price and volumetric risks. Since I initiated BP's derivatives activity in 1987, I have seen the energy derivatives market evolve from the simplest of futures and swaps markets, to one in which a firm's specific risk exposures across commodities, currencies, and beyond can be managed in a well-targeted way. Risk management techniques have evolved away from methods inherited from the financial industry towards energy-specific instruments that truly reflect the physical flexibilities and constraints presented by the physical consumption and production of commodity.

This innovation didn't arise from the flights of fantasy of Wall Street rocket scientists, but by understanding the fundamentals of the energy business. This evolution continues apace in BP, in banks, trading houses and funds; BP sees value in being a part of this business due to its presence in both the physical and derivative markets, allowing it to benefit from its diverse global network of physical assets and risk management capabilities, and to offer access to those same capabilities to third parties.

Creativity in the energy market shows no sign of slowing down. As new markets deregulate in power and gas, as new sources of physical supply come on-stream, and as new opportunities open in carbon trading and renewable generation, risk management will continue to adapt in response to these challenges. This report will set you well on the way to understanding what this evolution means for your company.

Vivienne Cox
Chief Executive
BP Gas, Power & Renewables
and Integrated Supply & Trading

Acknowledgements

Subdue the I[1]

This guide is the result of the knowledge I've gained working with, and knowing, the very best people in the energy business. I hope that with this report I'll succeed in some small way in offering a wider audience some of the insight I've gained from my acquaintance with these individuals. Any mistakes in the report are, naturally, my own.

My career in energy derivatives started in the late 1990s as part of Vincent Kaminski's Enron Research Group; there can't have been a better place to learn the technicalities, or the vagaries, of the energy business. In addition to Vince himself, thanks and acknowledgements are due to Grant Masson, Stinson Gibner, Vasant Shanbhogue, Krishnarao Pinnamaneni and Zimin Lu for their expertise, insight, and time, in showing me the ropes. Other figures from those Enron days who gave me great insight into the energy markets are Simon Hastings, Richard Lewis, Tani Nath, Dale Surbey, and especially Joe Gold, who taught me more about commercial focus than I ever realised at the time.

My time working in Paris for Société Générale was made possible by Christophe Petitmengin, and my time working first for Christophe, then subsequently for Edouard Neviaski at Gaselys, taught me huge amounts about the wide world of risk and energy derivatives modelling. I'd like to thank Christophe and Edouard themselves, as well as Mustapha Akhmouch, Nick Bate, Arnaud Cruiziat, Mehdi Loukili, Jean-François Maurey and Claude Philoche, all of whom aided my understanding of, and shaped my approach to, energy derivatives.

In my current role as head of bp**risk**manager's Global Structured Products Group (GSPG), I'd like to thank my boss, Daryl Schofield, for his support in the writing of this report, my GSPG colleagues Abdelatif Abada, Michael Bertuccio, Christine Cordel, Jerome Fitzgerald, Tony Hughes, Srikaran Rajasingam and Matthew Sullivan for the valuable debate that has shaped the report into its current form. I'd like to thank also our options traders Frederic Levinger and Claude Lixi *pour les bonnes discussions*, and my quant colleagues Anna Aslanyan, Bob Doubble, Milos Krkic and Hauke Schrempf for their debate and support.

Other academic and industry figures I've learned from (and enjoyed arguing with) over the years deserving of especial mention are Ehud Ronn, Helyette Geman, Les Clewlow, Chris Strickland, Fabio Cannizzo, Viacheslav Danilov, Alice Rogers, Lane Hughston and Mihalis Zervos.

My *Sifu*, Christopher Lai Khee Choong, taught me the meaning of the opening quotation in each chapter, and much else besides. Finally I must thank Rita for her patience in putting up with me during the long process of writing this guide.

Note

1 The quotations at the heads of chapters are taken from Shaolin System Nam-Pai-Chuan, the Precepts and Tenets of the System, copyright Christopher Lai Khee Choong.

Biography

Dr Steve Leppard is Head of bp**risk**manager's Global Structured Products Group, with global responsibility for the origination and structuring of cross-commodity and hybrid derivatives products for bp**risk**manager's clients. Steve's prior roles include working for Société Générale in Paris, where he was the Senior Strategist for the Gaselys JV with Gaz de France, and head of the quantitative analysis groups for Enron Europe and BP. Dr Leppard publishes and speaks regularly on the subjects of structuring, risk management and derivatives pricing in the energy industry. Steve has a PhD in mathematical physics from King's College London and a first class honours degree in mathematics from Imperial College London.

1 Introduction

Energy Risk Management

Teach with passion

Recent world events and booming economic growth in the East have thrown a spotlight on security of energy supply, energy costs and price volatility. There is now a widely held acceptance that energy costs are a significant source of uncertainty for budgeting purposes, and feed directly through to a company's bottom line – the need to understand energy market risk has never been greater.

Fortunately, a mature industry in energy price risk management has evolved, and, with a proper understanding of the nature and mitigation of energy price risk, a company's management can make well-informed decisions about whether, and how, to deal with this source of uncertainty. This report aims to inform its readers about how to identify, categorise and quantify sources of energy risk, what hedging instruments are available and how they can be employed to achieve a company's risk management aims.

Physical energy market participants may be broken into the three broad categories of producers, consumers and transformers. Examples of these are:

- *producers*: oil producers, gas producers, renewable-power generators;
- *consumers*: commercial and industrial users, domestic users, municipalities, transportation and shipping companies; and
- *transformers*: power generators, oil refiners, natural-gas liquefiers.

This report shows how the varied activities these energy users engage in can be viewed through the common "lens" of risk analysis, helping to identify which risks can be mitigated through hedging activity (as opposed, say, to better legal drafting of contracts), and assisting readers in formulating risk policies appropriate to their investors' wishes.

The discussion is presented in as non-technical a way as possible, using no abstract mathematics but plenty of numerical examples, diagrams and graphs. The reader is, however, required to do some work in understanding the concepts presented; we can assure you that the effort will be worthwhile!

The Risk Management Process

It is assumed that readers of this report are interested in understanding their energy portfolio, and assessing what tools are available for controlling its fluctuations in the face of market uncertainty. Such readers will need to engage in a risk analysis of their company, defining what they hope to achieve, and creating an appropriate control framework to ensure this happens in a measured fashion. The usual steps in designing and implementing a risk programme may broadly be listed as:

- identification;
- quantification;
- definition of control framework;
- monitoring; and
- management and response to changing circumstances.

Readers will gain a better understanding of each of these steps as they proceed through the chapters of this report. The report is designed to be read from beginning to end, though readers familiar with commodity market and derivatives concepts may like to skim through earlier chapters, checking only the "Chapter review and look ahead" section at the end of each chapter to ensure they haven't missed anything important.

This report is primarily concerned with the risks associated with commodity and associated market uncertainty. The physical nature of energy trading means that other physically based risks are mentioned when appropriate (eg, volumetric, technical and *force majeure* risks); a number of risks are skimmed over or ignored completely since they are considered to be out of the scope of this market-based work, and would need an entire volume in their own right to do them justice.

This report is intended to equip its readers with:

- the ability to identify risks and their interactions;
- techniques to express these risks clearly;
- an understanding of risk measurement techniques;
- an appreciation of trading activity and its role in risk management;
- a good understanding of energy risk management (derivative) instruments, and their relationship with physical supply and off-take agreements;
- insight into how risk management solutions may be constructed to offer varying levels of protection against market price movements at differing costs; and
- the ability to identify flexibilities in physical operations and to recognise their value.

This Executive Report is intended as no more that an introduction to this diverse, rich and ever-changing field. There is no substitute for working with specialists if you are serious about managing your risks, though this report should equip you with the ability to engage these experts in a more meaningful and challenging way.

Introduction

> In commercial and industrial companies the people most likely to need a good understanding of energy market risk management are:
>
> - treasurers
> - CFOs
> - procurement managers
> - risk managers.

This report is aimed primarily at such readers, together with the accountants, auditors and consultants who advise such companies.

> In specialist energy and trading companies there are a wide range of specialist roles devoted to the management and quantification of energy market risks. It is assumed that readers are less familiar with their job titles, and offer definitions here:
>
> - *Marketers.* Individuals engaging in the sale and purchase of physical commodity and/or risk management contracts with a customer base. In practice many marketers also engage in origination activity (see below).
> - *Originators.* A job similar, or even identical, to that of a marketer. In some companies origination may involve an element of identifying new prospects, sectors or the negotiation of larger structured transactions, rather than servicing a well-defined range of clients or sectors.
> - *Structurers.* A job similar, or even identical, to that of an originator. In some companies structuring may involve a significant amount of quantitative analysis and derivative modelling. Structurers will tend to be involved where a deal is especially large or complex.
> - *Traders.* Individuals who manage a portfolio of commodity, financial or combined contracts in real time, aiming to optimise the purchase and sale of contracts to exploit market volatility and liquidity.
> - *Quantitative analysts ("quants").* Mathematical specialists who carry out statistical analysis of market price movements, and create tools for the valuation of commodity market physical and risk management contracts based upon mathematical models of market dynamics.
> - *Risk managers*:
>   1. Those who assess, monitor and control the aggregate of a company's commodity and financial market activities, policing traders' actions, and providing independent assurance to management that risks are being controlled well.
>   2. An alternative name for a marketer, originator or structurer who works with their clients to achieve those clients' risk management aims.

> Does your company have a corporate-wide programme for managing commodity price, currency and interest rate risk?

Style of Presentation in the Report

Most guides on energy derivatives and risk management adopt a mathematical approach to the subject, showing the underlying mathematical themes, and exploring the various statistical and quantitative approaches to the pricing and management of risk. This report has been written for those who are not necessarily well versed in, and not inclined to learn, the specialist tools of stochastic calculus, partial differential equations or similar areas. Readers are assumed to be familiar with risk from a corporate perspective, and to be comfortable with the basic tools of discounted cashflow analysis, the use of probability distributions in expressing uncertainty, and other general business scenario analysis principles.

The main text of the report discusses the subject of energy risk management at a fairly intuitive level, developing examples and presenting ideas using words, diagrams and numerical examples, without the use of abstract mathematical formulas. At various points in the text boxes are used to summarise important concepts; those readers skimming the text should consult these boxes in a chapter before moving on to ensure they are comfortable with the notions introduced.

From time to time "questions" are used in the text, where the reader is invited to pause and ponder a question before proceeding. Some of these questions have well-defined answers, which are presented immediately after the question point; others are intended to do no more than provoke a line of thought for the reader. A chapter summary is used at the end of each chapter to recap the important notions introduced in that chapter, and to show how they lead to the material in the following chapters.

In some chapters there follow technical appendices, which give more quantitative detail about important concepts encountered in the text. This material is not necessary to understand the text, but those readers more comfortable with quantitative modelling may wish to read this material, and ponder how they might apply it to their own business.

Readers will benefit from following the main text, and stopping at question points. For subsequent reference the boxes, chapter summaries and technical appendices will refresh, extend and deepen the reader's appreciation of the subject.

Since I believe that a picture is worth a thousand words, various forms of diagram are used to explain and summarise key concepts in commodity and hedging transactions. The main forms of diagram used are:

- *block diagrams*, showing the entities involved in an energy market trade, and the flows of cash or commodity between them;
- *contractual timeline diagrams*, showing how a contract evolves from its inception through to final financial settlement; and
- *payoff diagrams*, which indicate how a commodity market contract or portfolio pays out in relation to the underlying market prices.

When the diagrams are being put to a new use, or to explain new concepts, they will be developed in explicit detail. Later use of the same concepts will employ the diagrams with less explanation, and so it is important that readers unfamiliar with these devices should follow the text.

Chapter Review and Look Ahead

In this chapter readers were introduced to a way of categorising the players who participate in the physical energy markets, producers, consumers and transformers. After a first look at the risk management process and its aims, a brief summary of the kinds of specialists who operate in the energy risk management space was given. More attention was given to those who work in energy trading and risk management divisions, since it is assumed the intended readership of this report is less familiar with such roles.

Finally, the style of presentation of this report was explained, and a summary of the various illustrative and teaching devices employed was given. Now the scene has been set all that remains is to proceed straight to an examination of energy risk and markets.

2 Risk in Energy Markets

Behave with fortitude

Financial and Commodity Markets

We are bombarded every day with news on the financial markets, discussions of their importance for measuring the health of the economy, and easy-to-digest measures of key indexes (FTSE100, CAC40). Since those readers who keep up to date with current affairs will be familiar with many of these concepts it is instructive to start by contrasting commodities markets with their purely financial counterparts.

When we talk of financial underlyings, we typically consider assets such as shares, bonds and currencies; delivery of these assets is almost an academic issue, generally involving little more than the exchange of data between computer systems. These underlyings trade because investors wish to gain an exposure to the capital gains or dividends afforded by possession of the securities, or because there is a need to possess the underlyings as a hedge for other market exposures.

By contrast, trading in physical commodity markets involves the buying and selling of material goods, including agricultural products, metals and various energy products. Such assets are fundamentally not investment, but consumption, assets, which means that they are bought or sold by many players as a consequence of some real physical needs.[1] This brings a strong psychological element to the behaviour of commodity prices, for example the "fear" of a refiner running out of oil and being forced to shut down operations.

Physical delivery of commodities is necessarily a non-trivial issue involving time, cost and the practical issues surrounding the arrangement of insurance, storage and freight. The fact of physical delivery, together with its attendant constraints, means that the pricing of commodity contracts is much more subtle than the pricing of less tangible financial underlyings.

> At some point buying and selling becomes trading activity. How many forms of trading activity can you think of? How many forms of trading activity does your own company engage in?

Trading activity in energy markets may be grouped under the following broad headings:

1. *Asset, commercial or industrial optimisation*: Trading activity intended to balance real-time needs in the operation of physical assets, commercial or industrial processes, buying additional supply or selling excess production when demand and production levels require, and making optimal choice of feedstocks to service the operations.
2. *Hedging*: Trading activity intended to reduce the riskiness of a portfolio.
3. *Arbitrage*: Trading activity resulting in a riskless profit, usually arising from participants exploiting inefficiencies in a market. The forces of supply and demand usually ensure these price mismatches subsequently disappear as a result of the trade being executed.
4. *Speculation*: Taking risky positions in a market with the intention of exploiting market price movements.
5. *Investment*: Investing cash through positions in energy markets, with the intention of earning returns on these positions.

Here we shall concentrate on hedging activity in the service of an energy risk management programme, meaning that we are concerned primarily with asset, commercial and industrial optimisation and hedging activities. Arbitrage activity imposes a certain discipline on the way we interact with the market, even if we are not ourselves arbitrageurs.

> Types of energy trading:
> 1. asset, commercial or industrial optimisation
> 2. hedging
> 3. arbitrage
> 4. speculation
> 5. investment.

> How does arbitrage govern a traded market?

Arbitrageurs seek to exploit price discrepancies between physical and derivative commodities between different locations, across physical grades and through different times to delivery. This arbitrage activity tends to keep the markets in related commodities aligned, with any pricing disparities quickly exploited and hence closed. The ability to exploit some arbitrages relies on the arbitrageur having access to a network of physical assets, and the logistical, operational or scheduling expertise to put on the trade.

Examples of arbitrage:

- *Cross-commodity 'arbitrage': an industrial optimisation example.* A European industrial company consumes a significant amount of power to run its production facility, and has the choice of buying from the traded power markets, or buying gas and using it to supply its own on-site generation. A large new order for their products has arrived, meaning they need to increase their production in three months' time. They estimate that they will need an extra 4,000 MWh of peak-load power in three months' time, and look first at the power forward market, where they discover the three-month forward price for peak-load power is currently trading at €60/MWh. Next they look at the gas forward market, where, once accounting for the efficiency of their on-site power generation, they find that gas is trading at the equivalent of €58/MWh. They therefore decide to buy gas forward, and generate the electricity themselves, thus saving €2/MWh × 4,000 MWh = €8,000. Purchase of this gas may put some upward pressure on the forward gas price, tending to close the gap between the gas and power prices.
- *Cross-commodity arbitrage, trading example.* A merchant power generator would have a different take on the previous cross-commodity arbitrage example, since they wouldn't necessarily need the power to service their own demand. They could buy the gas from the market (putting some upward pressure on the gas price), while simultaneously selling forward the power, putting downward price pressure on the electricity price. The merchant power generator will be able to lock in this spark spread of €2/MWh, and the market prices will be pushed closer together. The constant balancing of energy production and consumption, together with varying power generation efficiencies, give liquidity to, and relate, the power and gas markets through such spark spread trading.
- *Location arbitrage, trading example.* A large oil trader watching the relative prices of crude oil across the Atlantic Ocean notes that the six-month forward price for US light sweet crude oil is currently at US$60/bbl, while they are able to source an equivalent grade of European crude at US$54/bbl, and ship it for an equivalent of US$5.50 bbl for delivery in six months' time. They therefore buy the European crude, charter the shipping capacity, and lock in a risk-free profit of US$0.50/bbl. Exploiting such "real optionality" requires that the trader have access to the oil and shipping markets, and significant physical logistical support and expertise.
- An oil products trading company has access both to the traded markets and to distribution and physical oil storage facilities. The latest weather forecasts indicate that the month of December will be colder than previously expected, leading the company to predict that there will be higher-than-expected heating oil demand and thus higher heating oil prices. They note that heating oil for October delivery is currently priced at US$1.80/gal, for December delivery is US$2.00/gal, and they have access to two months of storage for the equivalent of US$0.17/gal. They therefore buy October heating oil, book the storage capacity, and sell December heating oil, locking in a risk-free profit of 3 cents per gallon. The storability of heating oil means that forward prices between different maturities are linked, with storage limiting the discrepancies through

time. Access to oil storage is another example of a "real option", namely a physical asset that derives its value from its ability to exploit price discrepancies and volatility in commodity markets.

The geographical dispersion of participants in commodities markets means that different prices for nominally the same physical commodity may exist in different regions due to local supply and demand, and the effects of imperfect and non-instantaneous transportation. As an example of the wide variety of physical grades traded, the box below lists the various grades of crude listed on platts.com at the time of writing. The need for physical balancing in some markets, especially regulated energy markets, adds complexity to these often-volatile price behaviours.

> Crude oil grades, as listed by platts.com:
> Arab Berri, Arab Heavy, Arab Light, Arab Super Light, Arab Medium, Amna, Ardjuna, Arimibi, Arun cond, Attaka, Azeri Light, Bach 17, Basrah, Bekapai, Belayim, Bombay Hi, Bonny Light, Bonny Medium, Brass River, Brega, Brent, Bu Attifel, Bunyu, Cabinda, Canolimon, Cinta, Daqing, Dubai, Duri, Ekofisk, Escravos, Es Sider, Forcados, Forties, Flotta, Gippsland, Handil, Hout, Iran Light, Iran Heavy, Isthus, Khafji, Kirkuk, Kole, Kumkol, Kuwait, Labaun, Leona, Lower Zakun, Mandji, Maya, Minas, Miri, Montros, Murban, Ninian, Oman, Oriente, Pennington, Qatar Land, Qatar Marine, Qua Ibo, Ras Gharib, Saharan Blend, Salawati, Sarir, Seria Light, Shengli, Siberian Light, Statfjord, Suez Blend, Tapis, Tembungo, Tengiz, Tijuana Light, Tijuana Heavy, Umm Shaif, Urals, Walio, WTI, WTS, Wyo swt, Zarzaitine, Zuetina.

In order to ensure that trading is practical, commodities contracts usually offer standardised terms as listed in Table 1.

With these standards in place, the participants in a market are better placed to assess bids and offers on a like-for-like basis, and then need concern themselves only with the other issues of transportation, storage and so on. Many transactions going to physical delivery will not meet these standardised terms, but these terms will act to define a reference price from which the actual price is determined.

The price quoted in a market for short-term delivery is referred to as the spot price, which almost by definition is driven by short-term,

Table 1. Standardised features in commodity contracts

Cost
Volume
When delivered
How delivered
Where delivered
Quality
Acceptable errors in quality or volume

supply-and-demand balancing activity in physical markets. This need for balancing in some markets, most notably power that can reach high "granularity" (eg, delivery in a single half-hour, rather than over an entire day, month or quarter), and the difficulty of storing certain commodities mean that spot prices may be highly volatile. Clearly, an unhedged energy user forced into buying or selling at spot prices is exposed to highly uncertain cashflows.

Energy trading takes place both on organised exchanges and via the over-the-counter (OTC) markets. Exchanges trade a limited number of benchmark commodity prices and locations, and provide price transparency, protection from counterparty credit default risk and the like. Their level of standardisation means they are unable to service the wide range of actual physical commodity grades, locations, styles of delivery, which is where the OTC markets play their most important role. OTC trading may be conducted directly between counterparties or via brokers, who act as a centralised meeting point for market participants' trading activity. We shall be examining the use of both exchange-based and OTC derivatives contracts for hedging purposes in the following chapters.

Understanding Risk

> What is risk?

Most dictionary definitions of risk relate to hazard, exposure to misfortune, or other quite negative meanings. For the purposes of this guide I propose to define risk as

> Risk: exposure to an uncertainty.

We can refine our understanding of risk by considering a couple of cases:

- Is tomorrow's temperature in Buenos Aires a risk for me as a resident of London?

    While tomorrow's temperature in Buenos Aires is *uncertain*, few London residents would consider it to be a risk since they have no *exposure* to this temperature.
- I have spent 10 pounds on lottery tickets, and have been informed that I have one winning ticket. The payout is at least 10 pounds, maybe significantly more. Is the payout a risk for me?

    The payout is uncertain, and in this case I have an exposure to this uncertainty, so in accordance with the definition offered above the payout is risky. The fact that the risk is only upside risk (that is, to my benefit), means that in normal English usage we might say there is no risk, though I will stick to the former usage in this report.

Energy risk management, the subject of this report, involves analysing risks and creating a solution to:

- hedging energy market price exposures;
- hedging associated interest rate or foreign-exchange exposures;
- unlocking the market value of embedded flexibility in existing contracts or asset operations;
- releasing working capital to enable capital investment; and
- improving the company's effective credit rating by putting in place firm commodity delivery commitments which can be borrowed against.

These solutions make use of energy or financial derivatives, or sometimes a hybrid of the two. Energy risk management may form part of a larger capital structuring transaction in which finance is provided for projects through the loan or debt markets, special-purpose investment vehicles are created and so on. The subject of trade finance is outside the scope of this work.

Common to all of these activities is the need to have a rigorous understanding of a company's energy inputs and outputs, the industrial or other transformative processes they engage in, the nature of any currency exposures they are subject to, volumetric risks due, for example, to variations in client demand or environmental conditions such as wind speed or temperature, technical risks due to failure of physical plant, *force majeure* risks and so on.

In my professional life I work with a matrix of around thirty risks that I consider when analysing physical and derivative transaction. Table 2 shows an extract from my risk matrix containing the risks of most relevance to this guide.

We shall return from time to time to this matrix, while interested readers can consult a fuller list of risks in this box:

> Fuller list of risks:
> Accounting, compliance, counterparty concentration, country default, credit, currency curve construction, interpolation or extrapolation, *force majeure*, funding liquidity, geographical, index specification, interest rate, knowledge, legal, liquidity, mapping, commodity market, modelling, operational, political, position concentration, proxy, raw data, regulatory, reputational, settlement, sovereign, systems/procedural, tax, technical, technology, volumetric.

We can see the form of analysis required by considering a simple example. Suppose a small European airline buys V gallons of jet fuel per day priced at the prevailing daily spot price in the market. The situation can be represented in the financial block diagram in Figure 1.

> Can you identify how the transaction in Figure 1 exposes the two trading counterparties to the risks in Table 2?

Table 2. Extract from risk matrix

Risk	Description
Currency	Exposure to uncertainty in currency exchange rates
Force majeure	Exposure to an unforeseen or rare event for which there is no contractual mitigation
Commodity market	Exposure to uncertain market prices, volatilities or correlations
Proxy	Exposure to imperfect matches between a hedge and the exposure being hedged
Technical	Risk that a physical asset's performance makes one unable to meet delivery obligations, or fully realise the apparent optionality inherent in the asset
Volumetric	Risk arising from changes in the volume of commodity supply or consumption

Figure 1. European airline fuel purchases

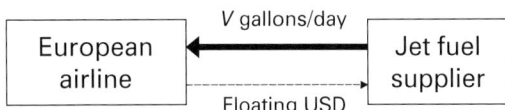

Using even just a few of the entries from the risk matrix up against Figure 1 we are forced to address the following issues:

- Where does the European airline get the dollars to pay for its fuel, and at what foreign-exchange (FX) rate?
- What happens if the airline requires more or less than the agreed volume of fuel on a given day?
- Is the airline happy to be exposed to the floating dollar price for jet fuel?
- Can it pass some, or all, of these costs through to its customers?
- What sort of protection could the airline receive to address these market, volumetric and currency risks?
- What policies does the airline have in place regarding these issues?
- Is fuel purchasing dealt with in isolation from currency management?
- Are the airline's risk managers looking to reduce cashflow volatility, minimise costs, hit a certain budget, or some combination of these?
- What level of insurance premium is the airline able and prepared to pay for protection against such risks?

Such analyses tend to raise similar concerns regardless of what energy derivative structuring transaction is being considered, and experience has shown that the following "risk management themes" arise most often:

- security of physical supply or off-take;
- achieving a specific budget;
- requirement to lock in energy prices or FX rates;

- protection from adverse price movements, while retaining some upside benefit;
- minimising the premium paid for protection, perhaps at the expense of some upside potential;
- volumetric flexibility; and
- ability to switch between different underlying commodities where substitutions are available.

These issues, and many others, are dealt with through the construction of appropriate packages of physical supply contracts and derivative-based hedges.

Designing a Risk Management Programme

In recent years there has been an increasing appreciation of the role of energy market risk management in industry, with competitive pressures forcing players to learn more about the area and to design and implement their own programmes. The term *risk management* means different things to different people, and in some quarters there is an imperfect understanding of just what risk management can achieve – indeed, the main motivation behind this guide is to improve the general appreciation of energy market risk management outside the trading community.

Since the mid-1990s the level of sophistication of risk management instruments offered in the energy sector has increased significantly, which has been a somewhat mixed blessing: on the one hand, correct use of these instruments has allowed energy players to mitigate their risks in a very controlled way; on the other hand, questionable behaviour by some derivative market participants has served to give derivatives in general a bad name. Derivatives are tools and, as with all tools, they can be used wisely or they can be abused.

What are you looking to achieve through your risk management?

Risk management programmes use hedging to achieve various aims, whether short-term tactical or long-term strategic, and managers need to be clear why they are instituting such a programme, and what range of risks they wish to consider, since there may be tensions between tactical and strategic hedging. Short-term hedges will often be put on:

- where customer demand has become better understood, and there is a need to purchase extra energy or currency;
- the hedger wishes to lock in the value of a specific delivery of commodity;
- stock levels need to be bolstered or shrunk;
- an opportunity to achieve a desirable budgetary level has presented itself;
- a natural opportunity to lock in a profit has presented itself; and/or
- there is a need to acquire some physical insurance, by buying or selling optional volumes.

By contrast strategic longer-term hedges are often put on:

- to achieve some agreed budget level;
- in project financing, where commodity sales or purchases are used to lock in values as a form of debt guarantee;
- to put some bounds around planning levels; and
- as a means of diversifying a company's global risk exposures.

Designing a risk management programme requires that a company's management carry out the following steps:

1. Identify the risks the company is exposed to.
2. Define the company's risk policy, setting the aims of the risk management programme, that will gain the approval of management and the investor community.
3. Quantify those risks that can be quantified to aid the risk management process.
4. Set authority levels, risk limits, targets and/or budgets that the company's risk managers will be judged against.
5. Design and implement the risk management programme making use, as appropriate, of derivative instruments.
6. Execute the risk management programme in a controlled way, consistent with the authority levels and risk limits defined above, in order to achieve the defined targets and/or budgets.
7. Monitor the programme.
8. Manage and modify the programme as the company's business and the market evolve.

The meaning of each of these steps will become clearer as the reader progresses through this report.

> One of your company's risk managers has a view of the market and puts on an unauthorised "hedge" using a derivative instrument that makes your company a large profit. Do you discipline the risk manager? What should you do with the profit?

A number of practical factors must be accounted for in designing a risk management programme. First among these is how "tight" the programme should be. Financial theory teaches us that without risk there can be no return, but bearing too much risk may not win the support of a company's stakeholders due to excess volatility of cashflows. Secondly, market liquidity can lead to significant challenges in some markets: positions that are easy to enter on a given day may be hard to exit (or "unwind") on a later occasion due to lack of players, or expensive to exit (due to wide "bid–offer spreads"). It is important to hedge using sufficiently liquid instruments, while still matching one's underlying risks.

Energy and financial market risk management services are available from banks and the risk management arms of oil majors, energy traders and utilities. Each company has its own strengths and weaknesses, including ability to provide access to differing markets, ability to make or take physical delivery or bundle the risk management with advisory, investment, financing or syndication services. Generally speaking, the larger the company, and the more diverse its asset portfolio, the more competitive and comprehensive its services should be.

Chapter Review and Look Ahead

In this chapter we have looked at energy commodity markets and compared how they differ from their purely financial cousins. The physical nature of these markets means there are many practical complexities encountered in the management of commodity market risk, though, as we shall see in later chapters, the financial markets have served as a rich source of inspiration for energy market risk management principles and tools. The forms of trading activity that take place in energy markets have many parallels with the financial markets, though the use of physical assets that produce, transform or consume energy introduce a multitude of other, volumetric, risks into energy risk management that are not so obviously present in the purely financial domain.

After defining risk, we considered what risk management themes a company's management may wish to consider in managing their energy portfolio; much of this guide is concerned with the derivatives tools available for the addressing these themes, and with the methods that might be used for monitoring and controlling exposures to market risks. All these considerations form part of the design of a risk management programme for an energy market player, and familiarity with the contents of this guide will set management well on the path to instituting such a programme for their stakeholders.

Note

1 Many investors now seek access to markets in commodities for their returns, which are considered to be relatively uncorrelated with traditional investment instruments.

3 Market Value of Physical and Financial Commitments

Focus on reality

Preamble

Marking to market refers to the process of reconciling asset values or obligations with a set of market prices even though the actual realisation of cash may not happen for some time to come. The use of mark-to-market (MTM) values for contracts is essential in understanding the cost of unwinding hedges in the market, how one is performing with respect to the market, and in gauging how well one's competitors may be doing in the same market.

This chapter introduces the most basic language and concepts one needs to understand before one is equipped to institute a risk management programme in one's company.

Commitments, Positions and Market Prices

Position

Before we are able to consider marking a commodity portfolio to market it is important first to understand what is in one's portfolio, and to express it in a way that it may be valued. We define a company's commodity position as shown in the box below:

> Commodity position:
> Aggregated volume of all commitments to produce, consume, buy or sell, all physical commodities, and financial contracts dependent upon such commodities, through time.

The position provides the basic data on what part of the company's contractual and physical asset portfolio will be affected by movements in the underlying commodity and financial markets.

Example: Jet Fuel Physical Position

The fuel purchasing manager for a small airline, ABCDAir, has just received the latest forecast for air fleet demand for the first quarter of

Table 3. ABCDAir Q1 jet fuel consumption

Q1 jet fuel position (kT)	January	February	March
Expected consumption by airfleet	24	27	29

Table 4. ABCDAir Q1 jet fuel consumption and supply

Q1 jet fuel position (kT)	January	February	March
Expected consumption by air fleet	(24)	(27)	(29)
Delivered from contracts	25	25	30
Net	1	(2)	1

next year. The position, expressed in thousands of tonnes per month, is shown in Table 3.

Suppose that the fuel purchasing manager already has some supply contracts in place, that will deliver the volumes shown now in Table 4.

With this jet fuel example in place we are now ready to learn the first pieces of terminology associated with marking to market. A net positive volume in the position is known as a *long position*, a net negative volume in the position is known as a *short position*. A balanced, or zero, volume is called a *flat*, or *net flat*, position.

> Is ABCDAir long, short or flat jet fuel?

This question cannot be answered without reference to the time periods over which the position is to be aggregated. Table 4 shows that the airline is long 1000 tonnes of jet fuel in both January and March, and short 2000 tonnes in February. Aggregated across the whole first quarter the airline is net flat. The variability and mismatches in monthly supply and demand mean that ABCDAir must make use of fuel storage facilities to smooth out the imbalances, and perhaps negotiate for some monthly volumetric flexibility in their physical jet fuel contracts too.

A company's physical commodity position is unlikely to be static, but instead will evolve as better data becomes available on supply-and-demand factors. In summarising a company's position the management must decide what portion of their expected supply and demand are certain enough to justify including in the position and therefore in any subsequent hedging programme.

Position sizes offer the first, and most basic, form of control that management can impose on their procurement department and risk managers. In laying down guidelines on what is considered sufficiently certain supply and demand to include in the company's position, those responsible for matching supply with demand can be required not to deviate from a match by more than some given amount. Any greater deviation will be either speculation on the certainty of the volume forecasts or speculation on market prices, neither of which is likely to be acceptable. Position limits will normally be imposed in some sort of hierarchy, and the limits at each level of the hierarchy must be consistent with each other.

Example: Position Limits for ABCDAir

ABCDAir's management have imposed the following position limits:

- monthly supply/demand imbalance not to exceed 1.5 kT; and
- aggregate quarterly supply demand imbalance not to exceed 3 kT.

We can see that the fuel purchasing manager has broken the monthly limit in February, even though the quarterly limit has been respected.[1] In order to respect the position limits at least 0.5 kT of fuel will need to be purchased for February, which will give management the comfort they need that supply and demand are sufficiently matched.

A hierarchy of position limits forces a disciplined approach to procurement and hedging, and an appropriately designed hierarchy gives sufficient flexibility to smooth out short-term imbalances subject to tighter aggregate controls over longer time frames.

Market Prices

Once we have a clear idea of what a company's physical commodity position is, we then wish to hold the longs and shorts up against the market and see what they are worth. In order to do this we must know where to find an appropriate set of market prices to use in the mark-to-market process. Clearly, it is necessary to use an objective set of market benchmark prices, since an employee's informal view on the market value of commodities is likely to be influenced by their position, and how they are incentivised to manage the position.

The principal sources of formal price data are:

- futures and options exchanges (eg, NYMEX, IPE);
- OTC market price reporting services (eg, Platts, Argus, Heren); and
- government price surveys (eg, the US Department of Energy).

These prices tend to take two main forms: price assessments or surveys of delivered commodities, and forward-looking assessments of prices for future delivery.

In exchange-based and OTC-traded markets, prices are expressed as a pair called the *bid–offer* or *bid–ask spread*. These express at what price players are prepared to buy (bid) or sell (offer or ask) the commodity. The bid–ask spread can be seen as a joint measure of market liquidity and sentiment, since wide spreads indicate that there is little competition, or no good consensus, on prices. Liquid markets with large numbers of active participants tend to have narrower spreads due to competitive pressure and arbitrage activity.

> Market price quotations:
> *Bid price*: The price at which a participant is prepared to buy commodity.
> *Ask or offer price*: The price at which a participant is prepared to sell commodity.
>
> (Continued)

Energy Risk Management

> *Mid-price*: The average of the bid and ask prices.
>
> *Closing price*: The final traded mid-price at which a commodity traded on an exchange.
>
> *Forward curve*: The market's view of prices for future delivery that can be locked in today.
>
> *Contango*: A forward market where longer-maturity forward prices are higher than shorter-maturity prices.
>
> *Backwardation*: A forward market where longer-maturity forward prices are lower than shorter-maturity prices.

For official mark-to-market purposes companies tend to use the closing price from an exchange, or the mid-price from a price survey. In ascertaining the market value of future contractual commitments, the *forward curve* is used. The forward curve is the market's view of prices for future delivery that can be locked in today. This should not be confused with a price forecast, which is an economic or statistical view of what spot prices are likely to be in the future, cannot necessarily be locked in today, and therefore cannot be considered a market value.

Commodity forward prices tend to reflect the value of commodity to be delivered over a period of time. A July price of 25 pence per therm for UK natural gas, for example, is the price that can be locked in today for a delivery of a determined volume of natural gas on each day of the month of July. Some commodity markets quote their prices for different lengths of delivery period, with shorter periods at shorter maturities (or the *front end* of the curve) with longer pricing periods at longer maturities (the *back end* of the curve).

Example: Natural Gas Forward Curve

Suppose that in December 2005 the forward price curve for UK natural gas is:

Month	Price (ppth)
January 2006	35
February 2006	34
March 2006	30
April 2006	25
May 2006	20
June 2006	19
July 2006	18
August 2006	19
September 2006	21
4Q06	32
1Q07	36
2Q07	24
3Q07	20
4Q07	31
1Q08	35
Summer 2008	23
Winter 2008	34
...	...

Figure 2. UK natural gas forward curve

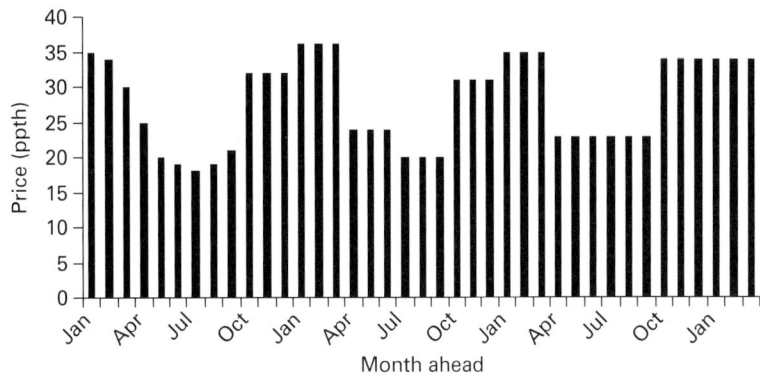

These prices may be assembled into the graphical representation in Figure 2, which clearly shows the seasonal nature of natural gas prices.

As time advances, contracts that were previously quoted as, say, quarters *cascade* into their component months. Even where the liquid market doesn't quote individual months, days or hours in a longer period, market makers may take a view on their likely interrelationships and quote these higher-granularity prices.

A forward curve where the short end is higher (ie, more expensive than) the back end is said to be in *backwardation*, while a curve where the back end is higher is said to be in *contango*.[2] Pure storage cost economics would dictate that commodities for delivery at some later time may be priced by buying immediately, then paying for storage, insurance and so on, until the commodity is required. Storage cost economics suggest, therefore, that forward curves should be in contango. In practice real-time physical needs and economic factors, together with psychological "fear" effects mean that there is often a premium for shorter-term maturities, leading to curves being in backwardation. This notion is expressed formally by talking of the *convenience yield*[3] of prices, in which the market assigns a monetary benefit to commodity deliveries at shorter maturities.

Contracts and Mark-to-Market Quantities

The process of marking to market involves understanding what obligations a commodity physical or derivative contract places on the holder or writer, and computing the net present value (NPV) of these commitments according to the market. In carrying out these discounted cashflow (DCF) calculations we assume that the commitments are binding, that the prices reflect the fair market price and that there is no further non-market risk involved in the transactions. These assumptions lead to the use of risk-free interest rates in computing the NPV.

Example: ABCDAir Mark-to-Market

Suppose ABCDAir negotiated to purchase its jet fuel at a fixed price of US$580/tonne; and that since negotiating this contract the market price of jet fuel has risen. On 1 December the market forward prices for each month's delivery in Q1 are as shown in Table 5. The mark-to-market value of this portfolio of contracts is equivalent to the value that could be derived from selling these contracts back to the market.

Table 5. ABCDAir Q1 jet fuel volumes and market data

Q1 jet fuel position (1 December)	January	February	March
Delivered from contracts (kT)	25	25	30
Contractual price (US$/tonne)	580	580	580
Jet fuel forward price (US$/tonne)	600	610	620
Days to settlement of contract	66	94	125
Risk-free interest rate (%)	3.5	3.6	3.7

Assuming that the interest rates are continuously compounding (see "Technical appendix: Interest rates and compounding conventions") the MTM of the January contract is found using the DCF calculation

$$\text{MTM}_{\text{January}} = 25000 \times e^{-3.5\% \times 66/365} \times (600 - 580) = 496845.61 \text{ US\$}$$

The MTMs for the February and March contracts are found in a similar fashion, giving a total portfolio MTM of approximately US$2424814.

We can see that the contracts will be delivering jet fuel for less than the current market forward price; in such a situation we say the contracts are *in-the-money* (ITM), and they could in principle be sold to another market participant for a profit. Unless ABCDAir has excess volumes to sell, this is only of academic interest to the airline, since they need the volumes to service their own demand.

In-, at-, out-of-the-money, or the "moneyness" of contracts:

In-the-money (ITM): A contractual commitment whose mark-to-market value is positive to the holder of the contract. The market has moved in favour of the holder, and the contract could in principle be liquidated in the market, realising a profit.

At-the-money (ATM): An MTM value that is exactly in correspondence with the market. Liquidating the position would only return exactly what was paid for the position. Commodities contracts are agreed (or *struck*) at-the-money at the contract inception – any difference from the current market value could be realised instantly, effecting an arbitrage.

Out-of-the-money (OTM): An MTM value that is negative for the holder of the contract. The market has moved against the holder of the contract, and liquidating the position would return less than the agreed amount of the contract.

Note that the use of risk-free interest rates is quite different from the use of interest rates in conventional planning and project management, where the interest rates are supplemented by some risk premium to reflect the uncertainties of the cashflows. Beyond credit risk, which will be dealt with by other means (eg, posting letters of credit), the cashflows arising from physical and derivatives contracts are considered to be certain, and therefore subject to risk-free discounting.

The ABCDAir example above shows how to find the MTM of a set of fixed-price physical "forward" contracts; these and other contracts will be discussed in later chapters, primarily for their role in hedging a company's

Figure 3. Flow of time in contractual timeline diagram

cashflows. While it is strictly a tautological statement, it is worth reiterating that marking to market can be used only where there is a market-based method for determining the value of something; if there is no market, then one is marking to a model, forecast or opinion.

Mark-to-market calculations assume that the market has infinite liquidity and depth, and that the market value of the contracts could be realised instantly, and without moving the market. This is obviously a strong assumption, and one that is especially difficult to defend where large volumes are concerned. In practice, traders adjust the price at which they are prepared to buy or sell according to the volume being traded, market liquidity, amount of time likely to elapse during which they are required to hold their prices "firm", and so on.

> You are responsible for computing the mark-to-market for a utility that supplies gas and electricity to industrial clients. Your customers are on one-year supply contracts, which you attempt to renew with them each year, but which they are not certain to renew with your company.
>
> 1. Should you mark-to-market their expected demand beyond the contract expiry?
> 2. Economic studies show that wholesale power prices are expected to rise significantly over the coming year. Your risk managers feel that the next two years' power purchases should be locked in now, even though there are no firm customers beyond the one-year horizon. Should you mark-to-market these long-term power purchases, even though there are no matching firm customer volumes?

These issues, and several others raised in this chapter, are best answered by consulting your accountants and auditors to receive industry- and jurisdiction-specific advice.

When discussing physical and derivative commodity contracts it is useful to have some way of illustrating the flow of time, and showing when various events (contract initiation, delivery, settlement and others) occur. With this in mind we now introduce the "contractual timeline diagram". In contractual timeline diagrams time is represented as flowing from left to right across the page, with contract initiation or the trade as the first event on the timeline, as shown in Figure 3.

The events and time periods of most interest to us are:

- trade date/contract initiation date;
- pricing period, the period of time during which the price is set for the contract;

Figure 4. Contractual timeline for physical natural gas forward contract

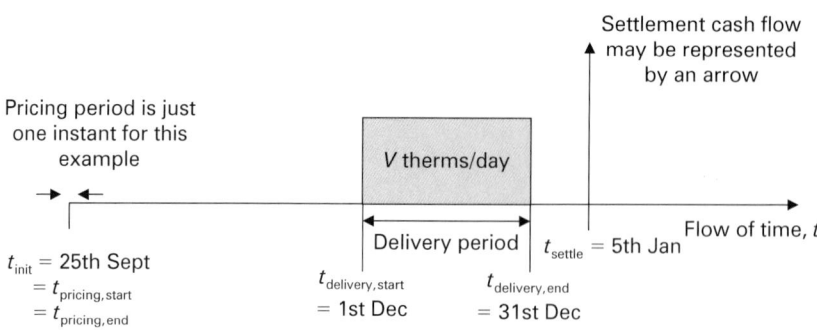

- delivery period, the period of time during which physical delivery of the contract is made; and
- settlement, the date or dates on which cash is exchanged in payment of the delivery.

Let's consider the diagram for the example of a physical forward contract bought by a participant in the natural-gas market. On the diagram we represent the following features:

- The contract is initiated (ie, traded) on 25 September. We represent the contract initiation date by t_{init}.
- The fixed price to be paid on delivery is fixed on that day too. Pricing period start and end dates will be represented by $t_{pricing,start}$ and $t_{pricing,end}$ respectively.
- Delivery of the natural gas is due during the month of December, with the same volume, V therms, being delivered on each day. The delivery period start and end dates will be presented by $t_{delivery,start}$ and $t_{delivery,end}$ respectively.
- Settlement of the contract takes place on 5 January. The settlement date will be represented by t_{settle}.

The corresponding contractual timeline diagram is shown in Figure 4.

Similar diagrams will be used throughout this report to represent physical and derivative commodity contracts.

In the ABCDAir example above the airline had a series of monthly forward contracts, all identical except for their month of physical delivery and settlement dates. Such a series is known in financial and energy trading as a *strip* of contracts, a notion we shall encounter often in the remainder of this guide.

Mark-to-Market is Valid only for an Instant

Example: ABCDAir Mark-to-Market Revisited

Suppose that on 2 December ABCDAir re-conduct their mark-to-market exercise for their strip of fixed-price physical forward fuel contracts. The new data from which they'll derive their mark-to-market is shown in Table 6.

Using the same NPV analysis as ABCDAir conducted on 1 December the mark-to-market value of the portfolio of forward contracts is now approximately US$2766483.

Market Value of Physical and Financial Commitments

Table 6. ABCDAir Q1 jet fuel volumes and market data, 2 December

Q1 jet fuel position (2 December)	January	February	March
Delivered from contracts (kT)	25	25	30
Contractual price (US$/tonne)	580	580	580
Jet fuel forward price (US$/tonne)	605	614	624
Days to settlement of contract	59	87	118
Risk-free interest rate (%)	3.55	3.65	3.75

> Why is the new mark-to-market significantly different from the previous value if ABCDAir haven't bought or sold any physical volumes?

In the case of ABCDAir the reasons the mark-to-market value of their portfolio has changed so much are:

- the jet fuel market has moved;
- the interest rates have moved; and
- the time to settlement of each of the contracts is now one day shorter.

This example raises a fundamental point about marking a portfolio to market: *mark-to-market values may change significantly even if the portfolio composition doesn't.*

In traded markets it is common to follow the combined effect of buying and selling contracts, market price and rate movements and the passage of time using a daily profit-and-loss (P&L) figure. This is based upon the difference between consecutive days' mark-to-market portfolio values. Suppose we denote the mark-to-market value of the ABCDAir portfolio on 1 December using $MTM_{1\,Dec}$, and the corresponding value on 2 December as $MTM_{2\,Dec}$, then the P&L for 2 December would be:

$$P\&L_{2\,Dec} = MTM_{2\,Dec} - MTM_{1\,Dec}$$
$$= 341668\ US\$$$

The value of the P&L depends therefore on the market prices and rates on the two days, the change in time to expiry of each contract, and any changes in the position due to trading activity.

> Position, mark-to-market and P&L:
> *Position*: Aggregate of all physical and derivative commitments to buy or sell commodity.
> *Mark-to-market (MTM) value*: The value of the position according to a set of market prices and rates taken at one instant. The MTM value of the portfolio assumes that the entire portfolio could be liquidated instantly, to realise the value, without moving the market.
>
> (continued)

> *Daily P&L*: The difference in two consecutive trading days' mark-to-market values, showing the combined effects of position changes, changes in commodity and financial market prices and rates, and the passage of time. Daily P&L usually also contains cashflows for premium payments, deal settlements, and so on.

Portfolios have various sensitivities to commodity and financial market prices and rates, times to expiry of contracts, and potentially many other sources of risk. These sensitivities can be expressed as a number of dollars' change in the portfolio value for:

- a dollar move in energy prices at various maturities;
- a one-basis-point move in interest rates or FX rates; or
- one day of time elapsing.

Such sensitivities, and their equivalents for other sources of risk, provide a way of controlling the risk exposures in a portfolio, and afford management a further way to place controls on the activities of their portfolio managers and traders.

Since the mark-to-market value of a portfolio is valid only for the instant at which the market price and rate data are taken, it is natural for management and traders to query how much their portfolio could change over the coming days, weeks or months. Mark-to-market is only a static measure of the value of a portfolio, and doesn't provide any indication of where the portfolio value may go. While the portfolio P&L is a measure of changes in MTM, it is a purely backward-looking measure of the impact of market dynamics and trading activity on the portfolio.

Two common tools used in energy risk management for examining the likely P&L impact of future market movements are *value-at-risk* (VAR) *analysis* and *stress testing*. These complementary techniques are intended to address:

- *Value-at-risk*: What is the worst-case scenario, at a certain level of confidence, the portfolio is likely to suffer due to market movements over the next time period?
- *Stress testing*: What is the likely P&L impact of a historically significant or rare adverse market event?

VAR is a probabilistic measure of uncertainty of future portfolio MTM values, while stress testing is a scenario-based analysis on the portfolio, and can't necessarily be related to a probability of occurrence. These methods for assessing possible future portfolio P&Ls are examined in greater detail in the later chapter, "Wider Risk Management Questions".

Chapter Review and Look Ahead

In this chapter, readers were introduced to the notion of a commodity market position, and encountered their first trading jargon in the shape of long, short and flat positions. After a brief examination of the different forms and sources of market price data, and how market prices are quoted, the notion of market liquidity was defined, and the role of bid–offer spreads as a measure of this liquidity was considered.

When contractual commitments are held up to the market, their mark-to-market value may be calculated. The MTM is valid only for the instant at which the prices are taken, and is not a dynamic measure of portfolio value. Contracts evolve along a natural timeline from inception through physical delivery to financial settlement, and readers were introduced to contractual timeline diagrams, which will be used in later chapters. The notion of a commodity market contract being in-, at- or out-of-the-money as a result of market movements was introduced, and the daily P&L was defined as the difference of consecutive trading days' MTMs.

Mark-to-market values vary due both to changes in the portfolio composition and to their sensitivity to various market parameters, including prices, forcign-exchange rates, interest rates and remaining time to financial settlement of contracts. Techniques exist to assess the possible changes in portfolio MTM due to these sensitivities, and the subjects of VAR and stress testing have their own chapter devoted to them.

Management may wish to put limits on the sensitivity of their company's position to market events, and this may be achieved in a static sense using a system of position limits. A more active form of portfolio sensitivity management involves the use of contracts that offset MTM changes, reducing the variance in portfolio P&L; this is known as *hedging activity*, and forms the subject of the following chapters.

Technical Appendix: Interest Rates and Compounding Conventions

In this chapter and throughout the rest of the report we use the continuously compounding interest rate convention. This convention is standard in discussions of energy derivatives but may be unfamiliar to some readers; in this Technical Appendix I explain how the convention arises.

Interest rates are conventionally expressed in an annualised sense, but this is not enough to compute how much interest one might earn across a one-year period – it is also necessary to know what the compounding period is. We start by discussing the computation of interest across a one-year period, with annual compounding, with an annual risk-free interest rate of, say, 10%. If US$1000 is placed in a risk-free account at the start of the period, then after one year the account will hold

$$1000 \times \left(1 + \frac{10}{100}\right) \text{US\$} = 1000 \times 1.1 \text{ US\$}$$
$$= 1100 \text{ US\$}$$

If this total sum is left in the account and invested again at the risk-free rate of 10%, at the end of the second year the account will hold

$$1000 \times \left(1 + \frac{10}{100}\right) \times \left(1 + \frac{10}{100}\right) \text{US\$} = 1000 \times 1.1^2 \text{ US\$}$$
$$= 1210 \text{ US\$}$$

This compounding behaviour may be carried across multiple years, and it is easy to see that after N years of compounding at an annual rate of 10% the account will hold

$$1000 \times \left(1 + \frac{10}{100}\right)^N \text{ US\$}$$

More generally, an initial amount a invested in an account at a risk-free annually compounding interest rate of $p\%$ for N years will have turned into an amount

$$a \times \left(1 + \frac{p}{100}\right)^N$$

Suppose now that instead of compounding annually the sum invested accumulates interest every six months. If again the annual interest rate is 10% then the six-monthly, or semi-annual, compounding of interest means that the initial investment will earn 5% every half-year. After six months US$1000 will have turned into

$$1000 \times \left(1 + \frac{5}{100}\right) \text{ US\$} = 1000 \times \left(1 + \frac{10}{2} \cdot \frac{1}{100}\right) \text{ US\$}$$
$$= 1050 \text{ US\$}$$

and after one year it will have compounded twice, turning into

$$1000 \times \left(1 + \frac{10}{2} \cdot \frac{1}{100}\right) \times \left(1 + \frac{10}{2} \cdot \frac{1}{100}\right) = 1000 \times \left(1 + \frac{10}{2} \cdot \frac{1}{100}\right)^2 \text{ US\$}$$
$$= 1102.50 \text{ US\$}$$

In more general terms, an amount a invested at an annual percentage rate of $p\%$ with a compounding period of $1/m$ years will have turned into

$$a\left(1 + \frac{p}{100m}\right)^m$$

after one year, and

$$a\left(1 + \frac{p}{100m}\right)^{m \times N}$$

after N years.

The continuously compounding interest rate convention assumes that the compounding period is arbitrarily small, and that interest accumulates continuously, which arises from allowing m to become larger and larger without bound. The convention is used because the formula used for computation of compounded interest employs a standard mathematical function: the exponential function, e^x or $\exp(x)$. The mathematically inclined reader will have encountered the result

$$e^x = \lim_{m \to \infty} \left(1 + \frac{x}{m}\right)^m$$

Market Value of Physical and Financial Commitments

and the link with compounding interest rates should now be clear following the discussion above. A continuously compounding annual interest rate of $r\%$ will turn an initial amount a, after N years, into an amount

$$\lim_{m \to \infty} a\left(1 + \frac{p}{100m}\right)^{m \times N} = ae^{pN/100}$$

We will usually write interest rates as decimals, $r = 0.10$, rather than percentages, $p = 10\%$, and denote the number of years the investment is held by T, where T needn't be a whole number. So with this final change of notation we state that an initial amount a invested at a continuously compounded annual interest rate of r for T years will have turned into an amount

$$ae^{rT}$$

An advantage of using continuously compounding interest rates is the ease with which one can move between computations where interest is accumulated, to those where future values are discounted at the same rate of interest. Suppose a cashflow of US$1000 is due in two years' time, the annual continuously compounding interest rate over this period is 10%, and we wish to compute the present value, PV, of this future cashflow. This means we are seeking the quantity PV satisfying the equation

$$PV\,e^{2 \times 0.10} = 1000$$

Rearranging this equation yields the value

$$PV = e^{-2 \times 0.10} \times 1000$$
$$= 818.73(2\ \text{d.p.})$$

where the quantity $e^{-2 \times 0.10}$ is known as the discount factor. In general terms the present value of a cashflow P due at some time T years in the future, if continuously compounding interest rates are r, is

$$PV = e^{-rT}P$$

Notes

1 Readers should note that this example does not consider the role of any fuel in storage on the position limits. In the case where storage is available, management are likely to include the level of fuel in storage on the supply side of the position, and declare that fuel storage levels may not drop below a minimum level.
2 Note that the terms *backwardation* and *contango* refer only to forward prices. They do not refer to spot prices increasing or decreasing through time.
3 Similar in spirit to the dividend yield in equity markets.

4 Physical Transactions and Basic Hedging Instruments

Learn always

Physical Transactions

Preamble

In this section I introduce some simple examples of physical transactions for producers, consumers and transformers. Readers are assumed to be familiar with their own company's use of physical energy, and so no attempt is made to categorise or describe the wide range of actual production, consumption or transformative processes. Instead, this section is intended to introduce readers to the tools of financial block diagrams, P&L diagrams and P&L tables in describing transactions. The notations and conventions established here will be used freely throughout the remainder of the report, and it is essential that readers are comfortable with the concepts introduced.

Physical Producer

We start the discussion by considering a producer of physical crude oil selling their output to an off-taker at some floating market index that is denominated in US dollars per barrel (US$/bbl), and that we represent by the symbol f; whatever the market index, that's the price the off-taker pays. This may be represented in a financial block diagram as shown in Figure 5.

From the producer's perspective the P&L table for this transaction is that shown in Table 7, where we assume there are no other costs incurred by the producer in this transaction.

These data can be summarised using a P&L diagram as shown in Figure 6.

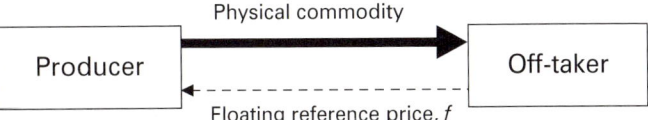

Figure 5. Physical producer floating reference block diagram

Table 7. Physical producer floating-reference P&L table

Market price index, f (US$/bbl)	...	30	40	50	...	80	...
Producer P&L (US$/bbl)	...	30	40	50	...	80	...

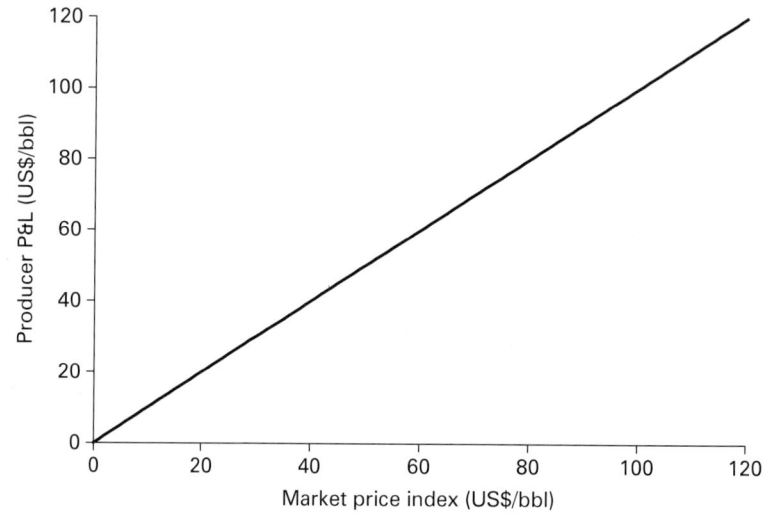

Figure 6. Physical producer floating-reference P&L diagram

Table 8. Physical producer fixed-price P&L table

Market price index, f (US$/bbl)	...	30	40	50	...	80	...
Producer P&L, F (US$/bbl)	...	50	50	50	...	50	...

In this situation, the producer wants prices to climb, the off-taker wants prices to drop, and neither player knows where the market index will be on delivery day.

Suppose now that rather than paying a floating market index the producer and off-taker have agreed some fixed price per barrel for the production. The block diagram, P&L table and P&L diagram now all need to be changed to reflect this new fixed price; the new block diagram in Figure 7 now shows the fixed price per barrel F, as do the P&L table in Table 8 and the corresponding P&L diagram in Figure 8.

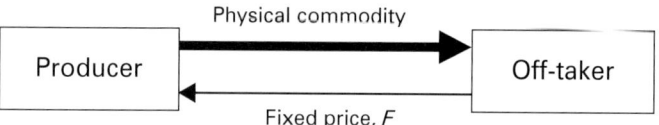

Figure 7. Physical producer fixed price block diagram

Physical Consumer

The illustrations and tables for a physical consumer naturally resemble those seen above in the producer example, though with costs rather than incomes arising from the commodity flow. We consider the case of an industrial consumer buying electricity in continental Europe at a floating market index priced in euros per megawatt hour (€/MWh), and represent this case in Figure 9.

Figure 8. Physical producer fixed-price P&L diagram

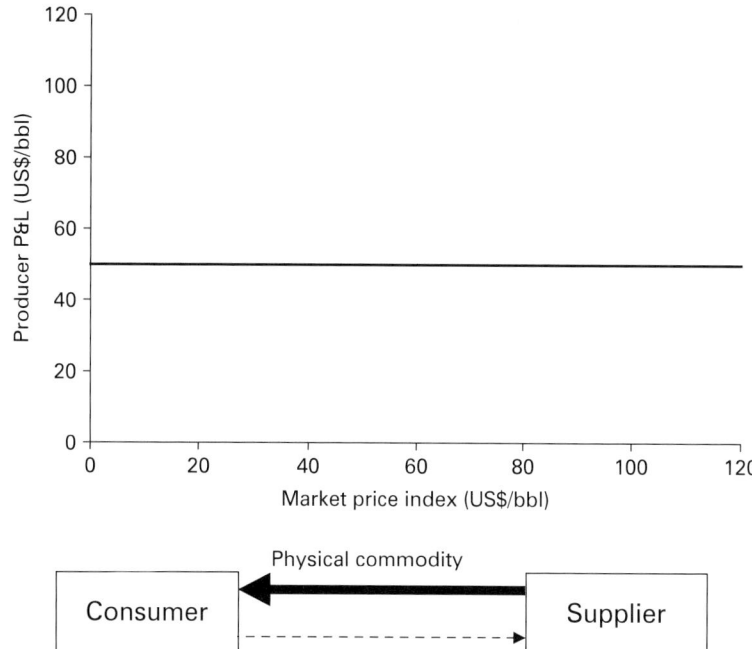

Figure 9. Physical consumer floating-price block diagram

How do the P&L table and P&L diagram look for the case of a physical consumer paying a floating-reference price?

Where previous discussions make the contents of the P&L table clear we may omit it and use the P&L diagram alone. For the power consumer we have the P&L diagram in Figure 10.

Figure 10. Physical consumer floating-price P&L diagram

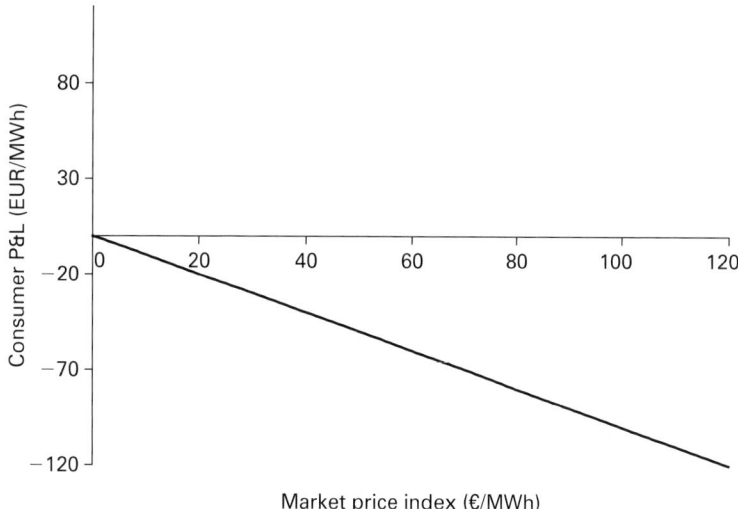

A physical consumer who has negotiated a fixed priced physical supply at, say, €30/MWh (represented in Figure 11) will have the P&L diagram in Figure 12.

Figure 11. Physical consumer fixed-priced block diagram

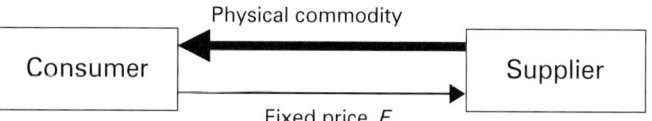

Figure 12. Physical consumer fixed-price P&L diagarm

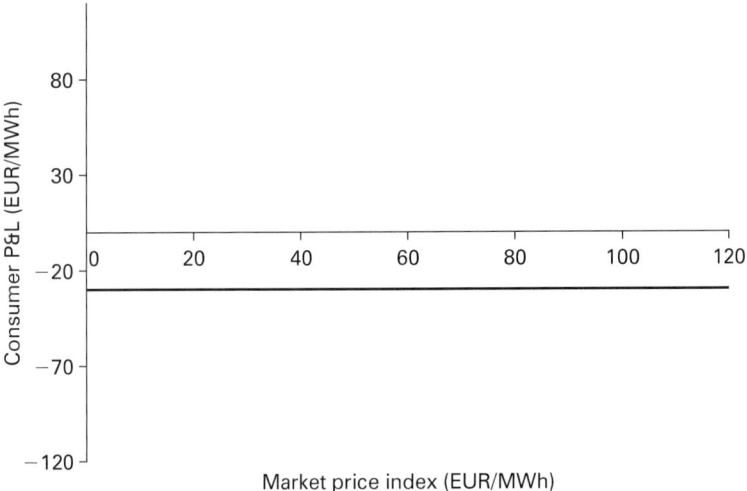

Physical Transformer

A physical transformer is exposed to at least two different commodity flows, and needs to account for the efficiency of their processes and internal costs, as well as market price dynamics, in running their processes. Having given explicit examples of floating- and fixed-price payments for the simpler producer and consumer cases above, we now consider only floating-price payments for the present example of an oil refiner.

We assume that the refiner is buying crude oil at some floating reference price, f US$/bbl, and producing a basket of oil products, which they sell to an off-taker and for which they are receiving a total floating price of g US$/bbl. We assume that the cost of processing each barrel of crude oil is some fixed amount C US$/bbl, and that there are no production losses. Every barrel in is converted into a barrel out.

> Draw the block diagram corresponding to this example. Don't forget to represent the production costs!

This refining example may be visualised as shown in Figure 13.

Understanding the P&L for the refiner is more challenging than for the producers and consumers above, since the transformer is exposed to two different price indexes in this simplified example: that for the crude oil input, and that for the basket of products.

> Draw the P&L table and diagram for this case of an oil refiner. Assume that the fixed production costs are US$2/bbl, and consider both crude and basket index prices between US$30/bbl and US$70/bbl.

To draw the P&L table we need to combine the crude and fixed production costs, $f + C$, and tabulate them against the basket prices, g. An example of such a table is shown in Table 9.

The corresponding P&L diagram probably less useful, and certainly less easy to draw, than the table since it is now in three dimensions, as shown in Figure 14.

Physical Transactions and Basic Hedging Instruments

Figure 13. Physical transformer floating-index block diagarm

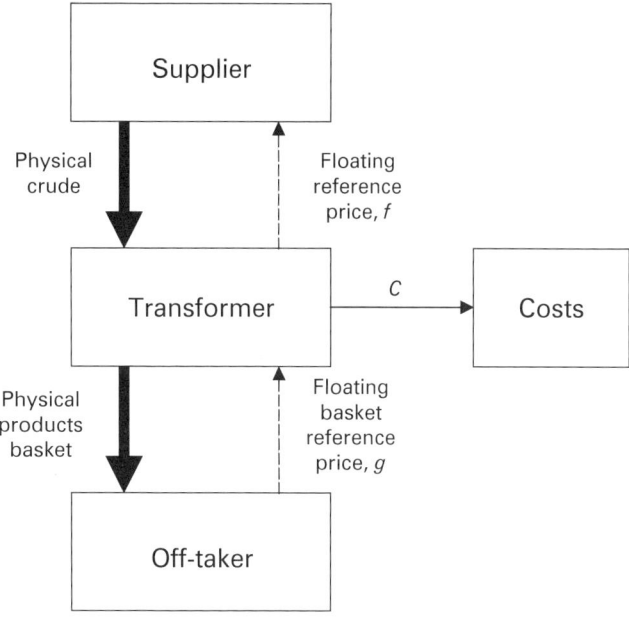

Table 9. Physical transformer P&L table

Refiner P&L (US$/bbl)							
	Crude oil price, f (US$/bbl)	...	30	40	50	60	70 ...
	Costs, C (US$/bbl)	...	2	2	2	2	2 ...
	Total costs (US$/bbl)	...	**32**	**42**	**52**	**62**	**72** ...
Basket price, g (US$/bbl)	...						
30		...	−2	−12	−22	−32	−42 ...
40			8	−2	−12	−22	−32
50			18	8	−2	−12	−22
60			28	18	8	−2	−12
70			38	28	18	8	−2
...							

Figure 14. Physical transformer P&L diagram

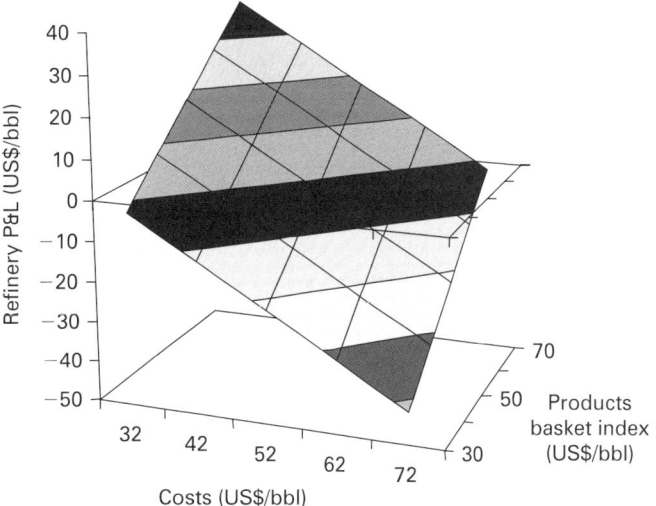

Risk Analysis

The discussion of physical transactions above has now exposed the reader to some of the tools we'll employ in this report for understanding risks, namely block diagrams, P&L tables and P&L diagrams. The simple cases we've examined so far already allow us to hold our risk matrix up against these transactions and ask the simple question, 'What could go wrong?' Let's do this for the floating index physical producer example.

Figure 15. Physical producer example, floating index, with lifted volumes

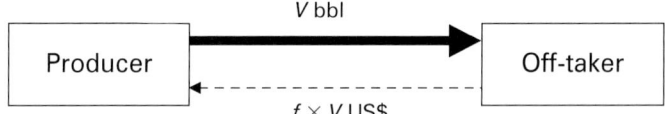

Table 10. Relevant risks to the producer example

Risk	Description
Currency	Exposure to uncertainty in currency exchange rates
Force majeure	Exposure to an unforeseen or rare event for which there is no contractual mitigation
Commodity market	Exposure to uncertain market prices, volatilities or correlations
Proxy	Exposure to imperfect matches between a hedge and the exposure being hedged
Technical	Risk that a physical asset's performance makes one unable to meet delivery obligations, or fully realise the apparent optionality inherent in the asset
Volumetric	Risk arising from changes in the volume of commodity supply or consumption

In the physical producer example shown in Figure 5, we assume that we are a producer supplying crude oil to an off-taker, for which we are being paid a floating market index f. We now assume that the transaction refers to a specific day, and refine the block diagram to incorporate the volume of crude oil being lifted by the off-taker on that day, as shown in Figure 15.

Looking again at the most relevant risks shown in Table 10, we can see immediately that there is commodity market risk: we are receiving a floating market index, f, and we have no idea what that will be until after the price fixings are published. The other risks require a little more thought before we are able to address them.

The presence or absence of the other risks requires specific knowledge about the physical off-take contract, the company's accounting currency, and so on. We address these risks in Table 11.

With our current knowledge of the arrangements we can state with certainty only that market risk is present.

> If commodity market risk is present, what must be done about it?

This question addresses the producer's risk policy. They may decide that they wish to be exposed to floating market prices since this is what their investors desire. In this case the producer may make the active decision to do nothing, and leave themselves unhedged. Other questions of why, when and how to hedge are left until later.

> Doing nothing as an active risk management decision:
> In risk management doing nothing *is* an active decision, provided the implications of this decision are well understood, and the company's stakeholders are in agreement with this policy.

Physical Transactions and Basic Hedging Instruments

Table 11. Risk analysis for physical crude production example

Risk	Assessment
Currency	Not present. We assume the producer is happy to receive payments in US$, and that this is consistent with their accounting
Force majeure	Contract-dependent. Does the contract allow for *force majeure* events? Do the producer and the off-taker agree on what constitutes such an event? Are the modifications to the arrangements in such an event clear and acceptable to both parties?
Commodity market	Present. Payment based upon floating market index that isn't known ahead of time
Proxy	Not present. No hedging being carried out in this example
Technical	Contract-dependent. Does the contract allow for technical outages forcing short-term stoppages in production? Are there limits to the number of such outages that are acceptable? Is the point at which *force majeure* is invoked clear, and its relationship to technical outages well defined?
Volumetric	Contract-dependent. Does the contract allow for variability in the volumes supplied or lifted? Does the payment follow the actual volume delivered barrel by barrel? What limits on variability are there? In case of undersupply, oversupply, underlifting or overlifting, whose responsibility is it to make up or take the volume difference?

Figure 16. Technical failure event, no supply

The other risks can be understood as modifications to the arrows present in Figure 15, with their attendant financial and physical impacts. We now consider a few simple scenarios, proposing what the impact of specific contractual terms would be.

We first consider the case of a technical production failure, and suppose that the off-take agreement requires that we as the producer provide exactly the contractual volume of V barrels every day without failure. In the case of this technical failure event our physical supply arrow disappears from the block diagram, as shown in Figure 16.

Since the contract requires us to provide V barrels of oil per day without failure, it is for us to source these barrels in the spot market to prevent breach of contract. We assume that this is possible, and that the cost per barrel is g dollars. This new situation is as shown in Figure 17.

We can now see the financial implication of such a physical event: the need to source the volume from the spot market will expose us to two different sources of market price risk. The original market index, f, is still present, but so too is the new spot market price g, which may be quite different from f. This sort of short-term physical supply optimisation in the face of technical

Figure 17. Technical failure event, physical supply sourced from the spot market

Figure 18. *Force majeure* event, accounted for in contract

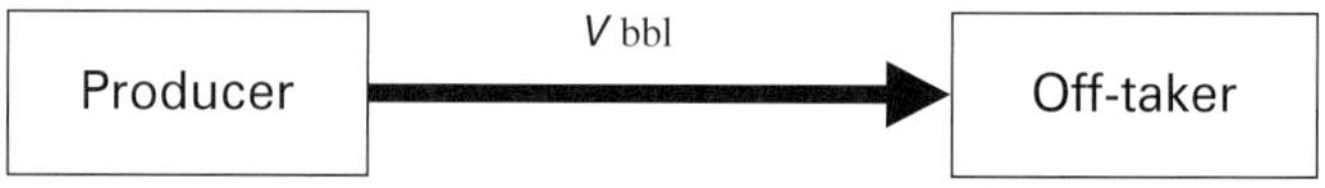

Figure 19. Producer risk event: which one is it?

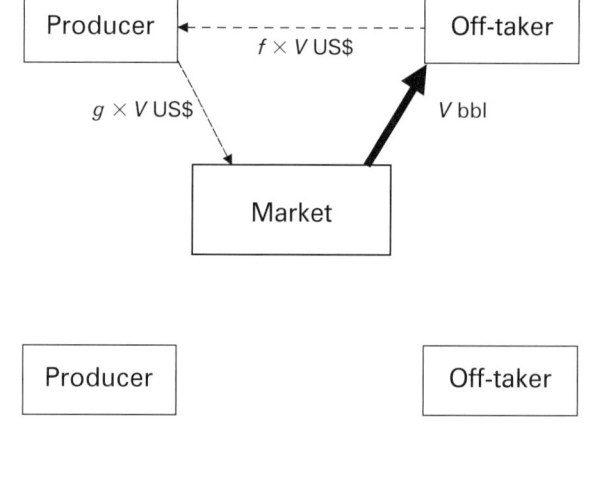

(and volumetric) risk events with respect to varying spot prices is one of the main activities of the trading floor in a company engaging in asset-backed trading.

Suppose now that there is a *force majeure* event: perhaps a major tropical storm has hit oil production and lifting facilities in the area where the physical supply contract was based. We assume that the contract contains *force majeure* clauses that account for such an event, and that in this case no volumes are due to the off-taker, and no payment will be made for the normal lifted volume. In this case we have the situation in Figure 18.

Here we are satisfied that we needn't carry out any market transactions to prevent breach of contract, we keep our volumes until the *force majeure* event has passed, and no payment is received from the off-taker.

This method of modifying arrows in block diagrams can also be used to reveal risks other than those in our reduced risk matrix in Table 11. Consider the block diagram in Figure 19.

> What risk is this?

In this case, while we have provided the contractual volume of V barrels to the off-taker, they have not paid us as agreed. This is a counterparty credit-default event, further analysis of which is outside the scope of this guide.

The risk analyses presented above form part of the responsibilities of a company's risk management and/or structuring function, and correspond to the initial steps in designing a risk management programme: identification and quantification. Having identified the risks present in an activity it is then necessary to define the company's appetite for such risks, and if appropriate implement some sort of risk control framework. We have already seen that doing nothing can be an active decision if the risks are well understood, and we turn now to some of the simplest, but most widely used, examples of risk management instruments in the physical markets: futures and forwards.

Figure 20. Futures contractual timeline

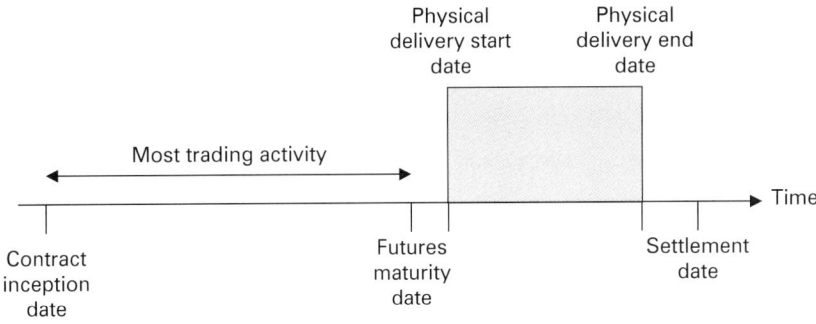

Figure 21. Flows at futures inception

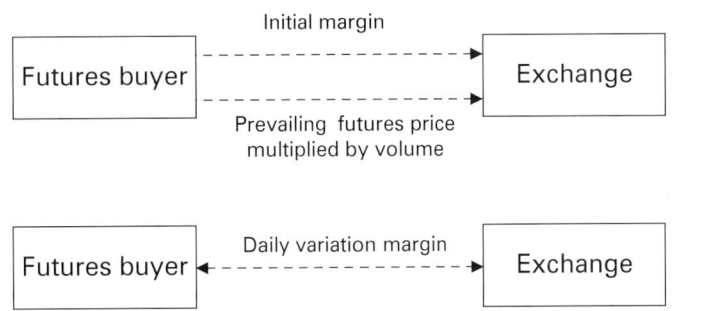

Figure 22. Daily marking to market of futures position

Physical Futures and Forwards

Futures Contracts

Energy futures contracts are commodity contracts traded on organised exchanges such as the NYMEX and the IPE. They are highly standardised contracts for physical delivery at some pre-agreed "strike" price, location, quality/grade, delivered over a defined period of time at a regular rate and so forth, and their degree of standardisation means that futures contracts are available on relatively few underlyings.

Despite their physical underlyings, futures contracts tend *not* to be used to receive physical commodity, but because their daily price variations track some physical commodity market price and can therefore be used in hedging; the majority of futures contracts are in fact "closed out" before physical delivery commences. Closing out a long futures contract, for example for September delivery, involves selling back to the exchange the same volume of commodity for September that was previously bought before the September contract matures some time in mid-August. The contractual timeline for a futures contract is shown in Figure 20, and the time period during which most trading activity is conducted as indicated.

Selling back the September volumes means that the physical position is net flat, and the profit or loss realised from the opening, then subsequent closing, of the September futures positions can be used to offset the price changes in some other transaction; that is, the futures have been used for hedging purposes.

On the contract inception date the buyer of a futures contract pays the exchange the prevailing futures price for the volume they are purchasing, together with an initial security margin that the exchange holds on account. This transaction is represented in the block diagram in Figure 21.

The exchange carries out a daily marking to market of all futures positions, and each day the profit or loss due to price variations is computed, and a variation margin payment is made, as indicated in Figure 22. This payment could be from the buyer to the exchange (if prices have risen), or vice versa if prices have dropped.

Figure 23. Closing of futures position

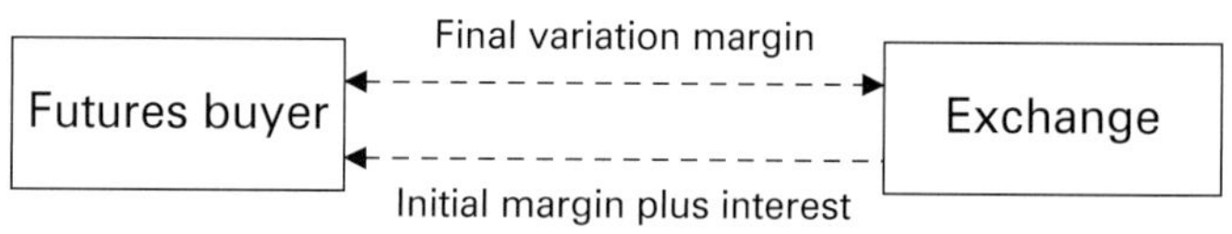

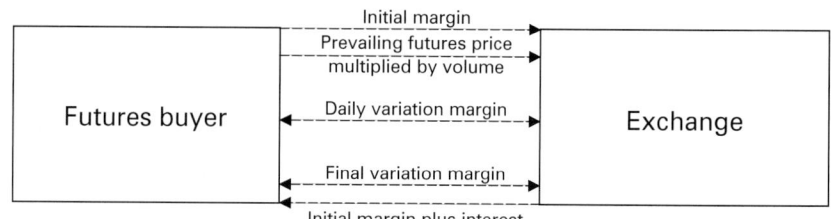

Table 12. Futures margining example

Date	Futures price (US$/bbl)	Payment made to/from exchange (US$)	Sum of payments (US$)
1 June	58.00	Initial margin (IM) + 580000	580000 + IM
2 June	58.50	5000	585000 + IM
3 June	58.75	2500	587500 + IM
4 June	57.75	−10000	577500 + IM
...	...	...	...
30 June	61.02	−(IM + interest) + final variation margin	610200

Figure 24. Futures cashflows summary, closing out before contract maturity

Finally, on closing out the position, a final variation margin payment is made, and the exchange returns the initial security margin payment with interest, as shown in Figure 23.

Example

Suppose that on 1 June a futures buyer buys 10000 barrels of Brent crude oil on the IPE for September delivery, at an initial price of US$58/bbl (fictitious prices are used in this example, and we consider only exchange open days). They will pay the exchange the initial security margin, plus US$580000 for the futures contract (580000 = 58.00 × 10000), as shown in the first line of Table 12. As each day passes (shown in Column 1), and the prices change (Column 2), the daily variation margin payments due to the exchange are computed and shown in Column 3. The sum of all variation margin transactions is shown in Column 4, which is in fact the mark-to-market value of the futures contract at the prevailing market price.

The profit-and-loss account from this set of transactions is (US$610200 − US$580000) US$ = US$30200, or US$3.02 per barrel, which is of course the price change in IPE Brent crude oil for September delivery between the 1 June and 30 June (see the Technical Appendix "Futures margining" for a further explanation of daily variation margining).

The various diagrams employed in Figures 20 to 23 provide two different views of the flows involved in a contract in more detail than would be necessary for someone familiar with their use. The contractual timeline shows clearly the flow of time and, when events occur relative to each other, while the subsequent block diagrams are each snapshots of a specific point in time, and give detail on the cashflows occurring at that time. It is common to use a single block diagram to summarise all cashflows through all points in time once the flows are understood; in Figure 24 we summarise the cashflows for a futures contract closed out before expiry.

Figure 25. Futures contract block diagram with physical delivery

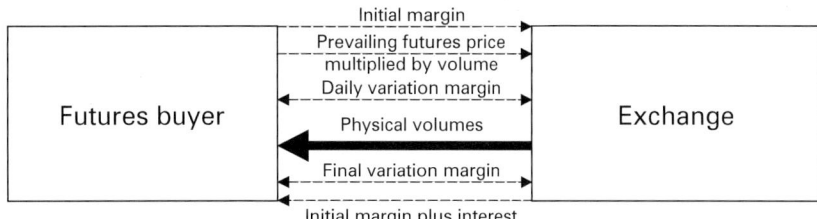

Figure 26. Futures P&L diagram

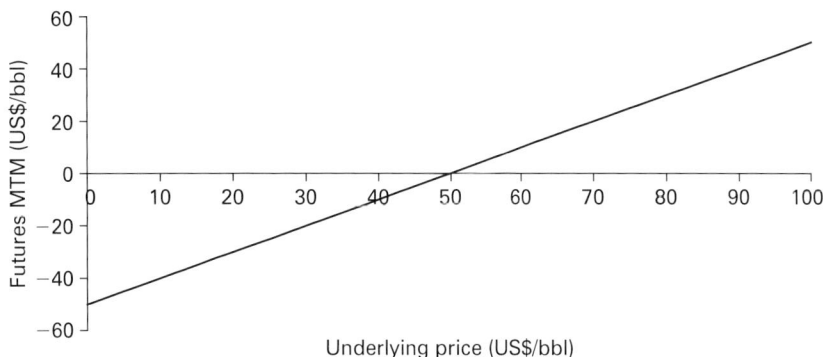

In the case where the futures contract is allowed to expire and the buyer is obligated to take physical delivery, the exchange continues to use a stream of daily variation margins through the physical delivery period. In this case the corresponding block diagram is shown in Figure 25.

As the example above shows the sum of the variation margins paid for a futures contract give the mark-to-market value of the futures position; they give the difference between the agreed "strike" price fixed for the futures contract at inception and the current market value of the same contract. The mark-to-market value of a futures contract may be summarised using a P&L diagram, such as that in Figure 26, which demonstrates the mark-to-market value of a Brent futures contract struck at US$50/bbl.

Futures contracts are used primarily as hedging instruments, rather than for taking physical delivery. The basic principle of hedging is that one takes a derivative position that is intended to offset the cashflows from a physical spot market position. In the case of futures contracts, hedgers expect the futures contracts to act as a hedge to the spot prices in the delivery month, and rely on this correlation. While realised spot prices in a given month may turn out to be different from the expired futures price[1] the risk is considered to be lower than going into the month unhedged or "naked". The imperfection of such hedges is known as *basis* or *proxy* risk, and is an important practical consideration in energy price risk management.

Example: North Sea Oil Producer Futures Hedge

Suppose that in February a North Sea oil producer has agreed to sell its July production of 10000 barrels of Brent-grade crude to a counterparty for the July posted price. This price will be posted on (say) 1 July, the futures market is currently around the US$50/bbl mark, and the producer is concerned about falling crude prices.

The producer may go to the exchange-traded futures market and seek the contract that best matches this price exposure. Since the July price will be posted on 1 July, it chooses to use the August futures contract, which expires in July. The producer therefore sells 10 lots (where 1 lot = 1000

Figure 27. Oil producer futures hedge

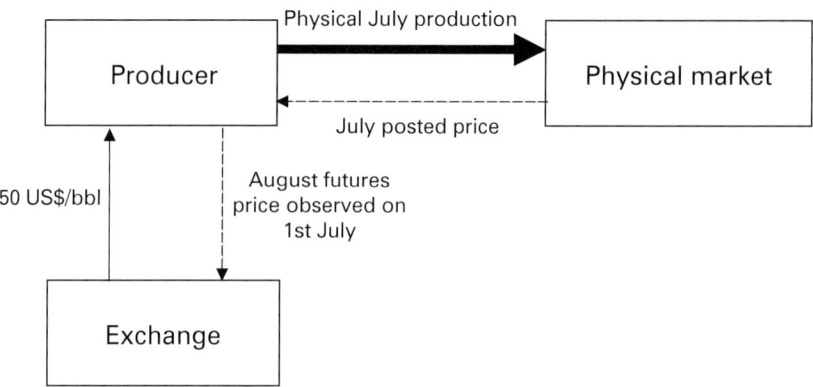

barrels) of August futures, and plans to liquidate this position on 1 July, when the July price posting is made; any deviation in the July posting between February and 1 July is expected to be cancelled by movements in the August futures contract. On closing the futures position, the net effect of daily margining is that the producer will receive US$50/bbl, and will pay the prevailing futures price at the time of closing out. The block diagram representing these transactions is shown in Figure 27.

In all cases the oil producer delivers their July physical oil production, and receives

US$ 50/bbl + July posted price − Aug futures price observed on 1st July

Let's see how this might work numerically:

- Case 1: Price decrease. Suppose that on 1 July the July price is posted as 47.25, and the August futures contract price is US$47.85/bbl. The August futures position is bought back at this level, and the producer receives

    47.25 US$/bbl + 50 US$/bbl − 47.85 US$/bbl = 49.40 US$/bbl

    This is near the US$50/bbl level they had intended to lock in with the futures, and the proxy risk will cost them US$6000, far less than the decline in prices from US$50/bbl to US$47.25/bbl.

- Case 2: Price increase. Suppose that on 1 July the price is posted as US$53.10/bbl, and the August futures price is US$53.90/bbl on this date. The August futures position is closed out, and the producer now receives

    53.10 US$/bbl + 50 US$/bbl − 53.90 US$/bbl = 49.20 US$/bbl

    Again this is close to US$50/bbl, and this time the proxy risk costs the producer US$8000.

Similar examples can, of course, be produced for energy consumers or transformers.

The liquidity and transparency provided by exchange-based futures trading means that high volumes of futures tend to trade. They also form an important part of much of the over-the-counter (OTC) bilateral and brokered markets, since many other commodities are priced at a "basis" to these

Physical Transactions and Basic Hedging Instruments

standardised commodity prices, and many types of OTC contracts (average priced options for example) settle on exchange settlement prices. Futures contracts carry no counterparty credit risk since the exchange acts as the counterparty to each transaction, making futures markets a safe place to transact from a credit perspective.

A special terminology exists to describe the maturity of futures contracts. The future with the nearest expiry date is called the *front line*, *first line* or *first nearby* contract, with subsequent contracts called the *second line*, *second nearby*, and so on.

Example: Futures Contract Expiries and Nearby Contracts

Brent crude oil futures contracts trading on the IPE typically expire around the middle of the month preceding the delivery period. At the time of writing the expiries for the 2006 Brent futures contracts were as shown in Table 13.

Thus, in early December 2005 the front line, or first nearby, contract is the January 2006 future; in the second half of that month the first nearby becomes the February 2006 contract; and so on.

The disadvantages of futures markets tend to lie in the fact that the high level of standardisation of their contracts means that the exposure being hedged may not precisely match the quality, location, timing (futures contracts are for a calendar month of delivery) or standardised lot sizes (volumes) available in the futures contracts. In such cases a hedger using futures would be exposed to proxy risk since the futures contract would be used as a proxy for a different physical market exposure that may not perfectly track the price of the standardised futures commodity. This proxy risk exposure could be avoided by going to the OTC markets, and buying a more tailored contract such as a forward (for physical delivery) or a swap (as a pure financial hedge).

Forward Contracts

A forward contract is the OTC cousin of a futures contract. Like futures, forwards are contracts for physical delivery at some pre-agreed "strike" price, location, quality and so on, though since they are OTC they can be tailored with a suitable counterparty to any quality, quantity, location, settlement date, etc. Forward contracts themselves don't require that any daily variation margins be paid due to daily marking to market,[2] and counterparty credit risk exists since these contracts are agreed bilaterally by a mutual agreement to deliver the commodity and make payment on the settlement date.

The complete contractual timeline for a forward contract is shown in Figure 28, with the corresponding block diagram in Figure 29.

If a forward contract is used to make or take delivery of the underlying commodity, then it has eliminated market price risk by locking in the price for the physical commodity. A long forward contract can effectively be

Table 13. IPE Brent futures contract expiries

Delivery month	Expiry date
January 2006	15 December 2005
February 2006	16 January 2006
March 2006	13 February 2006
April 2006	16 March 2006
...	...

Figure 28. Forward contract timeline

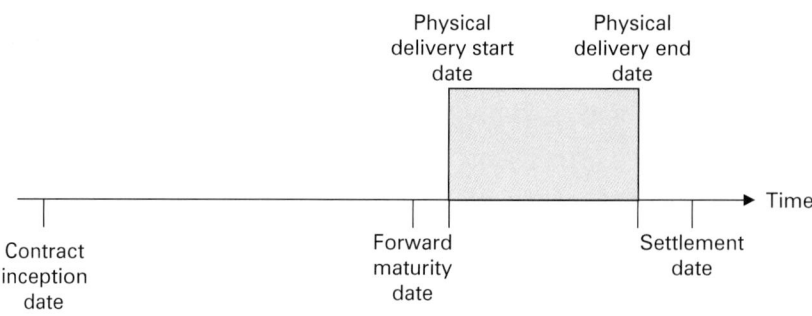

Figure 29. Forward contract block diagram

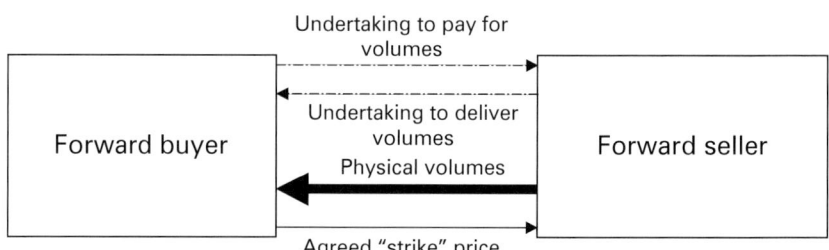

Figure 30. Opening, then subsequent closing, of forward contract of hedging purposes

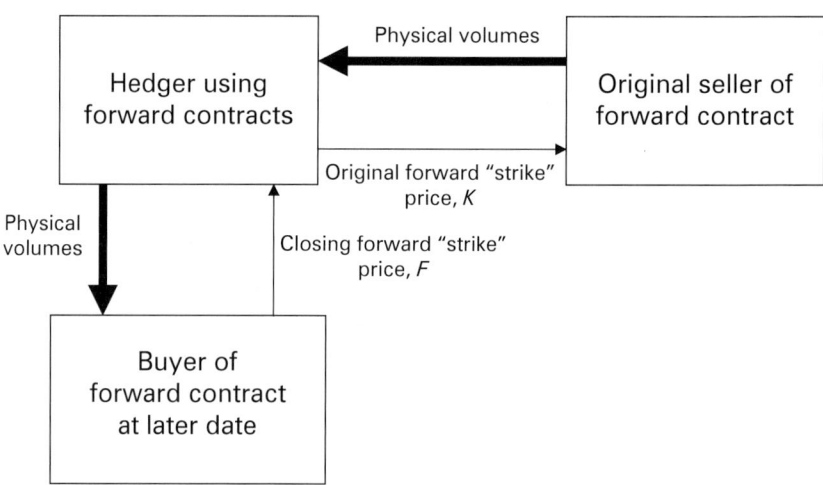

"closed out" by selling a contract for the same physical specification, location, volume and month before physical delivery commences; the mark-to-market value of a forward contract tells us the value of doing so at the current market level. Note that in closing out forward contracts the closing transaction may be with a different counterparty from that of the original opening transaction, in contrast with futures contracts, in which the counterparty is always the exchange. This situation is shown in Figure 30.

The profit realised by such a pair of transactions realises a profit of $F - K$ at settlement of the pair of contracts. In some cases it may be possible to replace the original hedging counterparty in the first forward contract executed with the new buyer in a process called *novation*. In this situation, physical delivery is made directly from the original seller of the forward to the new buyer of the forward, leaving the hedger with no need to schedule the physical flows.

How does a P&L diagram look for a forward contract?

Figure 31. Forward contract P&L diagram, at expiry, and present value

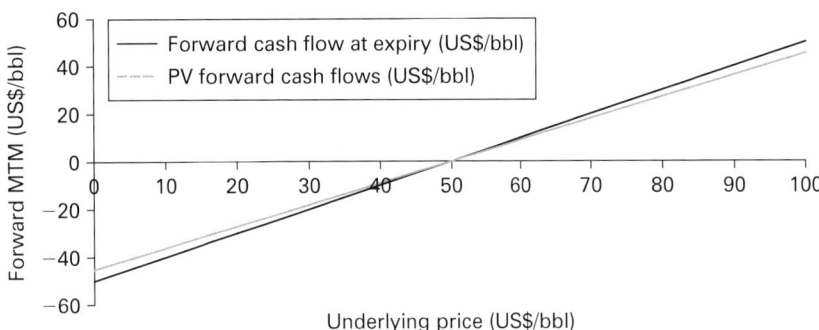

The mark-to-market value of a forward contract on settlement is the same as that for a futures contract, though since the only cashflows due for OTC forward transactions are at expiry we may also show the present value, discounted at the risk-free interest rate, of this future cashflow. The P&L at expiry, and before expiry, are shown in Figure 31.

Fixed-for-Floating Swaps

Swaps contracts are purely paper financial-style OTC transactions in which one cashflow stream is exchanged for another, with no expectation or possibility of physical delivery. The most common types of swap, which we'll examine first, are so-called *fixed-for-floating swaps*, in which regular payments of some agreed floating market index are exchanged for regular payments of a fixed quantity over the term of the contract.[3] Conventionally, only the difference between the two cashflow streams is exchanged at each settlement.

In agreeing a swap contract the two counterparties agree:

- which price index will be used for the floating cashflow stream, or *floating leg*, of the contract;
- which term of contract, and when it should commence;
- on which notional volumes the payments are to be computed; these volumes may differ across the contractual period, but will be agreed at inception of the contract;
- what fixed price will be exchanged for these floating cashflows, known as the *fixed leg* of the contract;
- how frequently settlement occurs (typically every month, quarter or year); and
- when these settlements should occur (eg, the fifth banking day of the month following the pricing period).

Conventionally we consider that the *buyer of a swap* is the party who receives the floating leg and pays the fixed leg of the contract, as shown in Figure 32.

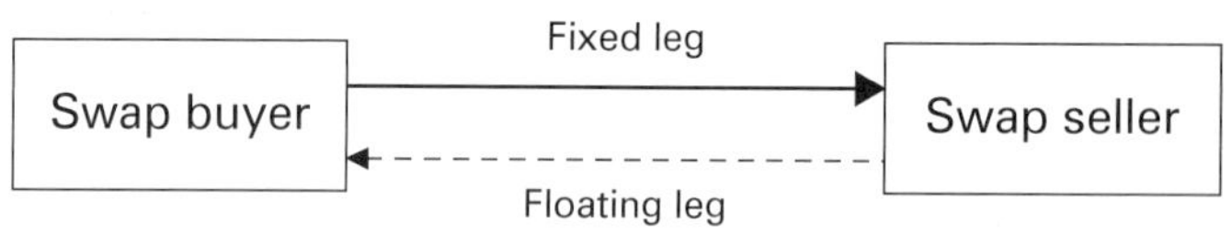

Figure 32. Fixed-for-floating swap block diagram

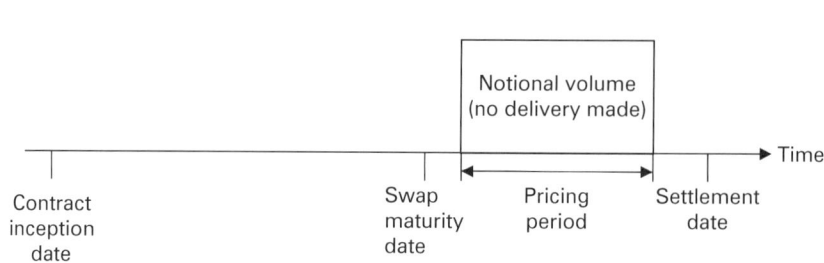

Figure 33. Monthly average price swap contractual timeline

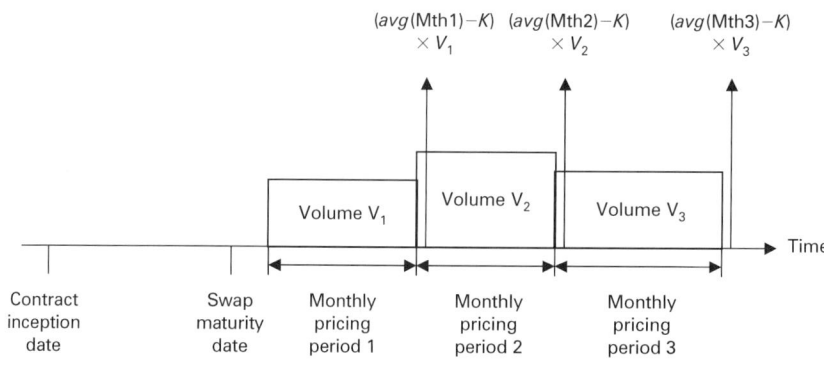

Figure 34. Variable volume swap

For the rest of this section we'll examine *monthly average price swaps*, in which the floating leg of the swap contract is based on the average of a month's index prices. These index prices will typically be either a standard industry benchmark price (eg, a Platts index), or the front-line futures contract from an exchange. The month over which the average is computing is called the *pricing period*, with the settlement cashflow occurring in the month following this period, as illustrated in Figure 33.

Example

Suppose a US power consumer buys a fixed-for-floating monthly average price swap from a power trader for baseload delivery of power during the month of February, agreeing a notional volume of 67200 MWh. The consumer and the trader agree a fixed price of US$40/ MWh, and agree the settlement date as 10 March.

On the first day of March the monthly average baseload power price is computed, and the average is found to be US$38.23/MWh. On 10 March the power consumer will pay a cashflow equivalent to (40.00 − 38.23) US$/MWh for each MWh of notional volume. They thus pay a total of US$118944 to the trader.

A swap contract may be negotiated for differing monthly volumes, though the contractual "strike" price chosen will be a fixed amount for all months of the swap. Figure 34 shows an example of a three-month swap, in which the buyer pays some fixed amount K per unit volume in exchange for the average of a monthly floating price index $avg(\text{Mth})$.

> How can a swap be used to hedge a physical supply agreement in which the supply is based upon a floating index? Draw an appropriate block diagram.

Figure 35. Long swap as hedge to physical supply contract

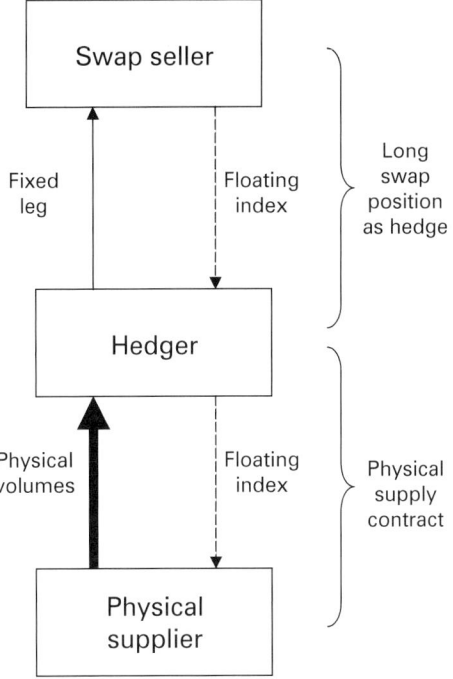

One of the most common uses of a fixed-for-floating swap contract is its use as a hedge against some commitment to buy or sell commodity on some floating price index: a swap is bought or sold in such a way that the floating leg cancels the expected variable cashflows of a physical contract. This is shown in Figure 35, where a purchaser of physical commodity on some floating price index buys a swap to hedge this floating position.

Example: Gasoline Reseller Hedge

Suppose a gasoline reseller has a physical supply contract in place to purchase unleaded gasoline during the months April, May and June, at the floating NYMEX unleaded gasoline front-line contract price, as summarised in Table 14.

Table 14. Gasoline purchasing commitment

Delivery month	Volume (gals)
April	420000
May	504000
June	504000

The reseller's expected costs for this gasoline fluctuate minute by minute in the traded markets, and so they elect to hedge these cashflows using a NYMEX gasoline front-line lookalike swap. The reseller contacts a range of institutions, and the best quotation they receive for the swap price at these volumes is US$1.70/gal.

After the months have passed, and the monthly averages have been computed, the prices on which settlement will be based are known. The cashflows with the physical supplier and the swap counterparty are shown in Table 15.

In this case the floating swap payments have cancelled the floating commitments of the gasoline supply contract, fixing the gasoline price at 1.70 US$/gal.

Table 15. Example gasoline hedge with swap

Delivery month	Volume (gals)	NYMEX front-line average price (US$/gal)	Paid to physical supplier (US$)	Paid to swap seller (US$)	Net (US$)
April	420000	1.68	1.68 × 420000	(1.70 − 1.68) × 420000	1.70 × 420000
May	504000	1.71	1.71 × 504000	(1.70 − 1.71) × 504000	1.70 × 504000
June	504000	1.78	1.78 × 504000	(1.70 − 1.78) × 504000	1.70 × 504000

Figure 36. Basic block diagram notation

> Notation in block diagrams:
>
> Many discussions of structured hedging transactions are simplified through the use of *block diagrams*. These diagrams show the *entities* involved in a transaction, which may be companies, departments within a company, or trading desks, or some notional source or sink of cash. Entities are represented by boxes with the entity's name written in each box. *Physical flows* of commodity between entities are represented by large solid arrows in the direction of the flow. These arrows may be annotated with the name of the commodity, or an indication of the total volume or rate of flow. *Fixed cashflows* between entities are represented by simple arrows with unbroken lines, while variable or *floating cashflows*, usually representing a sale or purchase at a market price index are presented by arrows with broken lines.
>
>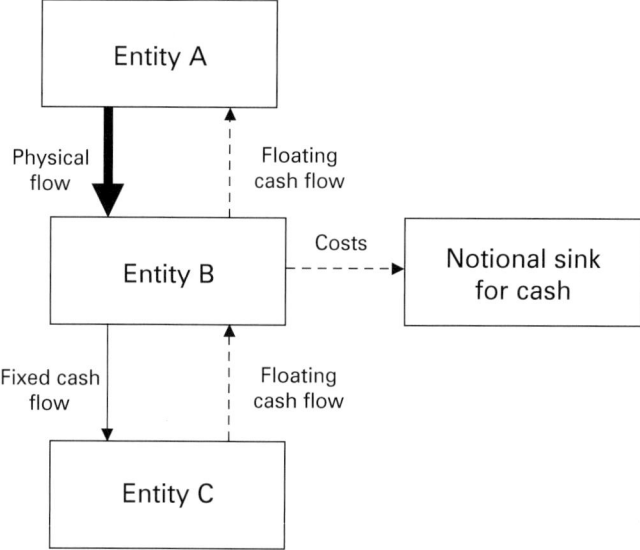
>
> The principal disadvantage of block diagrams (see Figure 36, eg) is their inability to show the time ordering of the flows; this may be circumvented by extensive annotation, or through using a series of diagrams, each corresponding to a different phase of the contractual arrangements.

Example: Refined Products Purchasing

Refined Products Company (RefPCo) negotiates gasoil purchases from a European refiner at fixed prices throughout the year, and sells the commodity into the Mediterranean market. RefPCo's sales into the market are priced off a monthly average Platts Med gasoil reference, and so RefPCo needs

Figure 37. RefPCo physical purchases, sales and costs

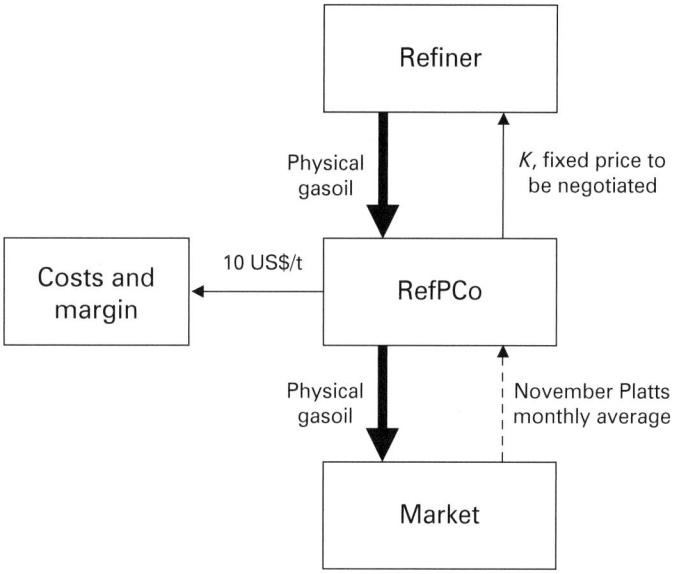

Table 16. RefPCo unhedged cashflows

Income	Expenditure
November average Platts GO 0.2% FOB Med, in US$/t	US$10/t costs US$$K$/t refiner's charge

to determine what will be an economic price to pay the refiner for the commodity.

Suppose that RefPCo is negotiating a fixed-price purchase of commodity that the refiner will be delivering in mid-October, and that RefPCo will sell into the market at the November Platts average. RefPCo's estimated costs plus profit margin needed amount to US$10/t, and they need to determine whether the fixed price for the commodity demanded by the refiner is economic. The situation is expressed in Figure 37.

Examination of Figure 37 shows that RefPCo's cashflows (ignoring discounting effects) are those in Table 16.

Written arithmetically the profit to RefPCo is

$$\text{Nov Platts average US\$/t} - 10 \text{ US\$/t} - K \text{ US\$/t}$$

Clearly RefPCo's cashflows are uncertain since in October the average November Platts fixing is completely unknown.

The refiner demands US$480/t for October delivery gasoil, and so RefPCo goes to the paper swaps market to determine the current November Platts gasoil Med price. The best price they are quoted is US$500/t, which they will choose to lock in if the refiner's demand of US$480/t is economic. The hedged situation is represented in Figure 38.

The cashflows through RefPCo are now indicated in Table 17, if the swap contract is in place.

Written arithmetically the profit to RefPCo would now be a locked in value of

$$\text{Nov Platts average} - 10 \text{ US\$/t} - 480 \text{ US\$/t}$$
$$+ 500 \text{ US\$/t} - \text{Nov Platts average} = 10 \text{ US\$/t}$$

This is positive, and therefore RefPCo concludes that the refiner's price is economic and agrees to transact at a level of US$480/t.

Figure 38. RefPCo's hedged cashflows

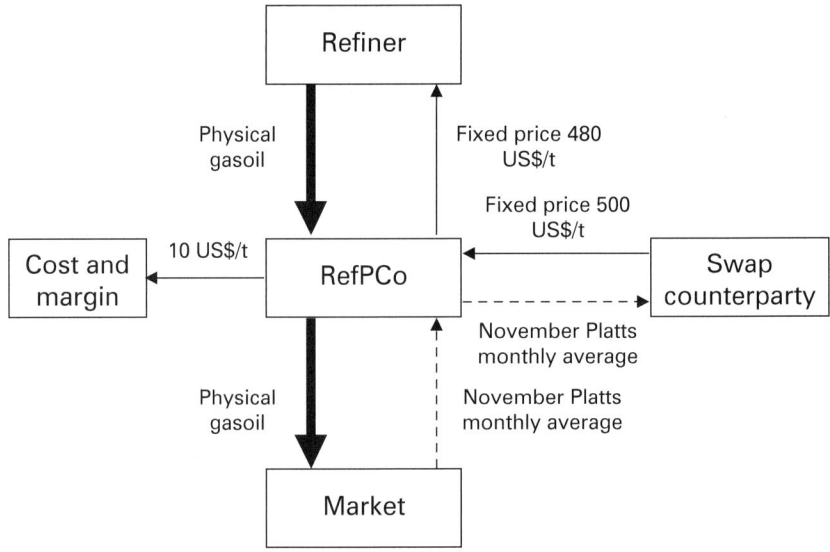

Table 17. RefPCo hedged cashflows

Income	Expenditure
November average Platts GO 0.2% FOB Med	US$10/t costs
Fixed price US$500/t	US$$K$/t refiner's charge
	November average Platts GO 0.2% FOB Med

Since there is no need to have the scheduling or logistical expertise associated with physical deliveries, many non-physical financial players such as banks and hedge funds are active in the OTC swap markets. These financial intermediaries add liquidity to the swaps markets, enabling physical producers and consumers to match their exposures at various locations, in a multitude of grades, distributing price risk among those market participants most willing to assume it. Swaps contracts may be written on single underlying indexes (as in the example above), or on a variety of different underlyings, for example:

◆ quality or grade differentials, for example sweet-sour crude oil price differentials or heating oil to jet fuel;
◆ location differentials, for example Brent to WTI crudes;
◆ spreads between associated commodities, especially in transformative industries, for example gas to power spreads (*spark spreads*), or crude oil to product spreads (*crack spreads*);
◆ baskets of more than two commodities, for example in oil refining, leading to so-called *basket swaps*; and
◆ swaps that allow price differentials between different future delivery times to be locked in, known as *time spread* or *curve lock swaps*.

Where might proxy risk arise in the use of monthly average price swaps?

Proxy risk arises wherever the underlying exposure and the hedge fail to match exactly. In the use of monthly average price swaps the most obvious sources of proxy risk are the following:

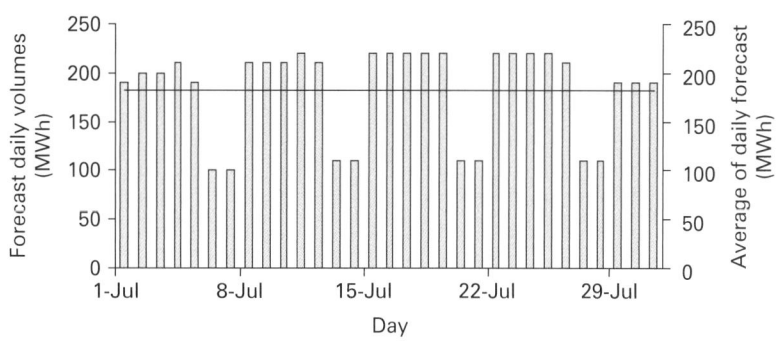

Figure 39. Forecast power consumption volumes

- There may not be a swap market in the precise grade or location of commodity being bought under the physical supply contract.
- The quantity of energy to be hedged may not match the common market lot sizes, or may be too small to hedge easily in the markets.
- The energy user may not be exposed to an entire month's prices, but only some days within a month.
- The energy user may not take or deliver the same volume each day in a month, while the swap contract will assume a fixed notional daily volume of commodity.

Example: Swap Proxy Risk Due to Lot Size and Volumetric Effects

Suppose a large UK industrial consumer of electricity buys baseload power at the prevailing market index. Its forecast daily volumes for the month of July are shown in Figure 39.

The average forecast consumption throughout the month is a little under 183 MWh per day, and the consumer decides to go to the swap market to hedge their exposure. The swap market quotes a price of £35/MWh, and offers liquid swaps in lots sizes of 25 MWh only. The hedger has two sources of hedge uncertainty:

- What will the actual volumes of power consumption be?
- Should they hedge 175 MWh or 200 MWh per day?

At the end of July the actual power consumptions are known, as are the power price indexes for each day in the month. The actual volumes and prices are illustrated in Figure 40, together with the forecast volumes for comparison.

The actual total cost of power during the month of July was £207245.

- Case 1: The hedger buys a £35/MWh swap on 175 MWh per day of power. The fixed-leg payment they make is therefore £35/MWh × 175 MWh/day × 31 days = £189875, and the floating-leg payment they receive

Figure 40. Actual consumption and prices

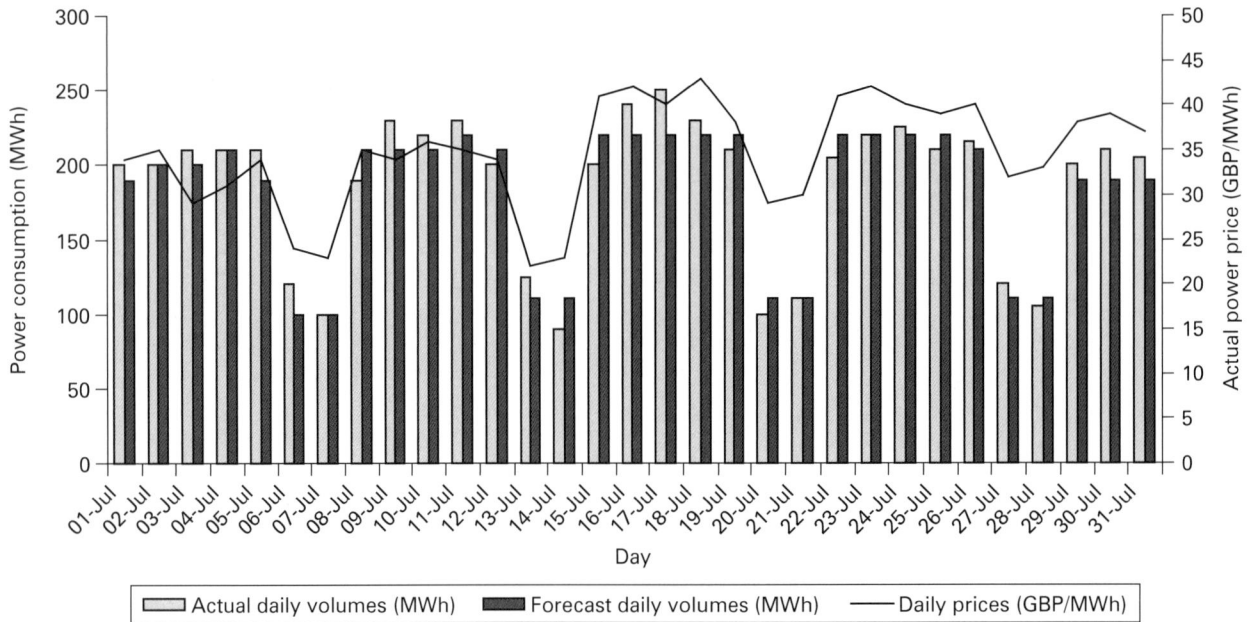

from the swap is £187775. The net cashflow to the consumer is therefore £(−207245−189875+187775) = £209345.

- Case 2: The hedger buys a £35/MWh swap on 200 MWh per day of power. The fixed-leg payment they make is now £35/MWh × 200 MWh/day × 31 days = £217000, and the floating-leg payment they receive from the swap is £214600. The net cashflow to the customer is therefore £(−207245−217000+214600) = £209645.

In neither case does the hedger find that the floating legs cancel perfectly. The hedger pays the fixed leg of either £189875 (in Case 1) or £217000 (in Case 2), together with a proxy error, which may turn out to be positive or negative. There is no good way of knowing in advance if one should under- or overhedge one's position to cover the proxy risk. In Case 1, as it turned out, the hedger paid more than the fixed cost, while in Case 2, by luck, they paid less than the fixed cost.

Example: Refinery 3-2-1 Basket Swap

Consider an oil refiner purchasing and selling their physical crude and products on floating market indexes. The forward market value of the refinery margins looks attractive, and so they decide to lock in a portion of their forward cracks (ie, the proceeds from refining). After assessing:

- their physical product slate;
- processing costs;
- the flexibilities, risks and constraints of their refinery operation;
- the indexes on which they purchase and sell their commodity; and
- the liquidity of the forward paper markets.

they elect to hedge their margin as a so-called "3-2-1 crack", using NYMEX front-line lookalike contracts. This is equivalent to considering their refinery

Figure 41. Basket swap for refinery 3-2-1 crack

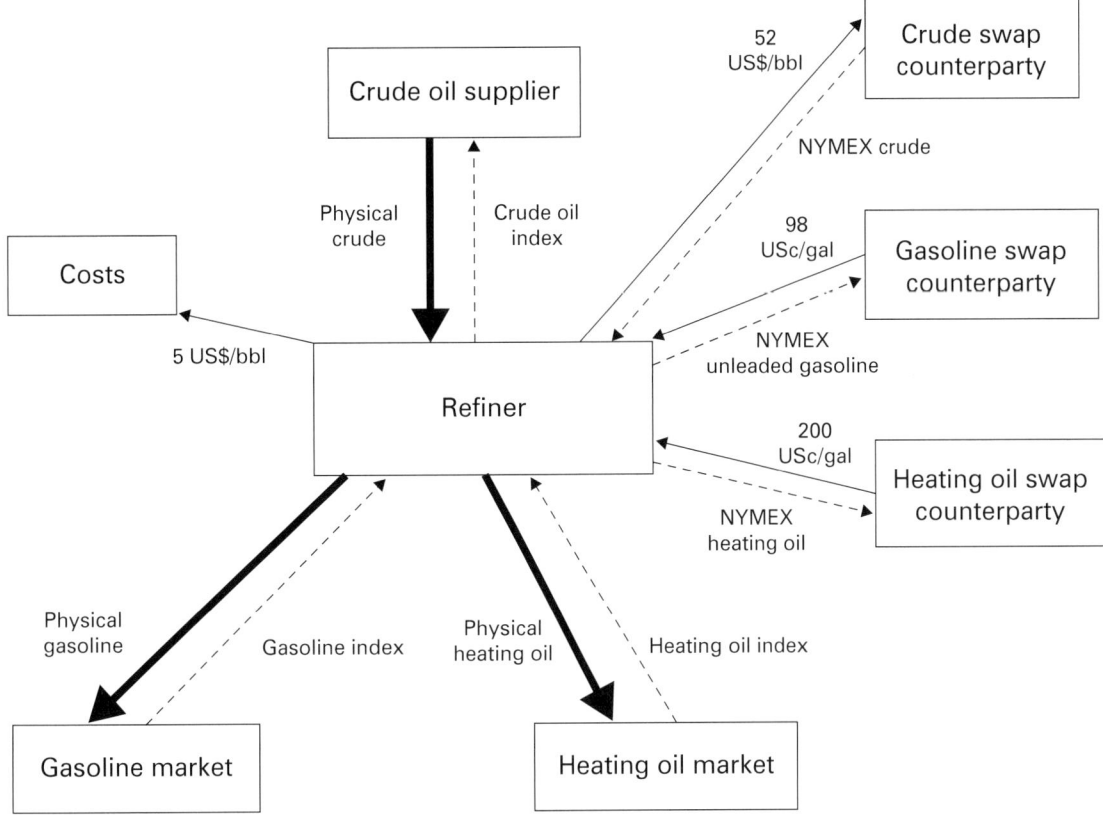

to transform 3 barrels of crude oil into 2 barrels of unleaded gasoline and 1 barrel of heating oil, and their assessment of their physical operational characteristics, risks, sales and purchase formulas leads them to believe they can exceed these simplified operational characteristics, putting an attractive lower bound to their profits in place. The hedged situation is illustrated in Figure 41.

What issues would a refiner need to consider in practice to arrive at such a hedge? (Clues: Consider the risk matrix in Table 2, and a "hedge table" of cost inputs and outputs. Try putting volumes against the flows to identify the simplifications involved in the 3-2-1 hedge, and the volumetric risks.)

The current NYMEX lookalike swap prices being quoted in the market are:

- crude swaps at US$52/bbl;
- unleaded gasoline swaps at 98 USc/gal; and
- heating oil swaps at 200 USc/gal.

and their processing costs are estimated to be US$5/bbl. The minimum refining margin they are able to lock in is therefore:

$$2 \times 98 \times \frac{42}{100} \text{ US\$/bbl} + 1 \times 200$$
$$\times \frac{42}{100} \text{ US\$/bbl} - 3 \times 52 \text{ US\$/bbl} - 5 \text{ US\$/bbl}$$
$$= (82.32 + 84 - 156 - 5) \text{ US\$/bbl}$$
$$= 5.32 \text{ US\$/bbl}$$

We have now seen a few examples of swap contracts and their use in hedging physical purchases, but we have yet to understand how swap contracts are priced. At any given moment the market's value for the floating leg of a month's swap contract in the future is the swap price for that month. Where the swap is an exchange lookalike index (eg, IPE Brent front-line lookalike) then a no-arbitrage relationship holds between the exchange futures prices and the corresponding swap price.

> What does the payoff diagram for a swap contract look like?

The payoff diagram for a swap contract looks similar to that for a forward contract, as shown in Figure 42, which considers a swap written on some index with a strike price of 50 (for general discussions I will henceforth omit mention of currency or volume units).

This similarity should not surprise us: the mark-to-market value of a forward contract for a given month is the value of liquidating a position in the market and not taking physical delivery. A swap contract achieves this same MTM value without any expectation or possibility of physical delivery – it is a paper contract only.

In practice, swap contracts are negotiated across a number of months, with one strike price for the complete strip, though possibly with differing nominal volumes in each of those months. The MTM of a swap is therefore equivalent to a strip of monthly forward contracts with this single strike price and set of volumes.

Swap prices are computed using the volume-weighted prices along the forward curve, where these volumes may cause some months' prices to be

Figure 42. Swap contract payoff diagram

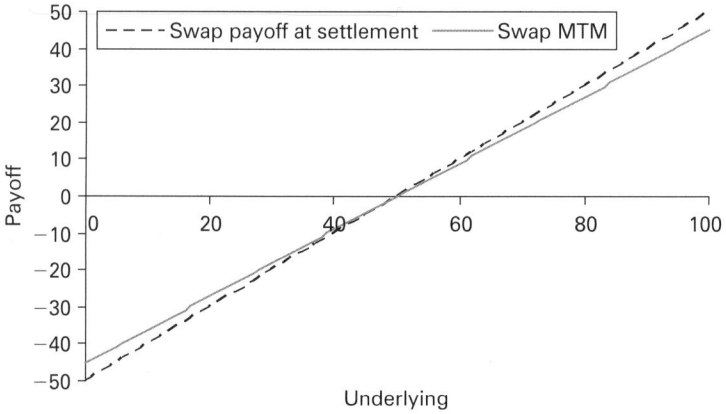

Table 18. Physical purchaser of commodity, with swap as hedge

Market index	Cashflow of physical purchase	Cashflow from swap contract	Total exposure of physical purchase plus swap contract
0	0	−50	−50
10	−10	−40	−50
20	−20	−30	−50
30	−30	−20	−50
40	−40	−10	−50
50	−50	0	−50
60	−60	10	−50
70	−70	20	−50
80	−80	30	−50
...	...	...	...

much more heavily represented in the strike price than others (for a quantitative explanation of swap pricing see the Technical Appendix: Technical appendix: "Pricing of OTC linear instruments").

For example, consider a heating-oil or natural-gas distribution company, where the company's physical monthly winter purchases may be multiples of their summer monthly purchases. A swap contract to hedge an entire year's physical purchases will have its strike price weighted more towards the higher-priced winter months than the cheaper summer forward prices.

Swaps prices are often formed by adding the price of a base commodity (eg, Brent crude oil or NBP natural gas), to various grade, quality, locational basis and maturity differentials. These differentials reflect the ways in which the markets trade, revealing the physical underpinnings and concerns of the markets, which are founded in transformative processes, physical transportation and so on. This style of pricing allows traders to price swaps in the market in their components without revealing the precise exposure they are hedging. This is important in maintaining the confidentiality of a company's physical and hedge positions, which could otherwise be used against them where liquidity is low.

The hedging effect of a swap contract can be illustrated in a very compelling way using payoff diagrams. Consider a purchaser of physical commodity, buying commodity at some market index, who decides to go long a swap contract to hedge this exposure. We suppose that the swap has a fixed strike price of 50, and so we write the physical contract price exposure, swap payoff, and total exposure of the physical purchase plus the hedge as shown in Table 18.

The swap has clearly combined with the physical purchase to fix the purchase price at 50 units of currency per unit of physical volume.

> Draw the physical price exposure, swap payoff, and the net exposure on a single payoff diagram. Identify where the total exposure is to the purchaser of physical commodity.

Plotting the numbers from Table 18 in a payoff diagram we obtain Figure 43.

> Draw the corresponding table and payoff diagram for a producer of physical commodity selling their commodity at a market index.

Figure 43. Purchaser of physical commodity with swap hedge

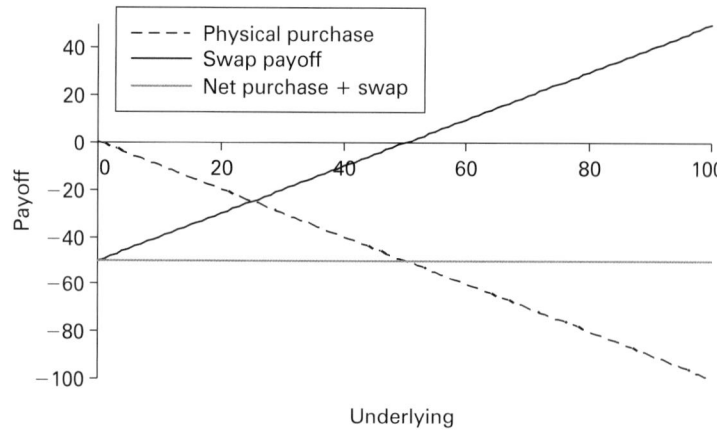

Table 19. SomeOilCo expected production profile

Month	Expected daily production (bbl)	FPP volume per month (bbl)
January	2000	49600
February	2500	56000
March	3000	74400
April	3000	72000
May	3500	86800
June	4000	96000

Example: Fixed-Price Physical (FPP) Contract

Companies that have both physical and risk management capabilities are able to offer their clients a *fixed-price physical* contract. These physical contracts deliver or off-take physical commodity at a single agreed price for the entire term of the contract. An FPP resembles a strip of forward contracts, though unlike a strip of forwards there is a single strike price agreed for all the months of the contract.

Suppose an independent oil producer SomeOilCo agrees an FPP with the structuring desk of the oil major BigOilCo for physical off-take of 80% of their expected production across a six-month period. Their expected production, and required off-take volumes, follow the profile shown in Table 19.

Since BigOilCo consists of a number of interacting businesses, each of which optimises its own physical and financial portfolios, it is necessary for the structuring desk to allocate flows and risks between:

- the physical off-take business, which operates in the short-term markets and likes to work with floating market indexes; and
- the risk management services desk, which prices and executes swaps with third parties.

Given the grade of the oil being extracted by, and the attendant physical risks of SomeOilCo, the physical off-take business in BigOilCo agrees to purchase the oil at a US$5/bbl discount to the floating dated Brent price, while SomeOilCo expects to receive a fixed price for the oil. The structuring desk will arrange the transactions shown in Figure 44 to create the FPP contract from SomeOilCo's perspective.

As Figure 44 shows, the single fixed price quoted to SomeOilCo is the volume-weighted discounted dated Brent swap price, plus a small sales

Figure 44. FPP example: SomeOilCo delivers crude oil to BigOilCo

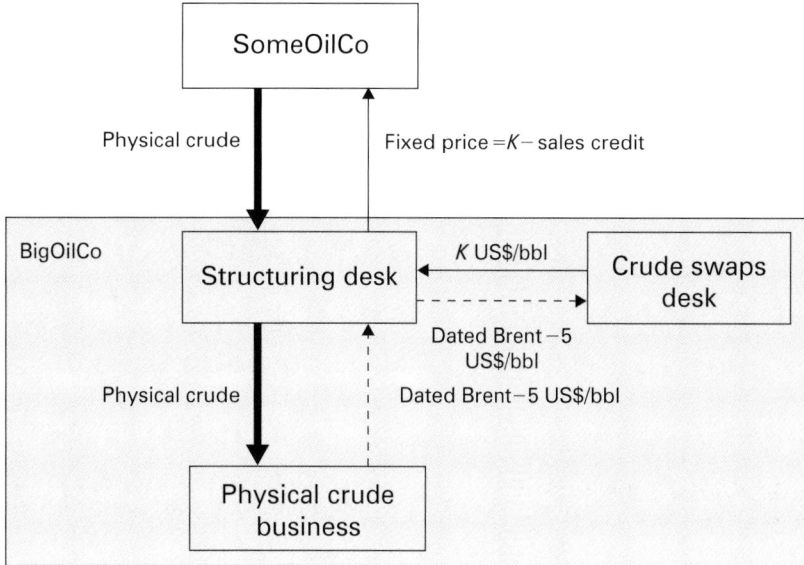

margin for the structuring desk for arranging the transaction. Checking the inward and outward flows of commodity and cash we can confirm:

- SomeOilCo delivers physical crude oil to BigOilCo, and receives a fixed price;
- BigOilCo's structuring desk receives a small sales credit, and passes all other flows through;
- BigOilCo's physical crude business receives physical commodity, and pays a floating index based upon discounted dated Brent prices; and
- BigOilCo's swap desk is long a discounted dated Brent crude oil swap.

1. Where does physical risk reside? For example, what happens if SomeOilCo delivers less than the nominal volume in a given month? Or if there is a forced outage due to a *force majeure* event?
2. What happens if the quality of the crude oil delivered is worse than expected, and the market value of the crude is lower than dated Brent minus five dollars per barrel?
3. What happens to the swap contract if the physical flows are interrupted?

These and others are the fundamental questions addressed by BigOilCo's originators. BigOilCo's diverse physical portfolio allows them to price the physical and quality risks, and these are reflected in the five-dollars-per-barrel discount to dated Brent. The contracts with SomeOilCo will specify physical lifting schedules, quality expectations, tolerances, penalties in cases of non-performance, definitions of *force majeure* and a host of other issues. It is the job of BigOilCo's originators to ensure that all risks are covered, and that no events can "fall through the gaps" between different groups' responsibilities. The risk of failing to identify and correctly price all risks is known as *mapping risk*.

> Why offer risk management services?
> Risk management services are offered in order to transfer risks between those with different risk appetites and capabilities. Physical energy users may not want the uncertainty of a floating market sales or purchase agreement, and will look to transfer some or all of this exposure to those who are willing to manage it. Energy price risk managers make their profits from:
>
> - aggregating all the flows they trade with counterparties, perhaps with their own exposures where they too have a physical presence, and
> - exploiting arbitrage opportunities where the arise, which will be more numerous the broader and more diverse is their portfolio, while
> - charging a premium for their judgement on market liquidity and ability to manage the risk in the real-time, volatile, traded markets, during which they may
> - make some proprietary trading decisions on the likely direction and size of market movements, which will determine the manner in which they lay their risk management flows off into the market.
>
> In some markets the exposure the counterparty has may not have a directly traded equivalent:
>
> - longer-maturity gas contracts, for example, may be based upon an entire year's or quarter's average price, while the customer's risk exposure may be to a single month within this period;
> - a power customer may have a highly variable intraday load shape that needs to be hedged using a cascade of contracts with increasing granularity: annual, quarterly, monthly, and so on down to hourly in the traded day-ahead market; and
> - a purchaser of physical oil may have a cargo price off a five-day loading window, while the only liquid hedge instrument may be a monthly swap.
>
> In all these cases the energy price risk manager will manage the increasing granularity of the traded instruments as they become closer to their pricing period. This requires judgement of market liquidity and a view of the likely rollover costs incurred from, for example, shifting volumes from month to month when a quarter rolls into its three constituent months. This activity demands a risk premium from the customer, and cannot be managed by those lacking access to, and experience in, the traded energy markets.

Other Types of Swap

Although most discussions of swaps contracts focus on fixed-for-floating swaps, other forms of swap can be constructed according to a counterparty's risk exposures. In this section we take a brief tour of the most important other forms of swap available, and refer interested readers to risk management

Floating-for-Floating Swaps

We start the discussion with so-called *floating-for-floating* swaps, in which one floating market price index is exchanged for another. The primary uses of such instruments are:

- to allow companies to tie their costs to their revenues; and
- to offer access to risk management instruments (such as options) on the swap holder's new floating leg exposure; such a swap may have been carried out to allow access to a new, more liquid, index, on which options may be written more cheaply and easily.

Example: Coal Mining Company Fuel Purchases

The coal mining company, CoalMineCo, buys significant amounts of diesel to power its road transportation fleet. Its revenues are largely related to the market price of coal, and it would like to tie its fuel costs to the same. The rationale behind this decision is that when coal prices are low it will pay less for its fuel, and when coal prices are higher it can afford to pay more.

CoalMineCo enters into a floating-for-floating swap with a bank, exchanging a liquid paper coal index for an IPE gasoil index to cover the major part of this exposure. It is happy to assume the proxy risks associated with the physical coal sales and the price of diesel.

The hedged situation is shown in Figure 45.

The CoalMineCo example motivates why a counterparty might want to enter into a floating-for-floating swap, but doesn't indicate how the transaction should be priced.

> How are the floating price streams arranged between such different commodities as coal and gasoil? On an equivalent-energy basis? According to how much gasoil is needed to transport one tonne of coal? Or is there something simpler?

Figure 45. CoalMineCo floating-for-floating swap

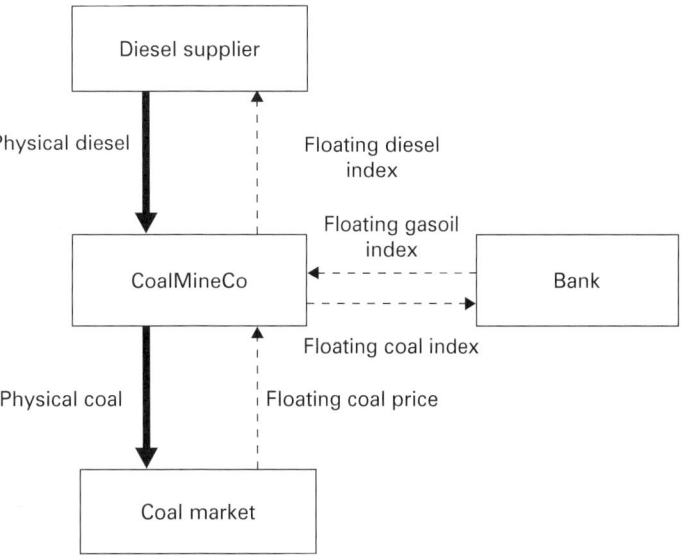

Floating-for-floating swaps can be viewed as a pair of fixed-for-floating swaps in opposite directions, arranged in such a way that the fixed legs cancel each other out. Once one of the fixed-for-floating swaps has been defined, the other swap is constructed to cancel the fixed leg on a cash basis only; there is no attempt to justify how the different commodities should relate to each other.

Example: Aluminium-for-Natural-Gas Floating-for-Floating Swap

Consider a US aluminium production company, AllyProdCo, which consumes large amounts of natural gas to generate power for its smelting activities. It decides it would like to buy some of its natural gas on a floating-aluminium basis for the third quarter of the year, and contacts its bank to arrange for an aluminium cash market for NYMEX Henry Hub front-line natural-gas swap.

The bank prices the aluminium swap at US$1600/t, and the natural gas swap at US$8.00/MMBtu, and AllyProdCo decides it wishes to hedge two NYMEX gas contracts (or 20000 MMBtu) per month. The fixed-leg payment for the natural gas would be

$$8.00 \text{ US\$/MMBtu} \times 20000 \text{ MMBtu} = 160000 \text{ US\$}$$

which corresponds to 100 tonnes of aluminium per month at the prevailing market rate; put in equivalent terms, one gas contract is worth the same as 50 tonnes of aluminium. The block diagram representing this hedge is shown in Figure 46.

Suppose the market prices of gas and aluminium in 3Q are as shown in Table 20.

The floating payoffs from the two legs of the floating-for-floating swap in each of these months would be as shown in Table 21, where the notional volumes are 20000 MMBtu for the gas leg, and 100 tonnes for the aluminium leg.

Since AllyProdCo is using this floating-for-floating swap to hedge its gas market purchases on an aluminium price basis, we need to look at the gas

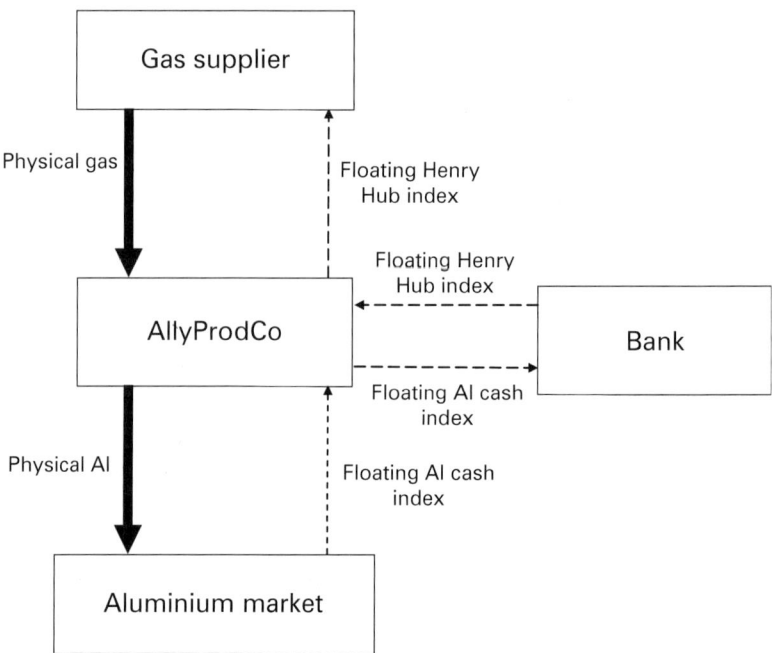

Figure 46. AllyProdCo gas to aluminium floating-for-floating swap block diagram

Physical Transactions and Basic Hedging Instruments

Table 20. AllyProdCo example: Gas and aluminium market prices

Month	Monthly average Henry Hub front-line natural gas price US$/MMBtu	Monthly average aluminium cash market price US$/t
July	8.50	1680
August	9.00	1700
September	8.20	1735

Table 21. AllyProdCo example: Gas and aluminium floating leg payments

Month	Monthly average Henry Hub front-line natural gas price US$/MMBtu	Monthly average aluminium cash market price US$/t	Gas floating payment, US$	Al floating payment, US$
July	8.50	1680	170000	−168000
August	9.00	1700	180000	−170000
September	8.20	1735	164000	−173500

Table 22. AllyProdCo example: Gas price exposure replaced with aluminium price exposure

Month	Gas floating payment, US$	Al floating payment, US$	Total floating-for-floating swap payoff, US$	Physical gas cashflow, US$	Physical gas purchase + float-for-float swap payoff, US$
July	170000	−168000	2000	−170000	−168000
August	180000	−170000	10000	−180000	−170000
September	164000	−173500	−9500	−164000	−173500

price exposure via the physical purchases, and the effect of the total swap payoff on these costs. This is shown in Table 22.

Examination of Table 22 shows that the physical gas purchase cost has netted against the floating-for-floating swap price, to give an effective gas price linked to the cash market price for aluminium. AllyProdCo is no longer exposed to gas prices for the 20000 MMBtu being hedged, and they pay a rate linked to their revenues; when aluminium market prices are higher and their revenues are stronger, they pay more for their gas, when aluminium revenues suffer, their gas purchases are cheaper.

Quanto Swaps

The next type of swap we consider is the *quanto swap*, in which payments are made in a currency different from that in which the underlying commodity is traded. Quanto swaps may be used where a company receives its revenues, holds its bank accounts or plans its budgets in a currency different from that in which their underlying commodity exposures traditionally trade. Examples of companies who might consider quanto swaps are:

- European transportation companies, who receive much of their revenue in euros or sterling, but who consume diesel, gasoline and jet fuel, which traditionally trade in dollars;
- Asian gas importers or consumers whose purchases of physical commodity are linked to a dollar basket of oil products, but whose customers pay in local currency; and

◆ Canadian oil producers who may wish to sell their oil forward at a locked-in Canadian dollar price.

Quanto derivatives offer companies the opportunity to manage their joint commodity and currency exposures in a predictable way.

> ◆ Does your company have a policy for the joint mitigation of commodity, currency and other financial market risk?
> ◆ Are your energy procurement managers incentivised only to manage dollar costs?
> ◆ Do you actively monitor the interaction between commodity market and financial market movements, or just adjust for them "after the fact"?

Example: European Airline, Fixed-for-Floating Quanto Swap

A European budget airline, CheapAirThanU, receives the bulk of its revenues in euros, while its jet fuel exposure is in dollars. CheapAirThanU's CFO has decided to implement a unified approach to managing the company's joint fuel price and foreign-exchange exposure, and she instructs her risk manager to compare the use of quanto swaps as hedge instruments to the company's current use of dollar instruments.

The risk manager reports back that, at present, the airline buys mainly dollar jet swaps from its energy risk manager (ERM), and uses its bank to translate its euros into dollars at its bank's prevailing spot rate at each monthly settlement. This situation is summed up in Figure 47.

Figure 47. CheapAirthanU airlines dollar swap hedges with spot market FX transactions

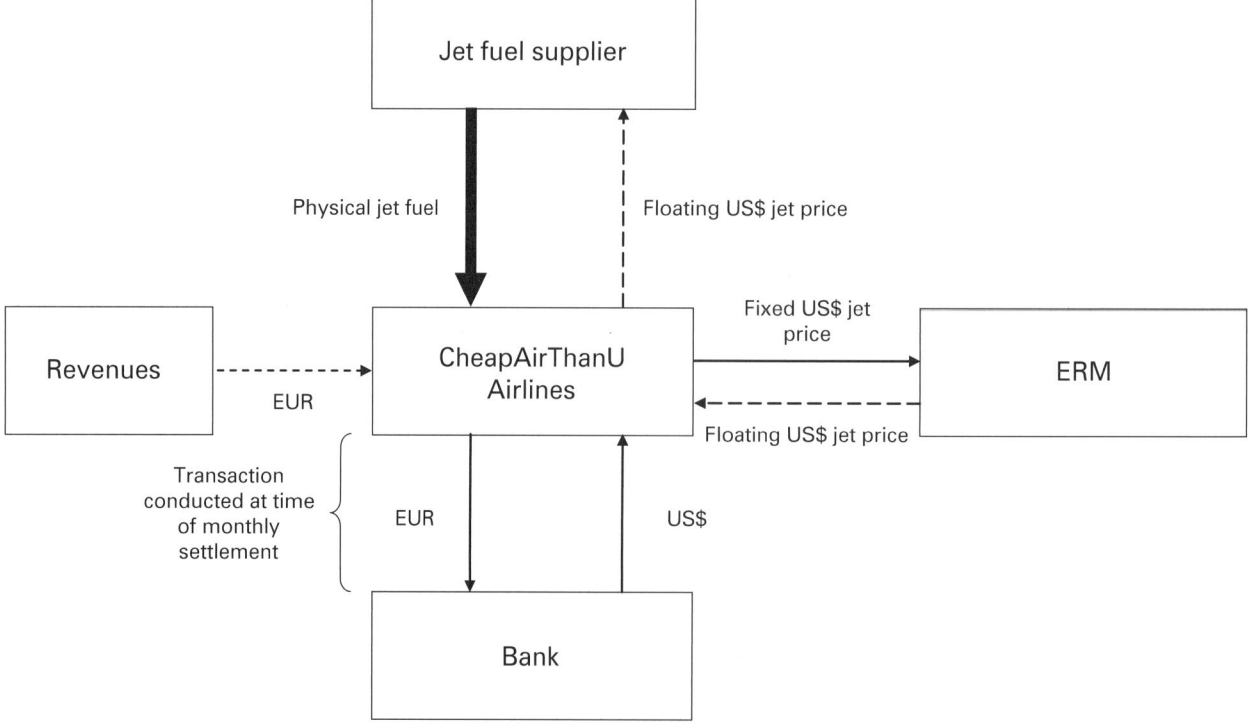

The CFO feels that, since a forward market exists in currencies, it must be possible to buy the fixed leg of the swap payments forward at the time of contract inception, fixing all cash outflows in euros up front. She draws the block diagram shown in Figure 48 to illustrate the concept to the risk manager.

The risk manager responds that, while CheapAirThanU could carry out this type of transaction, it could just let its energy risk manager look after this side of things for it, since it could presumably get a better rate in the FX markets. The risk manager reports that he has identified a range of simple quanto hedging products, and has also figured out how the ERM would structure the deal internally. He presents the cases to the CFO as a series of block diagrams.

Possibility 1: Fixed euro for floating euro jet swap: In this case ERM exchanges a stream of fixed euro payments for floating euro payments. Since CheapAirThanU usually buys its physical jet fuel in dollars, it will still need to go to the spot currency markets to pay for the physical. See Figure 49.

Possibility 2: Fixed euro for floating dollar jet swap: If CheapAirThanU had both dollar and euro accounts then it could pay a fixed euro price for the jet fuel, and receive back a floating dollar stream from the ERM, which pays directly for the physical jet fuel purchases. See Figure 50.

Possibility 3: Euro fixed-price physical supply: If CheapAirThanU find a suitable energy risk manager, such as a bank with physical supply capabilities, or an oil major, then it could negotiate new euro fixed-price physical supply contracts with this ERM. See Figure 51.

The CFO decides she needs some more time to assess the possibilities. She has a strong feeling that the dollar is likely to weaken against the euro,

Figure 48. CheapAirThanU airlines dollar swap with forward euro–dollar transactions

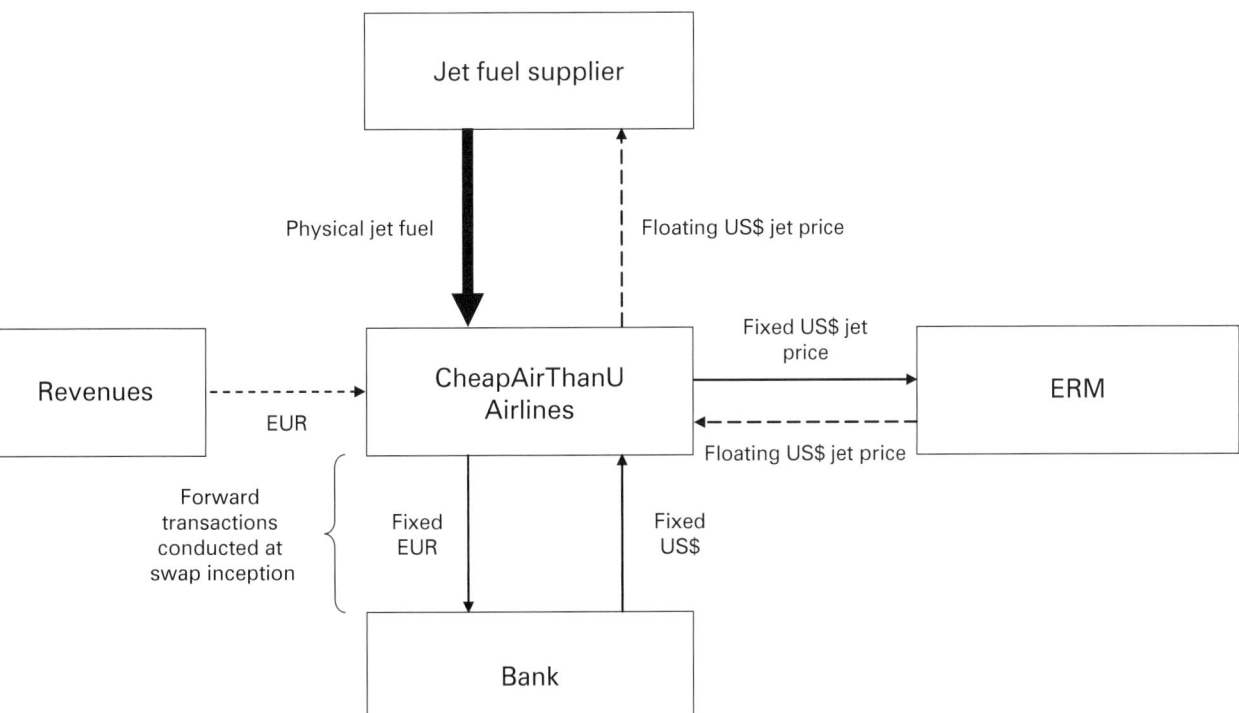

Figure 49. Fixed euro for floating euro jet swap, with dollar physical purchases

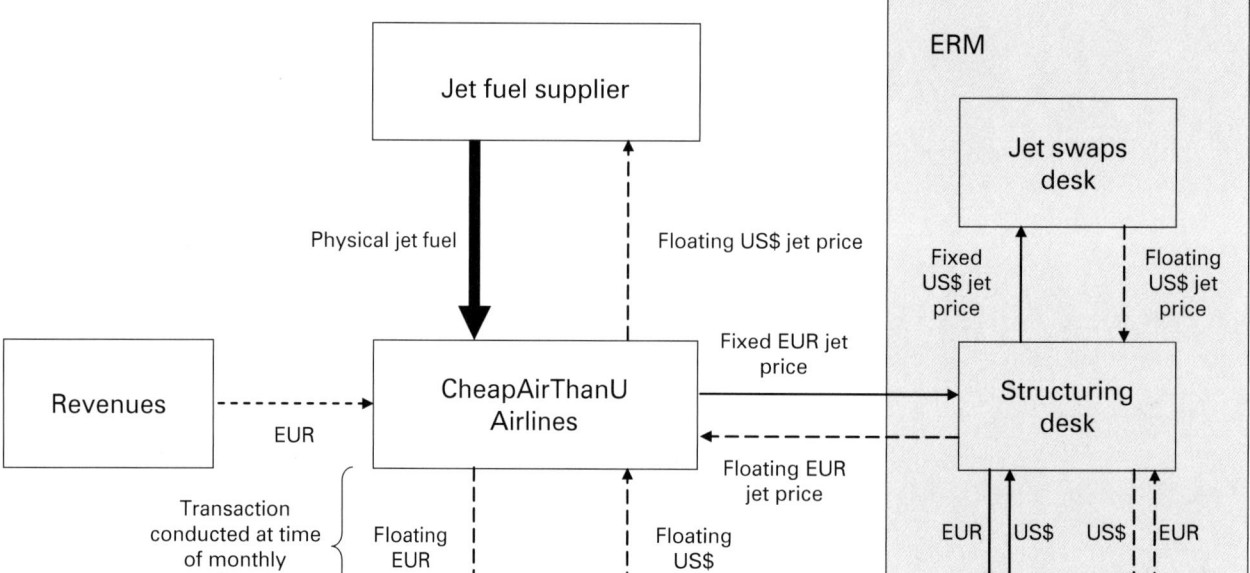

Figure 50. Fixed euro for floating dollar jet swap, with dollar physical purchases

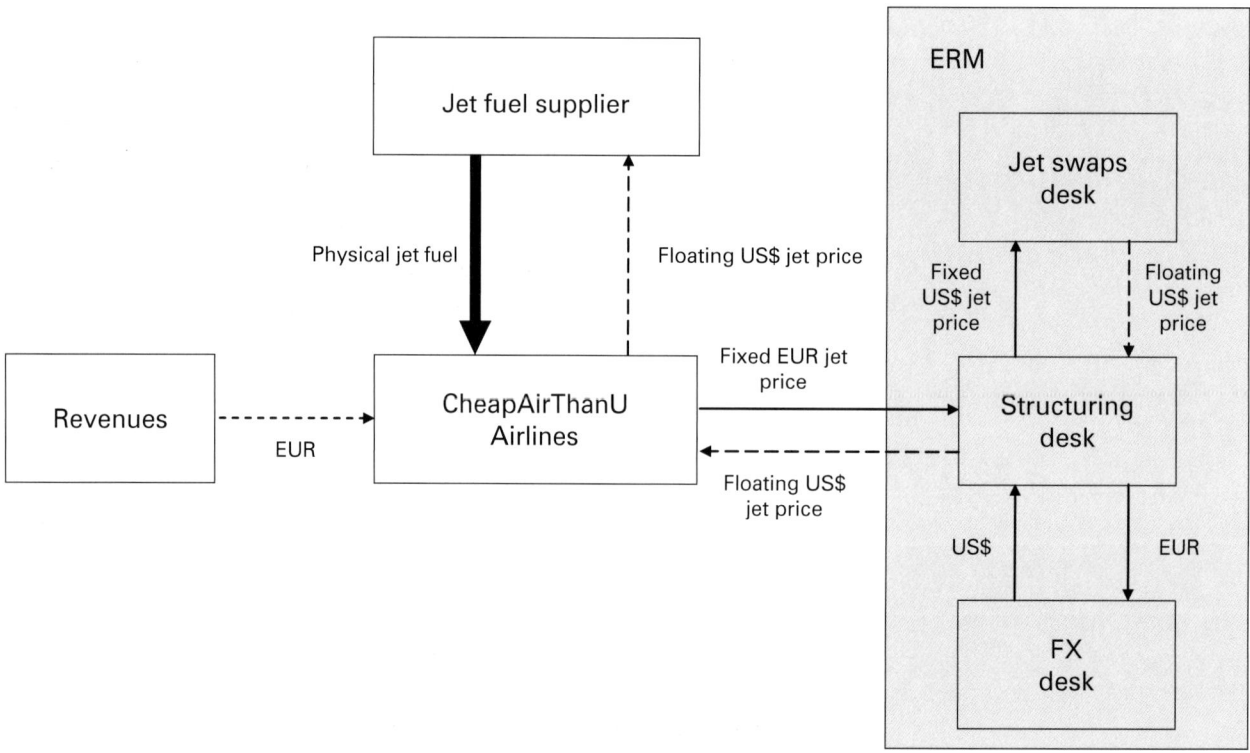

Figure 51. Euro FPP

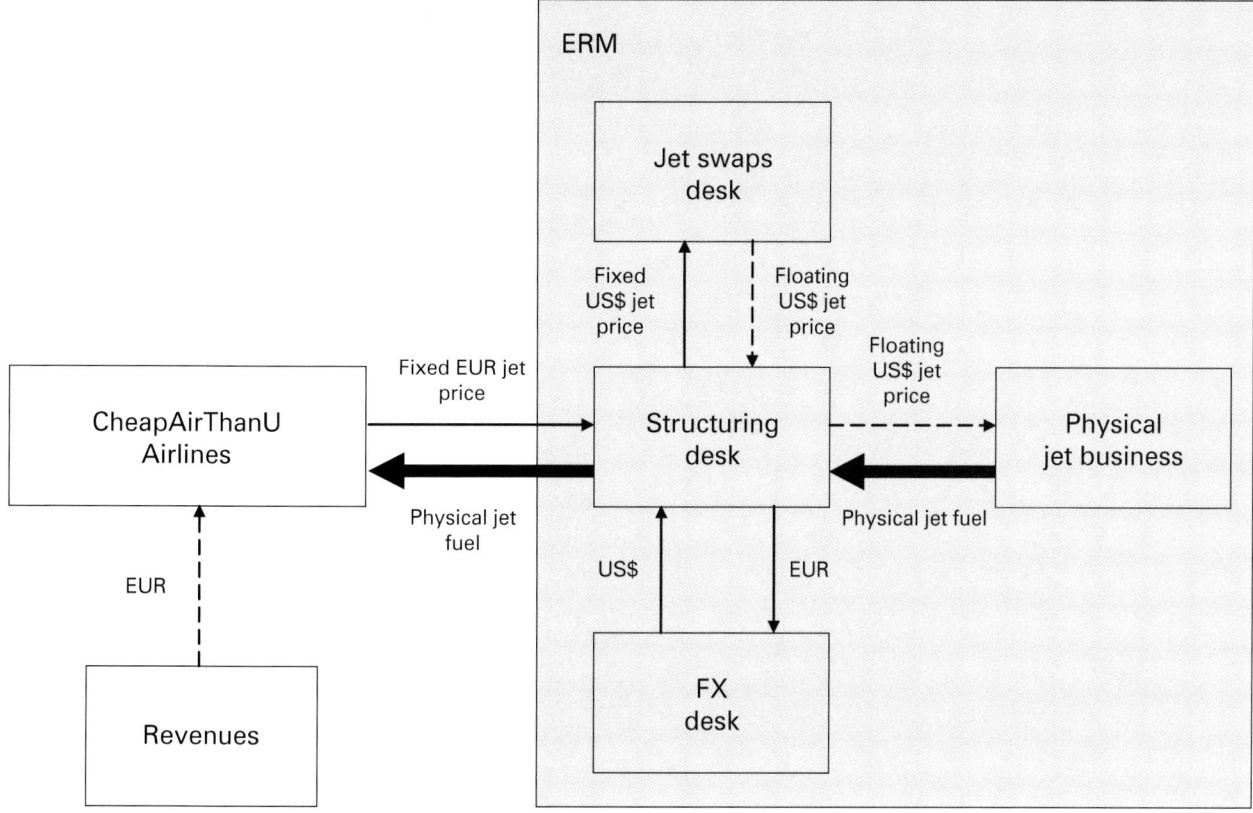

and feels therefore that jet fuel will be cheaper in the future if they continue to hedge in dollars only. The risk manager responds that this isn't hedging: it's speculation.

- Is the risk manager right that the CFO is speculating in this case?
- If hedging is defined to be activity to reduce portfolio variance, then will a quanto hedge always be better than a dollar hedge for a euro player?

In defining quanto swap settlement conventions it is necessary to pay attention to the precise way in which the commodity prices are adjusted by the FX rates. A few common conventions are:

1. The monthly floating price is computed as the average of each day's spot commodity index adjusted by each same day's spot FX rate. Put another way:

$$\text{floating price} = avg(\text{daily commodity index} \times \text{daily spot FX})$$

2. The monthly floating price is computed as the average of each day's spot commodity index, where the overall average is adjusted by the average of each day's spot FX rate. Symbolically:

$$\text{floating price} = avg(\text{daily commodity index}) \times avg(\text{daily spot FX})$$

3. The monthly floating price is computed as the average of each day's spot commodity index, where this overall commodity average price is adjusted at the last daily spot FX rate available in the month. This may be summed up mathematically as:

$$\text{floating price} = avg(\text{daily commodity index}) \times \text{last spot FX}$$

A variety of other averaging methods also exist. In understanding what method of averaging is most appropriate, readers should examine how often they purchase fuel in a month and on what basis they therefore need to make FX transactions. This joint exposure will determine the FX averaging convention to apply.

Indexation Swaps

In *indexation* or *Asian-style swaps* the floating monthly payment is computed not from just one month's average price, but on some moving average of a number of previous months' prices. The swaps can be written on a basket of different underlyings, each with its own averaging methods. Indexation swaps often arise in physical commodity sales or purchase agreements where the price is indexed to a basket of other replacement energy products, for example:

$$\text{Gas price} = a \times (\text{average Brent crude price}) + b \times (\text{average fuel oil price}) + c$$

where a, b and c are suitable weighting factors.

The averages are usually defined using three numbers (N, P, Q), where:

- N defines the number of consecutive monthly prices that form the moving average or the *averaging window*: for example, $N=3$ would mean that three months' average prices form the moving average;
- P defines the number of months' lag applying to the moving average; $N=3$, $P=0$ indicates that the three-month moving average is taken using the last three months' available prices with no lag; and
- Q defines the frequency with which the average "resets"; $Q=1$ indicates that every month the averaging window moves along by one month, and $Q=3$ means that the averaging window moves only once per quarter.

Example: (9,0,1) Swap

Here, each month's floating payment is defined to be the average of the preceding nine consecutive months' average prices, as shown in Table 23. The labelling convention (9,0,1) refers to:

- The number of months' average price fixings that are averaged, $N = 9$.
- The time shift before the present month before averaging starts. Here $P = 0$ indicates that the average is computed up to the latest month for which a fixing is available.
- The number of months for which the average applies, $Q = 1$, meaning a new average is computed every month.

Physical Transactions and Basic Hedging Instruments

Table 23. (9,0,1) calculation months

Application month	Payment based upon
January 2007	$1/9(P_{Apr06} + P_{May06} + \ldots + P_{Dec06})$
February 2007	$1/9(P_{May06} + P_{Jun06} + \ldots + P_{Jan07})$
March 2007	$1/9(P_{Jun06} + P_{Jul06} + \ldots + P_{Feb07})$
…	…

Table 24. (3,1,3) calculation months

Application month	Payment based upon
January 2008	$1/3(P_{Sep07} + P_{Oct07} + P_{Nov07})$
February 2008	$1/3(P_{Sep07} + P_{Oct07} + P_{Nov07})$
March 2008	$1/3(P_{Sep07} + P_{Oct07} + P_{Nov07})$
April 2008	$1/3(P_{Dec07} + P_{Jan08} + P_{Feb08})$
May 2008	$1/3(P_{Dec07} + P_{Jan08} + P_{Feb08})$
June 2008	$1/3(P_{Dec07} + P_{Jan08} + P_{Feb08})$
July 2008	$1/3(P_{Mar08} + P_{Apr08} + P_{May08})$
…	…

Example: (3,1,3) Swap

In this case the monthly floating payment is based upon $N = 3$ consecutive months' (averaged) prices, time lagged by $P = 1$ month, with the average applying for $Q = 3$ months at a time. See Table 24 for an example of such a swap.

Indexed swaps are often formulated as quanto swaps, in which each month's average price is translated into a local currency, before it is used in the moving-average calculation.

Other Swap Types

Having seen the basic linear instrument types in this chapter (see the box below), readers will have noted the way in which these contracts have been introduced in increasing order of complexity, or specificity to a particular type of risk. What all these instruments have in common is that they are so-called *linear instruments*; on the whole their payoffs depend directly on the difference between simple averages and some defined strike price, or just the difference between two averages.

The mark-to-market value of a linear instrument varies directly with these averages, and the value to the holder can be positive or negative in direct proportion to the relationships between the averages and the strike prices. The intention in using linear instruments to hedge is that this linear variability should directly offset the exposure introduced by physical contracts, effecting either a full locking in of price, or a complete swapping of two price exposures.

> Basic linear instruments summary:
> *Futures contracts*: Highly standardised exchange-traded contracts for physical delivery at some pre-agreed "strike" price, location, quality/grade, delivered over a defined period of time at a regular rate, etc.
> *Forward contracts*: OTC cousins of futures contracts, forwards are contracts for physical delivery at some pre-agreed "strike" price, location, quality and so on, though since they are OTC they can be tailored
> (continued)

> with a suitable counterparty to any quality, quantity, location, settlement date, etc. Counterparty credit risk exists since these contracts are agreed bilaterally by a mutual agreement to deliver the commodity and make payment on the settlement date.
>
> *Fixed-for-floating swaps*: Also known as contracts for difference, these are paper derivative contracts in which regular payments of some agreed floating market index are exchanged for regular payments of a fixed quantity over the term of the contract. Fixed-for-floating swaps come in various "flavours" including contracts written on a single underlying index, quality or grade differentials, location differentials, spreads between associated commodities such as spark or crack spreads, basket swaps of more than two commodities, and time spread or curve lock swaps that allow price differentials between different future delivery times to be locked in.
>
> *Floating-for-floating swaps*: Allow one floating market price index (or basket of indexes) to be exchanged for another, primarily to allow companies to tie their costs to their revenues or to offer access to risk management instruments (such as options) on the new, usually more liquid, floating leg exposure.
>
> *Quanto swaps*: Swaps contracts in which payments are made in a currency different from that in which the underlying commodity is traded.
>
> *Indexation* or *Asian-style swaps*: Swaps contracts in which the floating monthly payment is computed not from just one month's average price (or basket of prices), but on some moving average of a number of previous prices.

In this final section we now present a miscellany of other types of swap contract that readers may encounter. Readers are recommended to speak to their energy risk manager for further discussion and details.

- ◆ *Prepayment swaps*. We haven't considered the mechanics of swap settlement in this chapter, and have tended to assume that settlements are due monthly, shortly after a month's average prices have been computed (or the month has *priced out*) and settlement becomes possible. Many different settlement frequencies are possible (eg, quarterly, semi-annually or annual settlements), but an important further convention is the prepayment swap. In this case the fixed-price payer pays the entire NPV of their fixed-leg cashflows up front at or soon after contract inception. This may be used where the swap buyer is of low credit quality, and without the promise of upfront payment their counterparty would not be willing to trade.
- ◆ *Proxy swaps*. These are swaps contracts offered on indexes for which there is no liquid forward market. The energy risk manager needs to hedge as much of the exposure as they can in the market (using statistical correlation analysis), and charges the client a premium to cover the unhedgeable proxy or basis risk. Proxy swaps are especially popular for illiquid market indexes and for end users exposed to government price surveys for which there is no market.
- ◆ *Commodity-indexed interest-rate swaps*. These swaps, often used in project financing, expose the buyer to an interest rate indexed to the price of

an underlying commodity. For example, an upstream gas producer who has borrowed money at a floating market rate to fund the purchase of assets could swap the interest payments for one linked directly to gas or oil prices. If commodity prices are higher, and they are gaining extra revenues from sales of commodity, they can afford to pay a higher rate of interest. Where commodity prices are low, and revenues suffer, their interest payments are reduced by a corresponding amount.

- *Extendible, cancellable swaps.* These are swaps in which one of the counterparties has the right, but not the obligation, to either extend the term of the swap with the same strike price, or to cancel the remaining term of the swap. These structures may be used to provide extra flexibility where the swap buyer has the rights, or to lower the buyer's effective swap price where the swap seller has the optionality. Further discussion of such swap contracts is delayed until the Chapter "Derivatives Packages", since these contracts are built from packages of other simpler derivatives instruments.
- *Hybrids of the swap contracts seen above.* Many combinations and variations of the swaps seen above may be formulated. Consider, for example, a "quanto Asian floating-for-floating" swap, which might be used by a UK gas distribution company importing LNG on a dollar oil product indexation formula, who wishes to swap these purchases for a sterling NBP gas index.

> Which of your company's energy sales or purchasing formulas can be hedged with the simpler, or vanilla, fixed-for-floating, floating-for-floating, quanto or indexation swaps? Which exposures need to be hedged using more complex or hybrid products?

Chapter Review and Look Ahead

In this chapter we have looked at physical purchase and sale agreements indexed to a floating market price, and have met the most basic linear instruments that may be used to mitigate the price risk inherent in such arrangements. While we have seen numerous illustrations of how futures, forwards and the various flavours of swap can be employed to manage price risk, we need to be aware that the physical nature of the energy business means there is unlikely to be a perfect hedge.

The proxy risk introduced by imperfect matching of exposures and hedge instruments can arise in a multitude of ways, and it is critical that risk managers define their hedging objectives and monitor the hedge performance of their programme. Smart use of block diagrams in conjunction with the risk matrix can point out many pitfalls in the combined physical and financial hedge arrangements, and can be used to guide the contractual negotiations in physical supply or off-take agreements to bring them closer to "hedgeability".

The linear instruments encountered so far offer a locking in or swapping of two risk exposures. These contracts are costless to enter, and do not offer any price upside; if markets move in a favourable direction the linear instruments are intended to cancel the physical cashflows as directly as possible. Many hedgers would like to benefit from favourable price movements while eliminating exposure to unfavourable prices; instruments are available for such protection and they are asymmetric or *non-linear* in nature. The complexity of managing these contracts means they attract a premium for the directional insurance they offer, and they are known generically as *options contracts*. Options form the subject of the next, and subsequent, chapters.

> Risk management themes encountered so far:
> ♦ locking in of flat price;
> ♦ locking in of margin;
> ♦ tying costs to revenues;
> ♦ switching one price exposure for another;
> ♦ joint hedging of combined currency and commodity exposures; and
> ♦ managed price physical.

Technical Appendix: Futures Margining

Suppose that on Day 1 a hedger buys futures contracts in which they agree to pay US$ K per unit volume. On Day 2 the futures price will be different, F_2, and the hedger will pay a daily variation margin of $F_2 - K$. This daily margining process continues as shown in Table 25.

The net effect of paying the sum of these daily variation margins is that the hedger pays

$$(F_2 - K) + (F_3 - F_2) + \ldots + (F_N - F_{N-1}) = F_N - K$$

Technical Appendix: Pricing of OTC Linear Instruments

Here we consider two basic OTC instruments:

♦ physical forward contract; and
♦ paper fixed-for-floating monthly settled swap on a single underlying,

and examine their mark-to-market values.

A long forward contract is an agreement to pay some amount, K per unit volume, for receipt of commodity on some settlement date T_{settle}. We assume that the forward contract matures on date T_{mat}, after which taking delivery becomes an obligation, and we are interested in the mark-to-market value of liquidating this position on some date $t \leq T_{mat}$. We make the simplifying assumption that the settlement payment K and the income for the unwinding transaction are both due on the same settlement date, and the annualised continuously compounding interest rate $r_{t,T_{settle}}$ applies between the date of the marking-to-market exercise and the settlement date.

Table 25. Daily futures margining

Day	Futures price	Variation margin
1	K	None
2	F_2	$F_2 - K$
3	F_3	$F_3 - F_2$
4	F_4	$F_4 - F_3$
5	F_5	$F_5 - F_4$
...	...	...
N	F_N	$F_N - F_{N-1}$

If the market forward value for the T_{mat} contract on the date t is denoted $F_{t,T_{\text{mat}}}$, then the MTM for the long forward contract on day t is

$$MTM_t = V \times e^{-r_{t,T_{\text{settle}}}(T_{\text{settle}} - t)} \times \left(F_{t,T_{\text{mat}}} - K\right)$$

(where we assume all times are measured in years from some base date). The strike price, K, is chosen to be the market forward price at the time of contract inception t_0, that is $K = F_{t_0, T_{\text{mat}}}$. Readers can confirm for themselves that the MTM value of a forward contract is zero at contract inception:

$$MTM_{t_0} = 0$$

For a monthly, settled, fixed-for-floating swap contract, the strike price at the time of inception, t_0, is chosen to balance the volume-weighted average of the N monthly forward prices:

$$K = \frac{\sum_{i=1}^{N} \exp\left(-r_{t_0,T_{\text{settle},i}}(T_{\text{settle},i} - t_0)\right) \times V_i \times F_{t_0,T_{\text{mat},i}}}{\sum_{i=1}^{N} \exp\left(-r_{t_0,T_{\text{settle},i}}(T_{\text{settle},i} - t_0)\right) \times V_i}$$

where:

- the index i ranges over the N remaining months of the swap;
- each month's notional volume is V_i;
- the settlement date following each of these months is denoted $T_{\text{settle},i}$; and
- the risk-free annualised continuously compounding interest rate between t and $T_{\text{settle},i}$ is denoted $r_{t,T_{\text{settle},i}}$.

The MTM value of the swap is equivalent to that of a strip of forward contracts across the months with a single strike price chosen for the entire strip:

$$MTM_t = \sum_{i=1}^{N} \exp\left(-r_{t,T_{\text{settle},i}}(T_{\text{settle},i} - t)\right) \times V_i \times (F_{t,T_{\text{mat},i}} - K)$$

As for forward contracts, for swaps:

$$MTM_{t_0} = 0$$

Notes

1 Swaps contracts pay out according to realised spot prices, and trade OTC. There is important arbitrage activity between the exchange-traded futures markets and the OTC swaps markets.
2 It is, however, possible to establish OTC margining arrangements with one's trading counterparties to help mitigate OTC credit risk.
3 Fixed-for-floating swaps are sometimes known as *contracts for difference*, or *CFDs*.

5 Fundamental Option Concepts

Ever hope

The Language and Nature of Options

As mentioned many hedgers seek to benefit from favourable market price movements while eliminating or reducing their exposure to unfavourable prices, and so in this chapter we turn to an examination of basic *asymmetric* or *non-linear* derivative instruments or *options contracts*. There is a whole language associated with options and those readers new to options may find themselves somewhat overwhelmed at first. This chapter aims to introduce the basic concepts of options, and their associated language, in an intuitive way that we will build upon in later chapters.

The best way to get to grips with options is to consider them as forms of insurance contract that compensate their holder according to whether market prices cross a specified boundary. Like insurance contracts, options require that the holder of an option pay a premium for the protection they are offered, and as with actuarial practice the pricing of options contracts involves quantifying the level of risk inherent in such a contract.

Where options differ from insurance contracts is in the way that the premium is determined. In traded markets the value of an option's premium is usually the *fair market value* of the protection offered, rather than some statistical average based upon historical life, accident or event data. The option premium is invested by the *writer* of the contract, and is used to fund a dynamic trading strategy that ensures that, whatever the market outcome at contract expiration, the writer holds enough funds to pay the *holder* of the contract.

The standard definition of a simple or *vanilla* option contract is that it gives the holder the right but not the obligation to buy or sell an underlying instrument at some fixed price at or by some time in the future. As with the linear instruments above, we refer to the fixed price at which the transaction may take place as the *strike price* for the option. The decision to buy or sell is known as *exercising* the option, and the time at or by which the decision to exercise must be made is the *expiration* or *maturity date* for the option contract. In this guide we shall be concerned primarily with paper options contracts in which the holder of an option receives a cashflow equivalent to exercising their option, then liquidating their position immediately in the market, rather than delivering or receiving physical commodity.

An option contract that gives the holder the right to buy the underlying for an agreed strike price is known as a *call option*, while *put option* contracts give the holder the right to sell the underlying on exercise. In the financial literature, the classic definitions and discussions of options contracts consider the underlying to be shares, while in commodities markets we are concerned most often with options on futures contracts or realised values of market indexes. The market participant who holds the contract is known as the *option holder* or *long*, while the counterparty is known as the *option writer* or *short*. For the first part of this section we'll concern ourselves only with *European-style* options, where exercise may take place only at expiry, and not at any time before. This will allow us to see most of the basic concepts with few distractions.

Example: Call Option

The holder of a call option (on some unspecified underlying) has the right but not the obligation to buy the underlying for the strike price, which we suppose to be US$50, which they then sell immediately into the market. Their decision to exercise the option will be based purely upon the market price at the exercise time; if market prices are above US$50, they will exercise their option, receive the underlying for US$50, and sell the underlying immediately into the market realising a profit. If market prices are below US$50 they will choose not to exercise their option.

Example: Put Option

The holder of a put option has the right but not the obligation to sell the underlying for, say, US$50, which they simultaneously buy back from the market. As with the call option their decision to exercise the option will be based purely upon the market price at the exercise time. In this case if market prices are below US$50 they will buy from the market at this cheaper price, then exercise their option by selling this underlying for US$50, realising a profit. If market prices are above US$50 they will choose not to exercise their option.

> Compute the payoff tables and payoff diagrams for the call and put options in the examples above. Adopt the perspective of the holder of such an option.

Option payoffs may be represented naturally using the payoff tables and diagrams that were introduced for linear contracts in the previous chapter. A call option with strike price of US$50 has the payoff table shown in Table 26.

Unlike with swap contracts, the holder of an option contract needn't exercise if market prices are out of their favour. The payoff diagram for this US$50 strike call option is shown in Figure 52.

The put option with strike price of US$50 has the payoff table shown in Table 27.

The payoff diagram for this US$50 strike put option is shown in Figure 53.

Fundamental Option Concepts

Table 26. Payoff table for call option with US$50 strike price

Market price	Price at which underlying is bought by exercising option (US$)	Price for which underlying may be sold (US$)	Option payoff (US$)
...	...	...	...
20	(Wouldn't exercise)	(Wouldn't exercise)	0
30	(Wouldn't exercise)	(Wouldn't exercise)	0
40	(Wouldn't exercise)	(Wouldn't exercise)	0
50	50	50	0
60	50	60	10
70	50	70	20
80	50	80	30
...	...	...	...

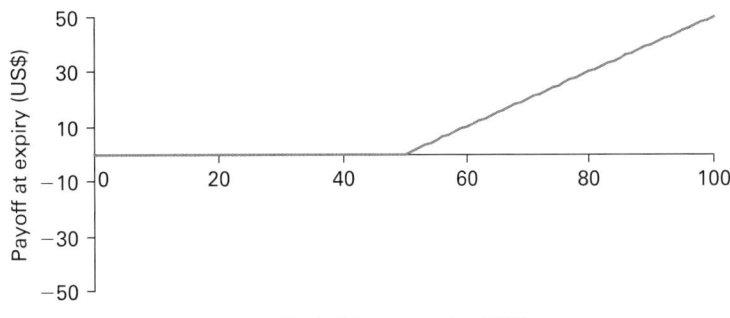

Figure 52. Call option with US$50 strike price

Table 27. Payoff table for put option with US$50 strike price

Market price	Price at which underlying is bought by exercising option (US$)	Price for which underlying may be sold (US$)	Option payoff (US$)
...	...	...	...
20	50	20	30
30	50	30	20
40	50	40	10
50	50	50	0
60	(Wouldn't exercise)	(Wouldn't exercise)	0
70	(Wouldn't exercise)	(Wouldn't exercise)	0
80	(Wouldn't exercise)	(Wouldn't exercise)	0
...	...	...	...

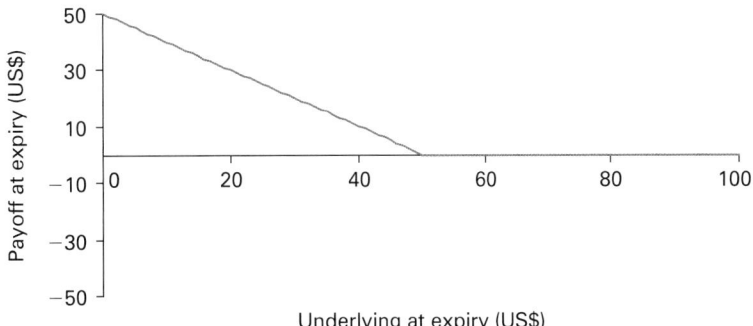

Figure 53. Put option with US$50 strike price

The call and put option payoffs shown in Figures 52 and 53 are no longer simple straight lines (as for swaps) but have a kink at the strike price. These forms of payoff are sometimes described as having a "hockey stick" form, and are *non-linear* payoffs. The flexibility to choose whether to exercise or not give the holder of an option the ability to "carve off" the desirable market price movements at a price.

The call and put option payoffs may be represented succinctly using the mathematical *maximum* function, which picks the larger of its two inputs:

$$\max(A, B) = \begin{cases} A, & \text{if } A \geq B \\ B, & \text{if } B > A \end{cases}$$

Using the maximum function the call option payoff may be written

$$\text{call payoff} = \max(F - K, 0)$$

where F is the market price of the underlying at expiry, and K is the strike price. The maximum function means that:

- if the underlying price is greater than or equal to the strike price the call option pays off the difference between these two values; and
- if the underlying price is less than the strike price the call option pays zero.

How does one represent the payoff of a put option using the maximum operator?

The put option pays off the difference between the strike price and the value of the underlying if the strike is greater than the market price. Thus the put option payoff is:

$$\text{put payoff} = \max(K - F, 0)$$

The existence of the upfront investment in the premium means that (in contrast with forward or swap contracts) the payoff from the contract is not the same as the profit-and-loss from the contract; the premium has been paid whether the option is subsequently exercised or not. It is by this mechanism that the writer of an option is compensated for the risk they bear, and the holder of the option is denied a "free lunch".

The basic option transactions we've considered so far may be represented using the block diagram shown in Figure 54.

Note that in Figure 54 we've introduced a new symbol to indicate an optional cashflow; the broken line indicates that the payment varies with the market,

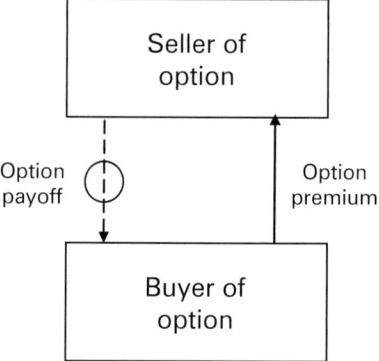

Figure 54. Basic option transaction

Fundamental Option Concepts

while the circle indicates that the payment is not compulsory. As the reader is aware block diagrams cannot show how the contract evolves in time, when payments are made, and so on. In Figure 55 we show the contractual timeline for a European option in which the decision to exercise is based upon one day's price only.

The payoff tables and diagrams given above do not account for the premium that is paid for the protection; while swap or forward contracts are costless to enter, option contracts are not. The payoff at expiry of an option is not the same as the final P&L of the option position due to this compulsory premium payment. We thus distinguish payoff diagrams, such as those shown earlier in Figures 52 and 53, from P&L diagrams which also show the financial impact of the premium payment.

> Compute the payoff tables, and draw the payoff diagrams, for US$50 strike call and put options, assuming that the holder of the options pays 5 US$ premium for each type of option.

The P&L table for the call option with strike price of US$50 is shown in Table 28.

The corresponding P&L diagram is shown in Figure 56.

The equivalent P&L table for the US$50 strike put option is shown in Table 29.

The put option P&L diagram corresponding to Table 29 is given in Figure 57.

All the option payoffs and P&Ls have been computed from the viewpoint of the long or the holder of the option. Clearly it is possible to derive the tables and diagrams from the perspective of the option writer who earns the premium in exchange for offering the protection.

Figure 55. Contractual timeline for European option

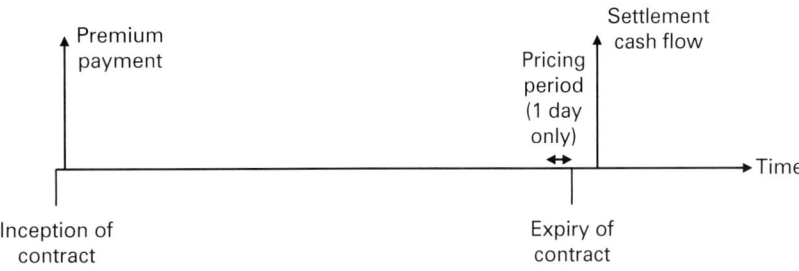

Table 28. P&L table for call option with US$50 strike price

Market price	Premium paid (US$)	Option payoff (US$)	Option P&L (US$)
...	...	...	...
20	5	0	−5
30	5	0	−5
40	5	0	−5
50	5	0	−5
60	5	10	5
70	5	20	15
80	5	30	25
...	...	...	...

Figure 56. Long call option P&L diagram with strike price of US$50

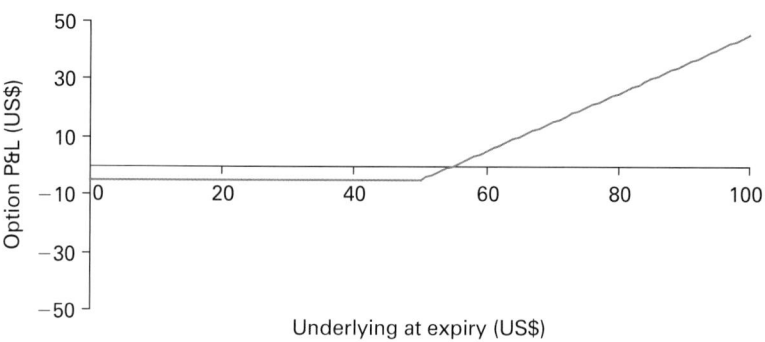

Table 29. P&L table for put option with US$50 strike price

Market price	Premium paid (US$)	Option payoff (US$)	Option P&L (US$)
...	...	...	...
20	5	30	25
30	5	20	15
40	5	10	5
50	5	0	−5
60	5	0	−5
70	5	0	−5
80	5	0	−5
...	...	...	...

Figure 57. Long put option P&L diagram with strike price of US$50

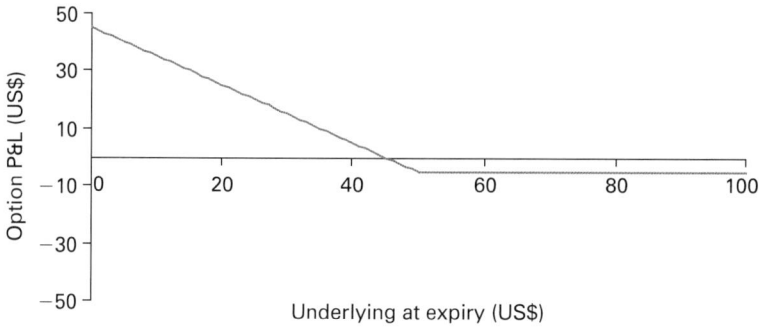

> Derive the P&L diagrams for the writer of a call option and of a put option. Assume again that the premium is US$5 for each of the option types.

The P&L diagram for the writer of a call option is shown in Figure 58. The P&L diagram for the writer of a put option is shown in Figure 59.

Basic option contracts tend to pay an amount that increases the further beyond the strike price the market has moved by expiration. This is intended to compensate option holders penny for penny in the direction they seek protection, while not demanding a payoff from the contract holder should prices move in the opposite direction. Options may be distinguished from

Figure 58. Short call option P&L diagram

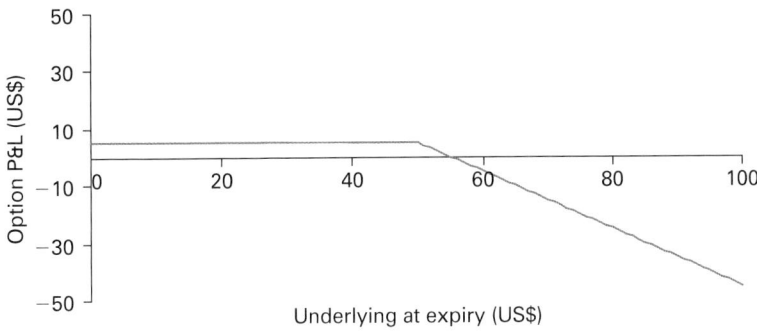

Figure 59. Short put option P&L diagram

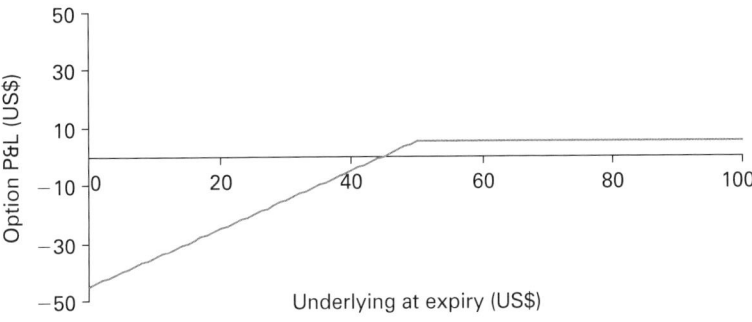

the types of insurance contract that most of us are familiar with in every day life by:

- the penny-for-penny increasing nature of the payoff beyond some strike price, where insurance contracts (and bets!) tend to pay off a fixed amount in the event of a claim; and
- the fact that the payoff is based on a market price, and not on the occurrence of a physical event such as a natural catastrophe, accident or mortality.

It is essential that readers be comfortable with payoff tables, diagrams and option P&L calculations before proceeding to later sections of this guide. The calculations seen in this section are the building blocks of energy derivatives risk management, and we will use these concepts extensively from now on.

Represent the option premium paid by p, the strike price of an option by K, and the market value of the underlying on expiry by F. Represent, using these symbols and the maximum operator, the P&Ls of:

- a long call option;
- a long put option;
- a short call option; and
- a short put option.

Using the symbols introduced we have:

$$\text{long call P \& L} = \max(F - K, 0) - p$$
$$\text{long put P \& L} = \max(K - F, 0) - p$$
$$\text{short call P \& L} = p - \max(F - K, 0)$$
$$\text{short put P \& L} = p - \max(K - F, 0)$$

Now we have examined the basic mechanics of computing option payoffs and P&Ls for long and short option positions we address the obvious questions:

- Why and how are options used?
- How much does the protection cost?

Why and How are Options Used by Hedgers?

Generically options are used to protect against downside (though not necessarily downward) price movements. Readers should note the distinction between price upside and downside, and price upward and downward movements. *Upside* and *downside* refer, respectively, to a market price movement that is to, or against, a market participant's advantage. For example, a consumer of energy prefers it when market prices drop, thus a *downward market movement is to a consumer's upside*, while a *rise in market prices is a downside market movement*. The converse case for energy producers is clear, and this precise terminology is extremely important to bear in mind when thinking about options products that exist to allow market participants some price upside. Finally a transformer is less concerned with absolute price movements in any given commodity, than with the relative price movements of the spread or basket of underlyings to which they are exposed.

An energy consumer seeking protection against market price movements may either:

- lock in their energy costs; or
- buy an option that compensates them should market prices rise.

What kind of option instrument will compensate this energy consumer?

Call options pay an increasing amount as market prices rise, so an energy consumer may buy a call option that will compensate them penny for penny as market prices rise.

Example: European Call Option as Consumer Hedge

Suppose a consumer of heating oil, with a physical supply contract based upon floating market prices, is concerned about market prices rising but wishes to benefit should market prices drop. They decide to enter into an OTC European call option on heating oil futures prices[1] with a strike price of 2.00 US$/gal for which they pay a premium of 30 USc/gal.

Figure 60. Eruopean call option as hedge for energy consumer

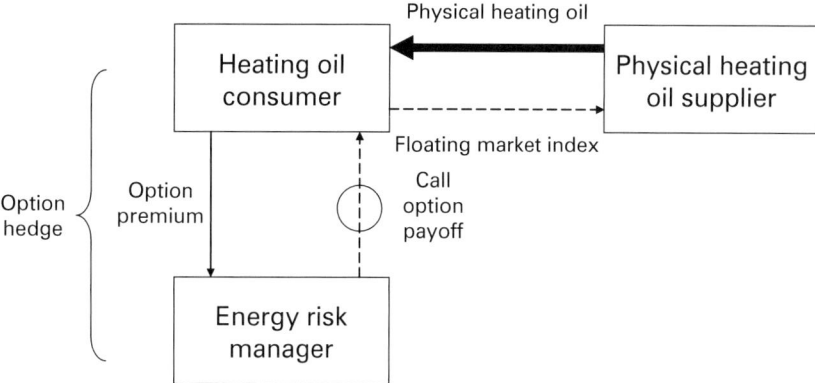

Table 30. European call option as hedge to physical heating oil purchasing contract

Market price (US$/gal)	Price paid for physical heating oil (US$/gal)	Premium paid (US$/gal)	Call option payoff received (US$/gal)	Total P&L (US$/gal)
...	...	...	...	...
1.60	1.60	0.30	0.00	(1.90)
1.70	1.70	0.30	0.00	(2.00)
1.80	1.80	0.30	0.00	(2.10)
1.90	1.90	0.30	0.00	(2.20)
2.00	2.00	0.30	0.00	(2.30)
2.10	2.10	0.30	0.10	(2.30)
2.20	2.20	0.30	0.20	(2.30)
2.30	2.30	0.30	0.30	(2.30)
2.40	2.40	0.30	0.40	(2.30)
...	...	...	...	...

The block diagram for the combined physical purchasing agreement and option hedge is shown in Figure 60.

The P&L table corresponding to the combined physical contract and European call option hedge is shown in Table 30.

As market prices rise beyond US$2/gal the call option compensates the holder of the option penny for penny. This has the effect of capping the consumer's heating oil price exposure, though they pay US$0.30/gal whether they exercise the option or not. The P&L diagram showing the exposure from the physical contract, the call option P&L and the total P&L, is shown in Figure 61.

Readers will note that the premium payment means that, if market prices remain relatively low, the consumer is paying above market price for their heating oil, and they'll never have the opportunity to exercise the option.

Energy producers have the opposite concern to energy consumers: they want prices to remain high, and may enter into a derivative contract to protect themselves against falling market prices. A put option compensates its holder in the case of market prices dropping below the strike price, and so energy producers often enter into puts to protect themselves against such downside movements.

Example: Crude Producer Hedge Using European Put Options

Suppose a producer of Brent crude oil is concerned about falling market prices, but doesn't want to sacrifice its upside if prices should rise. It sells its crude oil on a floating market index, and it decides to enter into a

Figure 61. Heating oil consumer European call option hedge P&L diagram

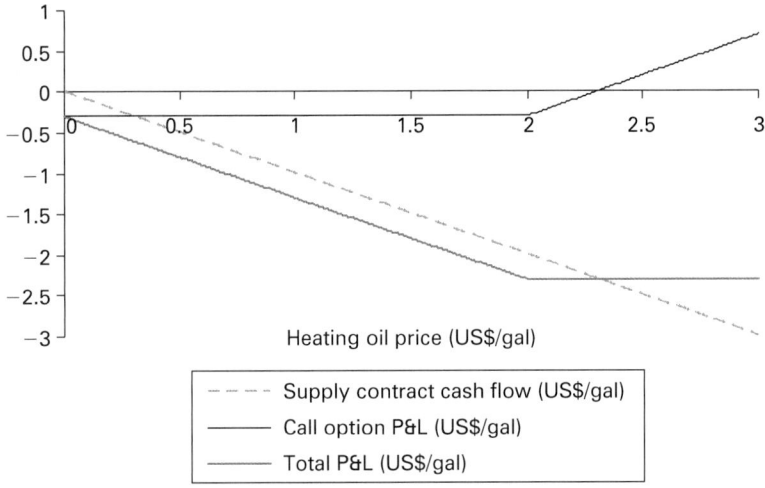

Figure 62. Oil producer put option hedge

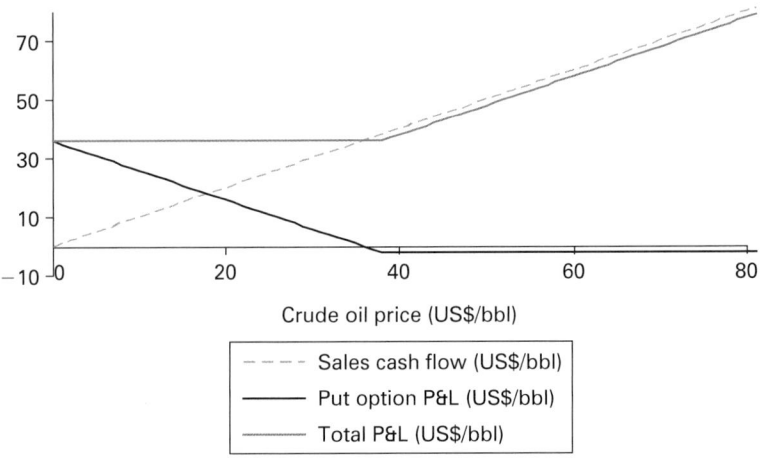

European put option on Brent crude oil to indemnify itself against price drops. It enters into a put option contract with a strike of US$38/bbl, and pays US$2/bbl for the protection.

The P&L diagram corresponding to its sales income, put option P&L and total P&L is shown in Figure 62.

As for the linear instruments above, one may buy a strip of options instruments. A strip of calls is known as a *cap*, and a strip of puts as a *floor*.

In this section so far we have looked only at option payoffs per unit of volume; clearly it is necessary to match the volumes of the option payoffs to some part of the physical exposure in order to achieve an effective hedge. This volume-matching consideration applies both to linear instruments, such as swaps, and to options. With swaps, which are costless to enter, the issue is mainly one of finding a good proxy hedge for the physical exposure. With options it is necessary to consider the additional factor that option positions cost money to enter; hedgers are therefore faced with the twin issues of identifying volumes and considering the cost of the protection being sought. In the next section we examine what factors impact option premiums.

"Moneyness" and Option Values

In the box, "In-, at-, out-of-the-money, or the 'moneyness' of contracts *In-the-money (ITM)*" in the chapter "Market Value of Physical and Financial Commitments", I introduced the notion of in-, at- and out-of-the-money contracts. These notions are very important for options and form part of the general language of options. For options we define, in loose terms:

- an option where the strike price is more favourable than the current market price is known as in-the-money (ITM);
- one where the strike price is less favourable than the current market price is out-of-the-money (OTM); and
- One where the strike price and market price are the same is at-the-money (ATM).

We will refine these definitions once we have examined option values in more detail.

Denote the current market price by F and the strike price of an option on this underlying by K.

- For a European call option is $F > K$ ITM, ATM or OTM?
- For a European put option is $F > K$ ITM, ATM or OTM?

A European call option gives its holder the right, but not the obligation, to receive the underlying for the fixed strike price K. If the market price is above the strike price, $F > K$, then the holder of the option may buy the underlying for a more favourable price than the current market level. A European call option is therefore ITM if $F > K$. Conversely, a European put option gives its holder the right, but not the obligation, to sell the underlying for the fixed strike price K. If the market is currently above the strike price the holder of commodity will choose to sell at the prevailing market price, rather than for the lower strike price. A European put option is therefore OTM if $F > K$.

Until now we have considered option payoffs at expiry of the option, where it is only necessary to compare the prevailing market price with the strike price. European options may be exercised only at expiry and the value of an option at expiry is trivially just the option payoff, which is either

---

- call payoff = $\max(F - K, 0)$; or
- put payoff = $\max(K - F, 0)$,

---

perhaps with some discounting to account for the fact that option settlement may take place after the option has expired.

A European option's value before expiry requires some thought. Although it is not possible to exercise the option before expiry, the contract may be sold on to another market participant, and so for mark-to-market purposes we need to know what the option is worth. The question of what the option is worth depends upon what the underlying price will be when the option expires – the only information the market offers is the price of the underlying today, and the value of the underlying at expiry is uncertain. Option values must therefore be derived from probabilistic models, which encode assumptions about how the market is likely to evolve from the present time until expiry of the option.

Example: Price Paths

Suppose that an energy hedger is holding a European call option with strike price of US$60, and that on 1 January the market is at US$50. Figure 63 illustrates the situation where the option expires in the money since the market price finishes above the strike price.

In Figure 64 we see a different situation where market prices fall, and the option expires out of the money.

Finally, Figure 65 shows that even options that expire out of the money may have spent some of their lifetime in the money.

Since European options offer no opportunity to exercise early there is no contractual way to take advantage of the situation illustrated in Figure 65.

Figure 63. Evolution of price such that the option expires in the money

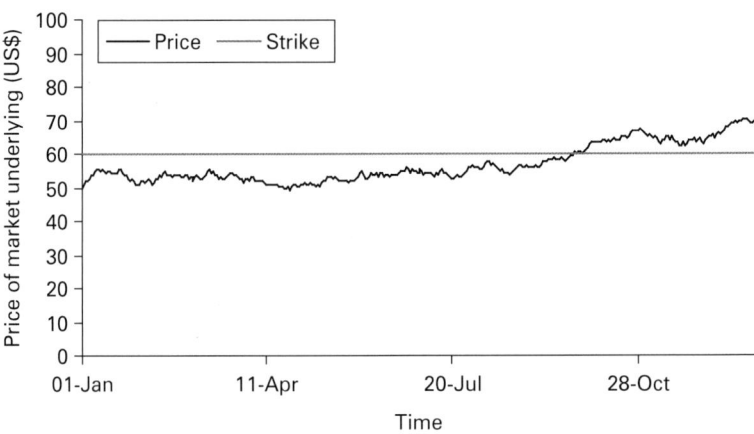

Figure 64. Evolution of price such that the option expires out the money

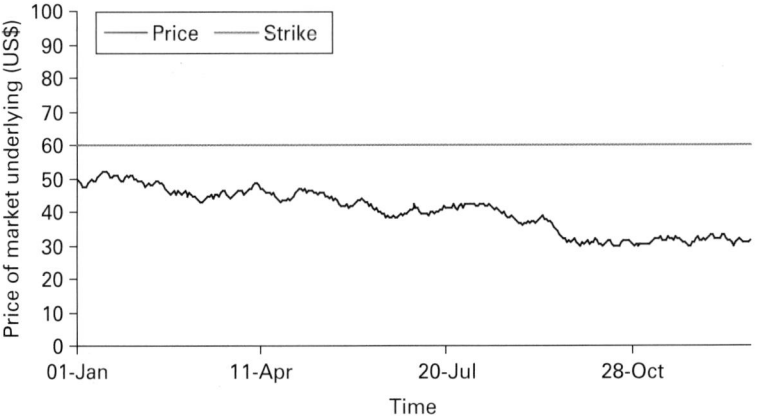

Figure 65. Evolution of price such that the option expires out-of-the-money, having spent some time in-the-money

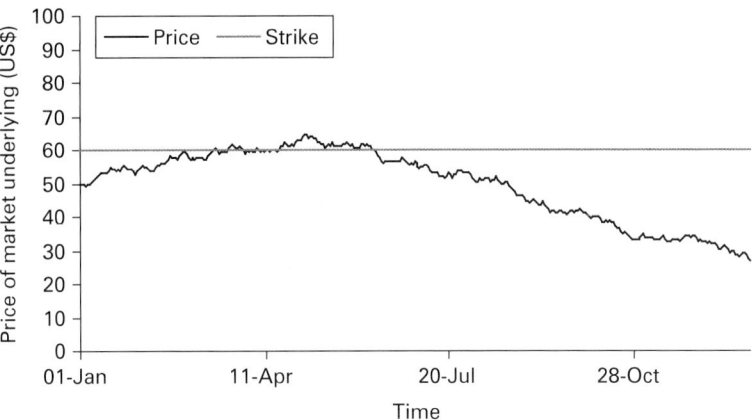

Figure 66. Call option value depending on final value of market price

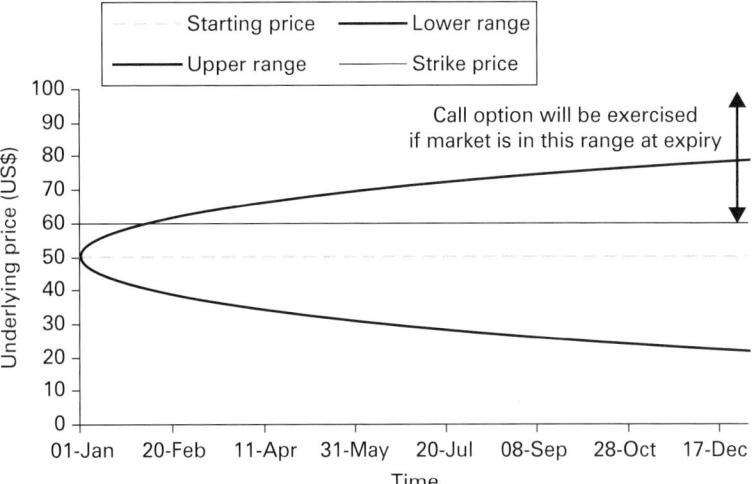

American options do offer this flexibility, and they will be examined later in this chapter.

It is useful to think of an option's value deriving from the range of possible prices that today's market may evolve into come expiry time, as shown in Figure 66.

The discussions above show that even an OTM option has some value before expiry since market price movements may bring the option ITM by the time expiry comes. The discussions above show that provided there is still some time to expiry, and still some volatility in the market price, the value of an option will never be zero. This fact is recognised by splitting an option's value into two components:

- the option's *intrinsic value*, which measures how in or out of the money the option is (the intrinsic value will be positive if the option is in the money, and zero if out of the money); and
- the option's *time value*, which measures additional value due to the possibility of the underlying market moving to a more favourable level (the time value will always be greater than zero if there is both time to expiry and volatility in the underlying market).

The option value can never be lower than the intrinsic value since there are potential gains to be made due to the existence of market uncertainty, and the option holder is not required to exercise until a later date. This right, but not obligation, is where option value arises in the face of market uncertainty.

The intrinsic value of an option is the present value of the payoff at expiry given current market prices. That is:

$$\text{intrinsic value of call option} = e^{-rt} \max(F - K, 0), \text{ and}$$
$$\text{intrinsic value of put option} = e^{-rt} \max(K - F, 0)$$

Figure 67 illustrates how a call option's intrinsic value is always less than or equal to the option's full value, while Figure 68 shows the equivalent picture for a put option.

As options near expiry we become more certain of the likelihood of exercise, and we find that the time value, the difference between the option value and the intrinsic, rapidly drops away to zero.

> Examine the graph in Figure 69 carefully. The graph shows a put option payoff at expiry and the option value before expiry.
>
> All data in the graph are correct, so how can the option value be less than the payoff at expiry (for underlying values less than US$30)?

Figure 67. Call option instrinsic value and option value before expiry

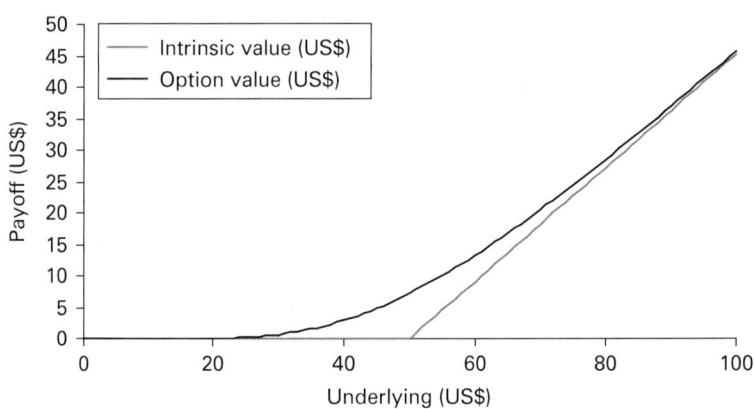

Figure 68. Put option intrinsic value and option value before expiry

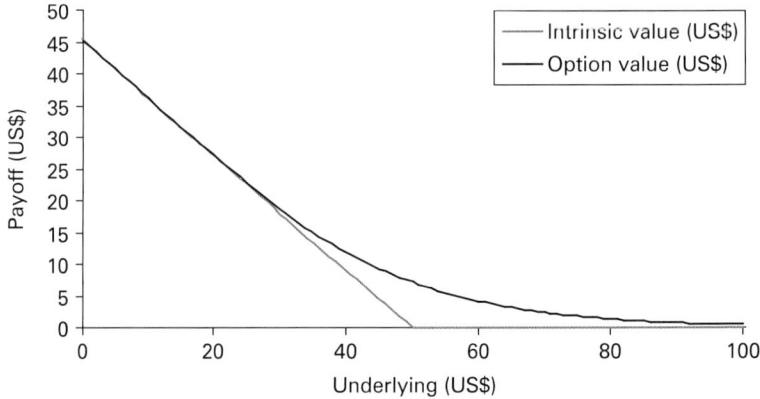

Figure 69. Put option payoff at expiry versus option value before expiry

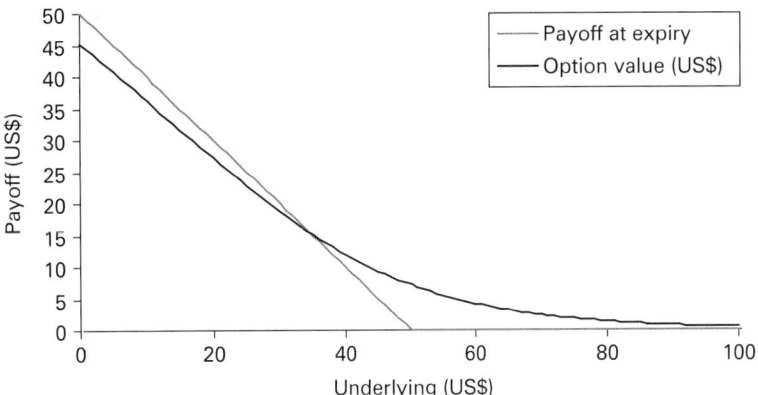

Figure 70. Time value of a call option as a function of underlying market price

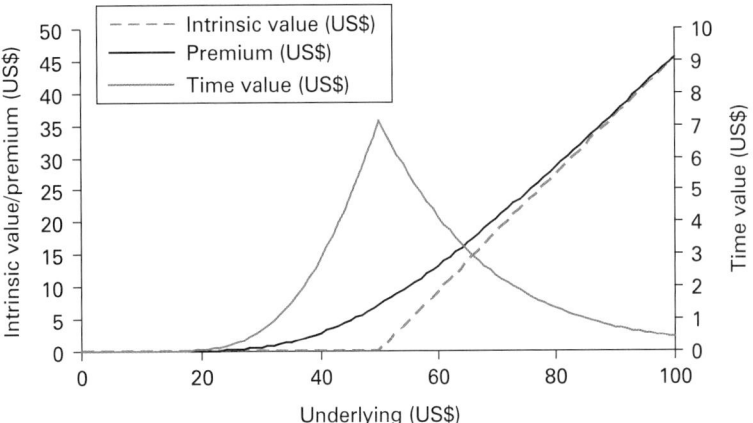

In Figure 69 we are not comparing like with like. The option payoff at expiry is an undiscounted value, while the option premium before expiry is the present value of an expected final cashflow. To compare similar quantities we need to find the present value of the option payoff at expiry, which is precisely the intrinsic value of the option. This, as we have already seen, is illustrated in Figure 68.

Examination of Figures 67 and 68 shows that the further in the money the option, the closer is its premium to its intrinsic value. This is because the holder is almost certain to exercise a deep ITM option. It would require a lot of time, or unusual market circumstances, for a deep ITM option to move OTM. Similarly, out-of-the-money option values also approach the option's intrinsic value, and deep OTM options are similar to holding no underlying at all, since there is little chance of exercising a deep OTM option.

Between these two extremes we can observe that time value is at a maximum where the underlying price is equal to the strike price, ie, the options are at-the-money. The time value of a fifty-dollar strike European call option is illustrated in Figure 70.

We now turn to a more detailed study of what impacts option values, and how.

> Basic option terminology:
> *Strike price*: Fixed price at which the transaction may take place.
> *Option exercise*: Act of buying or selling at the strike price.
> *Expiration* or *maturity date*: Date on, or by which, option exercise takes place.
> *Call option*: An option giving its holder the right, but not the obligation, to buy the underlying for the strike price.
> *Put option*: An option giving its holder the right, but not the obligation, to sell the underlying for the strike price.
> *Option buyer*, *holder* or *long*: The market participant who buys the option.
> *Option seller*, *writer* or *short*: The market participant who sells the option.
> *European-style*: An option that can be exercised on the expiry date only.
> *American-style*: An option that can be exercise any time up to the expiry date.
> *Asian*: Also known as an *average-price option*; an option whose payoff depends upon an average price.
> *In-the-money (ITM) option*: An option where the strike price is more favourable than the current market price.
> *Out-of-the-money (OTM) option*: An option where the strike price is less favourable than the current market price.
> *At-the-money (ATM) option*: An option where the strike price and market price are the same.
> *Intrinsic value*: That part of an option's value found by direct comparison of the market price and the strike price.
> *Time value*: That part of an option's value determined by favourable possible future price movements.

Factors Impacting Option Value

In this section we shall focus on cash-settled European options on futures or swaps contracts, where on exercise the option holder receives a cash settlement based upon the difference between a futures or swap contract price and the strike price – the underlying contracts themselves are not received on expiry. The price of such a vanilla option, whether a call or a put, depends upon five classic inputs, namely:

1. current market price;
2. strike price of the option;
3. time to expiry;
4. risk-free interest rates; and
5. volatility of the underlying market.

Fundamental Option Concepts

In intuitive terms these factors impact option prices in the following way.

- The current market price and the strike price may be combined to determine the moneyness of the option, and thus the intrinsic value.
- The time to expiry and the volatility of the underlying market combine to determine the "cone of possibilities" as shown in Figure 66. The greater the time to expiry, or the greater the market volatility, the more chance there is for an OTM option to move ITM, or for an ITM option to move even deeper ITM.
- Finally, the risk-free interest rate is used because in liquid markets we consider the option value to be a fair market value, with no place for an individual's risk appetite. The interest rate enters into the valuation due to the need to take the present value of the final expected cashflow; the greater the interest rate, the smaller the present value.

Of all the inputs above, the least familiar to those outside financial trading is the volatility, though in option pricing it is the key input, since without market volatility there is no time value. In generic terms *volatility* is a measure of uncertainty in market prices, and different forms of volatility exist for different applications. We can talk of:

- *historical volatility*, a measure of how variable market prices have been in the past; historical volatility is a backward-looking measure of variability; and
- *implied volatility*, a measure of how variable the market expects prices to be between now and the expiration of an option; implied volatility is a forward-looking measure of uncertainty.

Since we're examining options in much of this guide, readers should take "volatility" to mean "implied volatility" unless otherwise specified. Volatilities are usually quoted in an annualised sense, that is to say the volatility number indicates the variability over an annual period.

Example: Price Diffusion

Suppose crude oil is priced at US$50/bbl today – let's examine how the probability distribution of crude prices looks if price volatility remains constant at 20% for the next year. Today there is no uncertainty in today's crude price, that is to say with Probability 1 the price will be US$50/bbl, as indicated in Figure 71.

Tomorrow's price is uncertain, but with 20% volatility isn't expected to deviate too far from today's price of US$50/bbl. The Day 1 probability distribution is shown in Figure 72.

Clearly, as more time passes a wider range of crude prices is possible. Figure 73 shows the probability distribution of crude prices 100 days into the future.

Alert readers will have noticed that the probability distribution is not symmetric – this is to be expected since crude oil prices cannot become negative.[2]

Figure 71. Day 0 probability distribution of crude prices

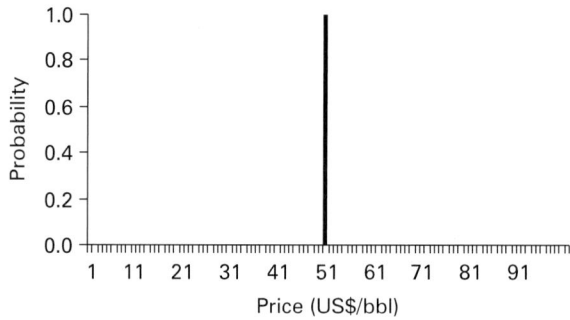

Figure 72. Day 1 probability distribution of crude prices

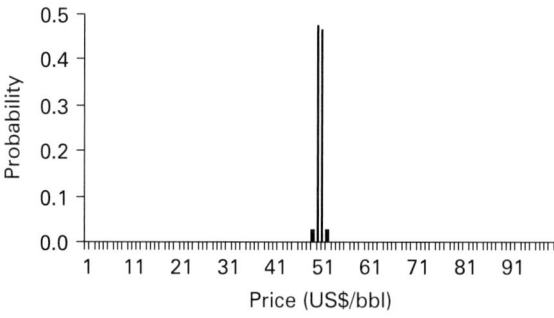

Figure 73. Day 100 probability distribution of crude prices

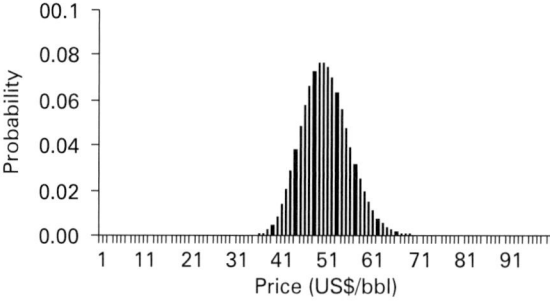

Figure 74. Day 200 probability distribution of crude prices

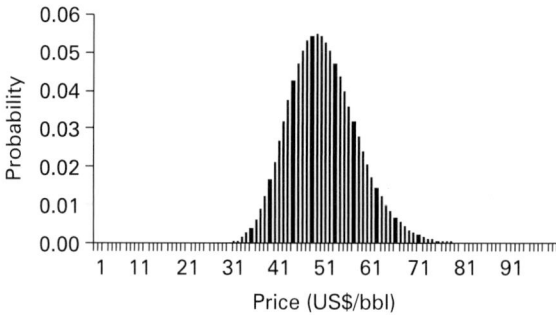

The interplay between volatility and time becomes even clearer as we consider the distribution of prices at 200 days (Figure 74) and 300 days (Figure 75) respectively.

This price behaviour, in which the probability distribution becomes wider with time, is known technically as *price diffusion*. The spreading out

Figure 75. Day 300 probability distribution of crude prices

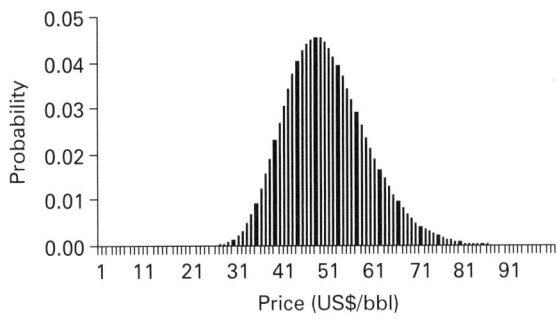

Table 31. Option value dependence on volatility

Volatility (annualised)	Option premium (US$/bbl)
0	0
10	0.006
20	0.351
30	1.221
40	2.356
50	3.616
60	4.940
...	...

of the range of possible prices over time resembles the diffusion of an ink drop in water through time, and in fact the same quantitative techniques underpin the analysis of both the physical and the financial phenomena.

The diffusion behaviour feeds through directly into the option price; all other things being equal the greater the volatility, the wider the range of possible prices in the future, the more likely it is that a favourable price will be achieved, and so the greater the value of an option.

Example: Option Value Dependence on Volatility

Consider an OTM cash-settled European option on a Brent crude futures contract. Suppose the current market price of Brent crude is US$50/bbl, the strike price is US$60/bbl, the time to expiry is six months, and the interest rate is 5%. The volatility impacts the option premium as shown in Table 31.

In Table 31 we see that when volatility is zero an OTM option has no value. This is true quite simply because if the option is OTM, and there is no market volatility, then there is no possibility of the current market price changing, which would bring the option into the money.

It is instructive to consider how volatility affects option prices for in-, at-, and out-of-the-money options. Consider a European call option on Brent crude oil, with the current market price at US$50/bbl, the time to expiry being six months, and the risk-free interest rate being 5%. We can examine the dependence of the option values on volatility for:

- strike price at US$25/bbl, in-the-money;
- strike price at US$50/bbl, at-the-money; and
- strike price at US$75/bbl, out-of-the-money.

Figure 76. Option premium sensitivity to volatility

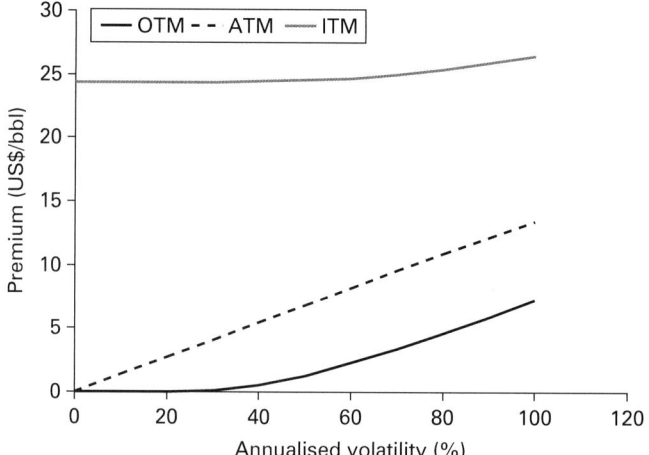

Figure 77. Time-value sensitivity to volatility

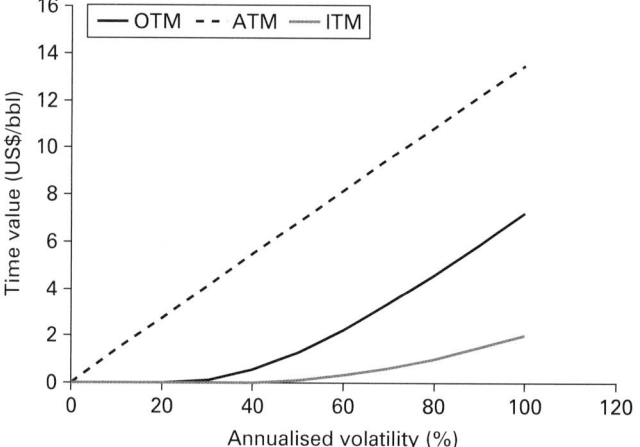

These are illustrated in Figure 76.
Readers should note that:

- the option value for an ATM vanilla option varies linearly with volatility;
- the ITM option value consists mainly of intrinsic value, and so proportionally there is less effect of volatility; and
- an OTM option premium consists mainly of time value, so proportionally there is a higher effect of volatility that drives time value directly.

It is clear from the discussions above that volatility impacts only the time value of an option, so let's examine the volatility dependence of time value only for ITM, ATM and OTM options. Figure 77 shows a graph equivalent to that in Figure 76, though with intrinsic value stripped out.

Time value is considered to "leak away" throughout the lifetime of an option – an out-of-the-money option is more likely to move into the money if it has more time to do so. In Figure 78 we see the time value leaking away from an option premium for an ATM option. Note that the time value leaks away more quickly as the option approaches its expiry.

Figure 78. Time value leaking away for an ATM option

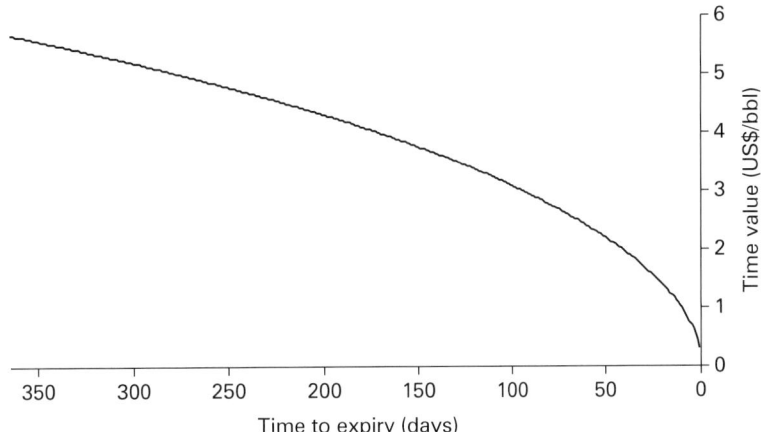

For any given option, the strike price and time to expiry are contractually defined, while the current market price and interest rate are a function of the market circumstances prevailing at the time of valuation. Given all these inputs to an option valuation, option premium and volatility may be used almost interchangeably – an option's value may be expressed directly in dollar terms per unit volume of commodity, or in terms of the volatility that would give the same dollar number. It is because of this equivalence that implied volatility is so named – it is the volatility that may be implied from the current price of the option in the market.

What is volatility?
Volatility is a measure of how much, and how quickly, market prices move. *Historical volatility* is a measure of how much prices have moved in the past, while *implied volatility* is a measure of how much the options market expects prices to move in the future.

Historical volatility is usually measured using historical day-on-day price returns, and a number of different methods exist. The most basic method is to compute the standard deviation of a set of price returns, where the trader or risk analyst makes their own decision as to how much history is relevant to their needs. Other methods use so-called *weighting methods*, in which more weight is given to recent historical price movements on the grounds that they have greater relevance to the near future.

Implied volatilities are computed by taking the option price and running an option pricing formula "backwards" to find what volatility would give this price. Since most option-pricing formulas make strong assumptions about how markets behave, it is likely that options with different strike prices will give different implied volatilities, even though the underlying market is the same. This phenomenon is called the *volatility smile*.

Example: Implied Volatility Calculations

Consider an OTC European call option on a Brent futures contract with 90 days to expiry and a strike price is US$60/bbl. The current market price is US$50/bbl, and the risk-free interest rate is 4%. Stating that the option premium is US$0.10/bbl is equivalent to stating that the implied volatility of

Figure 79. Volatility implied from option premium

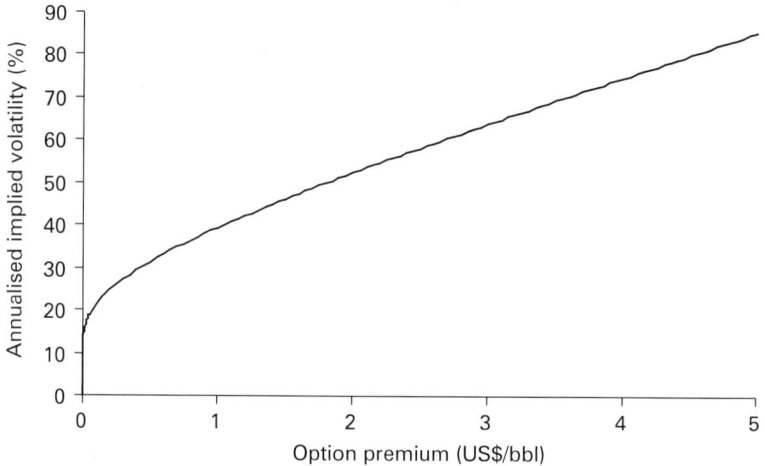

the option is 21.346%. That is, putting 21.346% into the appropriate option pricing formula will yield US$0.10/bbl as the premium of the option.

In Figure 79 we see the equivalent implied volatility for different levels of premium of this option.

More on Volatility

The implied volatility for options on energy tends to vary according to the maturity of the underlying. In broad terms, nearer months tend to have a higher volatility than further-out months, and seasonal effects can also contribute to volatility. These behaviours are due to the following factors.

- Nearby months tend to trade more heavily since players in the market know more about their positions, and need to engage in balancing of supply and demand.
- More fundamental information is available about global or regional supply, demand, transportation, weather and so on. Greater availability of information for these shorter maturities leads to a heavier volume of trading.
- Commodities with seasonal price behaviours often exhibit seasonal volatility behaviour too. This seasonal volatility can be attributed to the "fear factor" that commodities exhibit when the supply–demand balance is expected to be quite fine, leading to higher volatilities at times of greater uncertainty in market prices.

> Moneyness and option delta:
> An option that is deep ITM is almost certain to be exercised. A penny movement in the underlying market translates through almost directly to a near-penny move in the vanilla option price. Conversely, deep OTM options are quite insensitive to market price movements since they are highly unlikely to be exercised; a penny movement in the underlying market translates through to almost no movement in the vanilla option price.

Fundamental Option Concepts

> These option *price sensitivities* are formalised in the notion of an option's *delta*. The delta is a formal measure of how much the option price changes with the underlying market:
>
> ♦ OTM vanilla options have deltas near zero;
> ♦ deep ITM call options have a delta of near +1, since each penny increase in the underlying market translates nearly into an extra penny on the option premium;
> ♦ deep ITM put options have deltas near −1, since their premiums decrease as the market increases.

Figure 80 shows an example of a volatility forward curve, often known as the *term structure of volatility* (TSOV), showing how volatilities may be higher for shorter maturity contracts.

As a contract approaches maturity its implied option volatility tends to increase in a process known as "climbing up the vol curve", though this statement should be taken only in an annualised average or deseasonalised sense. In seasonal markets it is quite possible for a longer-maturity contract to have a higher implied volatility than a closer contract due to seasonal effects, as shown in Figure 81.

Implied volatilities are derived by taking a market price for an option, supplying all inputs except volatility, and essentially running the Black–Scholes machinery "backwards" to derive the volatility equivalent to

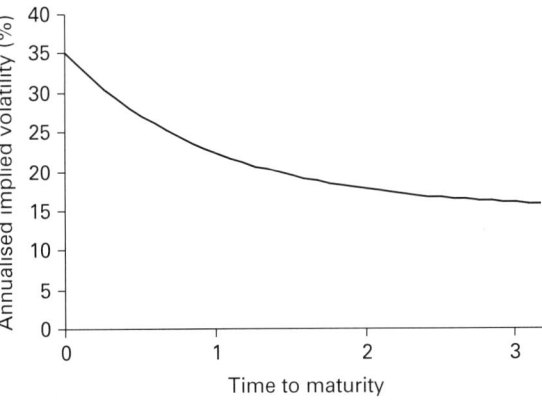

Figure 80. Term structure of volatility

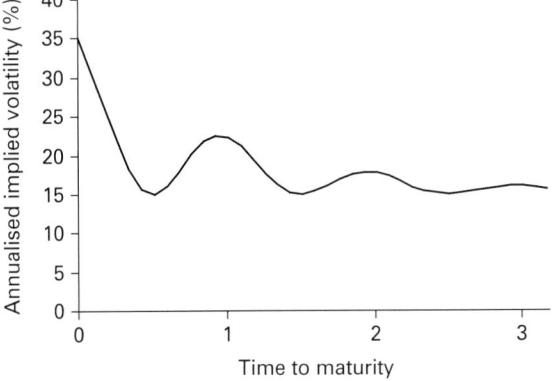

Figure 81. Seasonal term structure of volatility

Option pricing and fair option values using hedging:
Options may be priced using models based on probabilistic principles, the best known of which is the Black–Scholes model. The Black–Scholes model arrives at its value for an option by taking the five classic option pricing inputs:

- current market price;
- strike price;
- time to expiry;
- risk-free interest rate; and
- volatility;

and, based upon a number of strong assumptions about market behaviour, derives a so-called *fair market value* for the option.

This fair market value is based on a dynamic hedging strategy of continuously buying and selling quantities of the underlying instruments to ensure that, come expiration day, the option seller has enough underlying to deliver, should the option be in the money. Since anyone could in principle adopt the same strategy, all market participants should agree on what the option's value is, and anyone who makes a price different from this will be punished through the principle of arbitrage. The theoretical cost of adopting this hedging strategy is the theoretical price of the option.

The strong assumptions about market behaviour are necessary for the theoretical modelling to work, but in practice these assumptions don't hold. The assumptions are that:

- markets are efficient, with all information about price history summed up in the current price of an instrument, and with no arbitrage opportunities;
- markets are infinitely liquid, where it is possible to move any volume of underlying, however big or small, in or out of the market at any time, without moving that market;
- there are no transaction or frictional costs, meaning it is possible to buy or sell at the same price at any point in time;
- it is possible to sell short into the market, that is to sell an underlying one doesn't own, with the ability to buy back at a later time;
- trading is continuous, with no market closed days, 24 hours per day;
- interest rates are either constant or deterministic; and
- the underlying price dynamics are such that price returns are normally distributed.

In practice the Black–Scholes formula is a starting point for the analysis of option prices, and option traders need to make adjustments for the imperfections of the real world in deciding their pricing and trading strategies.

this price. To be precise the implied volatility is a volatility derived both from a market price and from *a particular option pricing formula*, and should perhaps be known as *Black–Scholes implied volatility*. One curious but important artefact of the near-universal use of Black–Scholes arises where one implies volatilities for options with the same maturity but different strike prices.

Example: Implied Volatility for Different Strike Prices

Suppose we are interested in understanding option implied volatilities for a one-year Brent crude oil contract. The current market price is US$50/bbl, the risk-free interest rate is 5%, and we receive the quotations for call and put options at a range of strike prices as shown in Table 32.

Putting these premiums into the Black–Scholes formula we may derive the implied volatilities shown in Table 33.

> Given that volatility is a property of the underlying market, why do different options *on the same underlying* give different implied volatilities? Does merely considering a different option somehow change the underlying market dynamics?

Clearly, merely considering different options cannot change the underlying market dynamics. The reason why implied volatilities vary for different option strike prices is that the probabilistic model assumed by the Black–Scholes formula differs from the true market dynamics. The phenomenon of different implied volatilities for different strike prices is known as the volatility *smile* or *skew* due to its often upward-slanting pictorial representation (see Figure 82).

This divergence between the Black–Scholes model and actual market behaviour can be accounted for by the observation that larger price movements are more frequent than the Black–Scholes model's normal

Table 32. Option prices for a range of strike prices

Option type and strike (US$/bbl)	Price (US$/bbl)
Put, $K=30$	0.50
Put, $K=40$	2.00
Call or put, $K=50$	5.00
Call, $K=60$	3.00
Call, $K=70$	2.00

Table 33. Strike-dependent implied volatilities

Strike (US$/bbl)	Price (US$/bbl)	Implied volatility (%)
30	0.50	36.72
40	2.00	32.46
50	5.00	26.43
60	3.00	32.38
70	2.00	36.77

Figure 82. Volatility smile

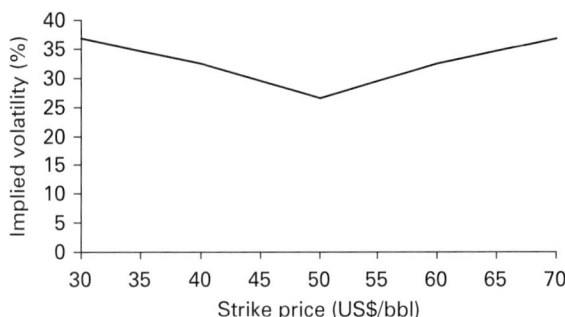

distribution assumptions would suggest. This fat-tailed behaviour is one of the most important factors that option traders need to consider when pricing and hedging their options positions.

> Implied volatility and the Black–Scholes model:
> Since implied volatility is a number implied from an incorrect model to match an observed market price, some people state that:
> "Implied volatility is the wrong number put into wrong model to get the right price".

Moving Beyond European Options

Asian Options

European options are a good way to learn the language and concepts of options, but most OTC energy hedgers employ option contracts that better hedge their exposure to energy prices over a period of time. Much as we started examining energy forwards and futures before moving to swaps, we now turn to *Asian option* or *Average Price Option* contracts, which hedge an energy user's realised price exposure.

Asian options have payoffs that depend not on a single price at expiry (eg, the price of a futures contract), but on an average of realised prices over some period of time.[3] Since Asian options look back at the past, and pay out on the basis of realised prices, they are a type of *look-back* or *path-dependent option*, which is a term readers may encounter from time to time in the financial literature.

The payoffs for Asian options may be written in a similar way to those for European options as follows:

$$\text{Asian call option terminal payoff} = \max(avg(F_t) - K, 0)$$
$$\text{Asian put option terminal payoff} = \max(K - avg(F_t), 0)$$

where it is understood that the average is computed as the mean of the prices F_t through some time period measured by t. The average prices on which Asian options settle are the same as those for swaps, namely market price surveys such as Platts and Argus, or exchange-traded futures settlement prices. Due to the similarities in computing the underlying settlement prices we can say informally, Asian options are the optional equivalents of swaps contracts.

Example: Asian Option Payoffs

Suppose an energy consumer is interested in hedging their exposure to daily NYMEX front-line heating-oil prices during the month of October. During this month the daily prices for NYMEX heating oil are as shown in Table 34.

Fundamental Option Concepts

Table 34. NYMEX front-line heating-oil prices

Date	Daily price (cpg)	Average price (cpg)
01-Oct	Exchange closed	Average not yet started
02-Oct	Exchange closed	Average not yet started
03-Oct	160.43	160.43
04-Oct	161.41	160.92
05-Oct	165.13	162.32
06-Oct	165.22	163.05
07-Oct	164.03	163.24
08-Oct	Exchange closed	163.24
09-Oct	Exchange closed	163.24
10-Oct	160.90	162.85
11-Oct	158.73	162.26
...	...	...
27-Oct	146.78	157.26
28-Oct	146.65	156.73
29-Oct	Exchange closed	156.73
30-Oct	Exchange closed	156.73
31-Oct	141.88	156.02

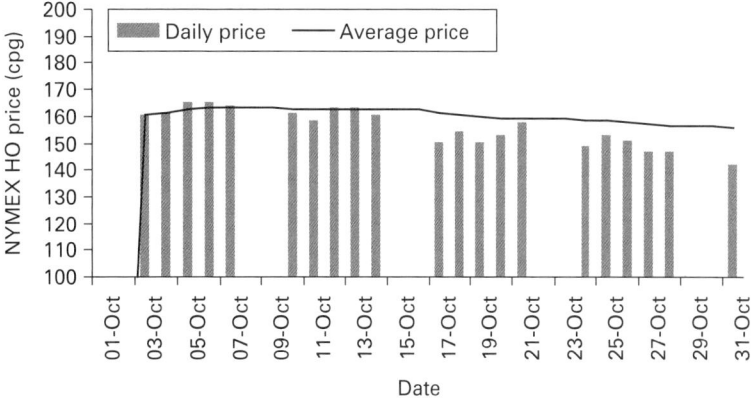

Figure 83. Asian price average

The corresponding graph of heating-oil prices in Figure 83 shows how the average price throughout the month becomes less sensitive to the daily price variations as the month proceeds.

Let's consider how this monthly averaging behaviour would have impacted various hedging strategies:

1. Suppose the hedger had entered a monthly average price swap contract when the monthly swap was at 145 cents per gallon. In this case, come month end the monthly average price is 156.02 cpg, and the hedger would have been due 11.02 cpg from their counterparty.
2. Suppose instead the hedger entered an ATM Asian call option on this monthly average with a strike of 145 cents per gallon. The premium paid for this protection would have been (say) 6.84 cpg, and again come month end the hedger would have been due 11.02 cpg. In this case the hedger would have realised a net profit of (11.02 − 6.84) cpg or 4.18 cpg.
3. Suppose the hedger had bought an OTM Asian call option with a strike price of 160 cpg, and a premium of 2.10 cpg. The option would expire out-of-the-money, and the hedger would have a fixed loss of the premium.

> Draw P&L diagrams for Asian call and put options. How do they differ from their European option equivalents?

The P&L diagrams for Asian calls and put options at expiry are identical to those for European vanilla calls and puts, with the exception that the payoff is computed from an averaged price, not a single price, and so we don't reproduce them here. Readers who want to refresh their memory of these graphs should refer to Figures 56–59.

The block diagrams for Asian calls and puts are instructive since they show in clear terms how an energy consumer or producer, buying or selling commodity at some index throughout a month, can use Asian options to protect their revenues, in exchange for a premium. These cases are shown in Figures 84 and 85 respectively.

The contractual timeline for an Asian option resembles that of a swap somewhat, though the actual formula for settlement is of course different. The timeline is shown in Figure 86.

In general Asian options cost less than their European counterparts, since the volatility of an average price across a period of time is lower than that of the individual price on the last single day of that period. The hedge costs for such an option are correspondingly lower, since as the averaging period proceeds the option trader hedging the position becomes increasingly certain of whether they need to hold the underlying, or not, at expiry. In fact due to this averaging behaviour, the longer the period over which the prices

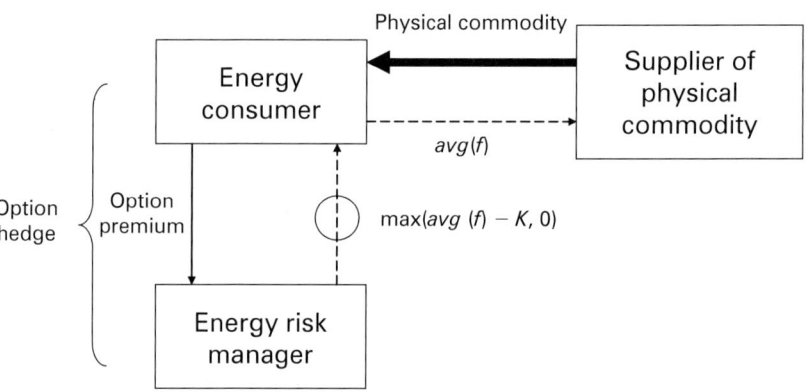

Figure 84. Energy consumer using Asian call option to hedge

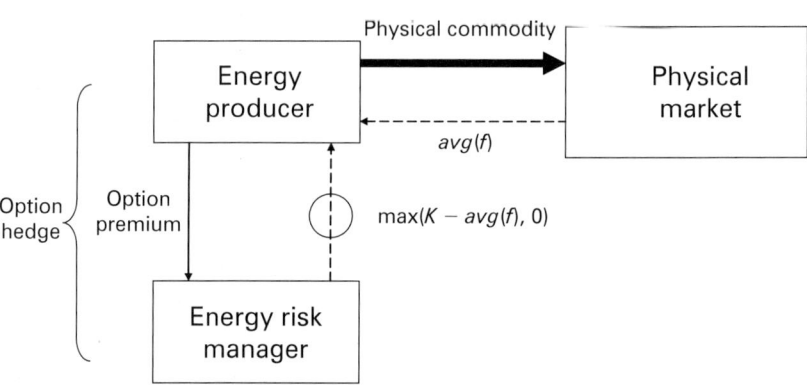

Figure 85. Energy producer using Asian put option to hedge

Figure 86. Asian option contractual timeline

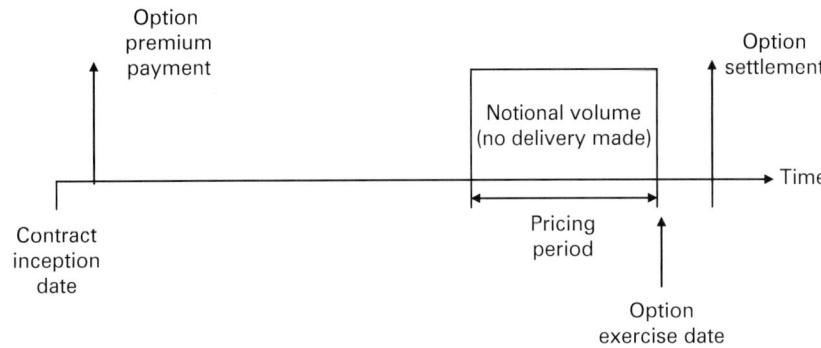

Figure 87. Comparison of European and Asian option premiums for different Asian averaging periods

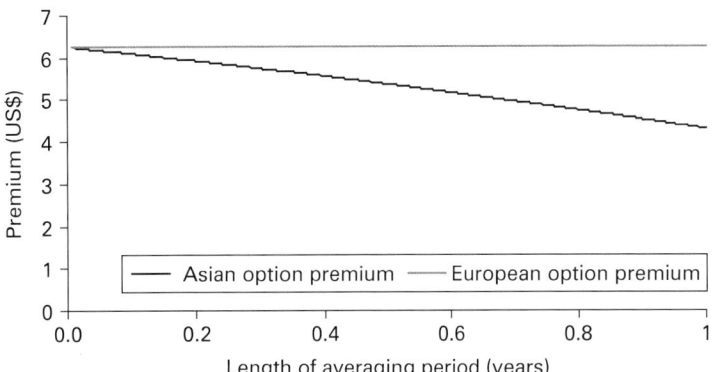

are averaged, the lower the Asian option premium compared with its European equivalent, as shown in Figure 87 for example.

It is common to use cash-settled Asian options on more liquid commodities than the underlying exposure – a jet fuel purchaser for example may choose to hedge using NYMEX lookalike heating oil options. As with swap hedging, proxy risk arises in Asian option hedges wherever the underlying exposure and the hedge fail to match exactly. As for swaps:

- There may not be an option market in the precise grade or location of commodity being bought under the physical supply contract.
- The quantity of energy to be hedged might not match the common market lot sizes, or may be too small to hedge easily in the markets.
- The energy user may not be exposed to an entire month's prices, but only some days within a month.
- The energy user may not take or deliver the same volume each day in a month, while the option contract will usually assume a fixed notional daily volume of commodity.

Greater market liquidity leads to lower hedge costs, and consequently to lower option premiums – this cheaper protection, with residual proxy risk, is often judged to be more cost-effective than a precisely tailored, though expensive, option on an illiquid underlying.

Integrated Physical and Risk Management Contracts

Having examined Asian options, we are now in a position to examine a couple of simple examples of physical contracts that integrate risk management into the settlement prices. These contracts may be offered by those energy risk managers who have access to physical supply or off-take capabilities, and offer clients the following advantages:

- the simplicity of dealing with one counterparty for both their physical and risk management needs, with one settlement through one invoice for both physical and financial legs; and
- potentially simpler accounting treatment, limiting the need to demonstrate that a set of hedges to a physical supply contract are effective.

We have already seen one example of such a contract in the previous chapter when we looked at fixed-price physical contracts. Generically, it is useful to refer to all such transactions as *managed-price physical* (or *MPP*) contracts, two examples of which we'll look at in this section: capped-price physical supply, and floored-price physical off-take.

We start by examining the *capped-price physical* (or *CPP*) contract, in which an energy consumer may receive physical supply at a capped price. This transaction may be represented by the diagram in Figure 88.

Note the flows in this diagram:

- The energy risk manager delivers physical commodity to the consumer.
- The energy consumer pays a premium for the protection.
- The consumer pays the minimum of the floating market price or the fixed cap, denoted by K, per unit volume of physical commodity.

The capped price paid by the consumer is represented most simply by the mathematical *minimum* function, which picks the smaller of its two inputs:

$$\min(A, B) = \begin{cases} A, & \text{if } A \leq B \\ B, & \text{if } B < A \end{cases}$$

Example: CPP Gasoline Supply

Suppose that in early February a gasoline reseller wishes to enter a physical supply contract to purchase unleaded gasoline during the months April, May and June. They consider:

- purchasing at a floating market rate equivalent to NYMEX unleaded gasoline front line contract prices – they discount this possibility since it will leave them fully exposed to floating market prices, and they are very concerned about their cashflows in the second quarter of the year;
- entering a fixed-price physical contract, fixed at the current swap price of US$1.70/gal – they consider this seriously, but fear being locked into a higher price should gasoline prices drop, putting them at a disadvantage to their competitors; and

Figure 88. Capped-price physical contract

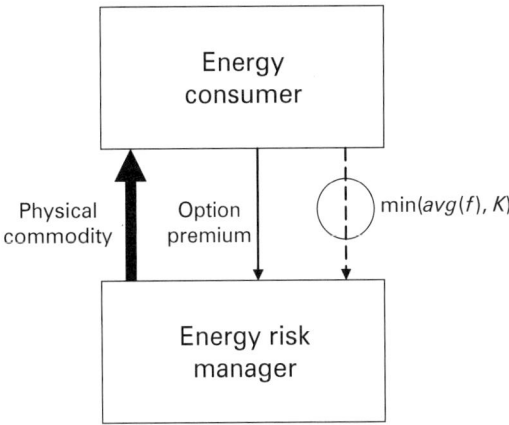

Table 35. Gasoline purchasing commitment

Delivery month	Volume (gal)	Price (US$/gal)	Risk-free interest rate (%)	Volatility (%)
April	420000	1.65	5	35
May	504000	1.69	5	32
June	504000	1.75	5	30

◆ entering a capped-price physical supply contract at the current market level of US$1.70/gal, subject to a premium. They choose to investigate this strategy more carefully.

Their gasoline purchasing commitments, and relevant market data, are shown in Table 35.

After running their option pricing calculations, the energy risk manager computes that the gasoline reseller will need to pay 11.2 USc/gal for this protection, equivalent to a total premium of US$15993600. This premium was computed from the theoretical Black–Scholes values in Table 36, adjusted for market liquidity.

The Black–Scholes option premiums are equivalent to an average of approximately 11.045 USc/gal. Note that, by choosing a single strike price for the entire strip, April and May are OTM options while June is ITM.

After the months have passed, and the monthly averages have been computed, the prices on which settlement will be based are known. The cashflows between the gasoline reseller and the energy risk manager are shown in Table 37.

> (A slightly quantitative exercise.) Can you write the minimum function in terms of the maximum function?

The minimum function may be expressed in terms of the maximum function as follows:

$$\min(A, B) = A - \max(A - B, 0)$$

To see this relationship in action consider the results in Table 38.

Table 36. Gasoline reseller hedge option calculations

Delivery month	Volume (gal)	Premium (US$/gal)	Premium (US$)
April	420000	0.0782659	32871.694
May	504000	0.1060587	53453.572
June	504000	0.1470377	74107.026

Table 37. Capped price physical settlements

Delivery month	Volume (gal)	NYMEX front-line average price (US$/gal)	Price paid for gasoline (US$/gal)	Premium paid (US$/gal)	Total price paid (US$)
April	420000	1.68	1.68	0.112	752640
May	504000	1.71	1.70	0.112	913248
June	504000	1.78	1.70	0.112	913248

Table 38. Relationship between minimum and maximum functions

A	B	min(A, B)	max(A − B, 0)	A − max(A − B, 0)
2	8	min(2, 8) = 2	max(2 − 8, 0) = max(−6, 0) = 0	2 − 0 = 2 = min(2, 8)
10	5	min(10, 5) = 5	max(10 − 5, 0) = max(5, 0) = 5	10 − 5 = 5 = min(10, 5)

It is an instructive exercise in basic financial engineering to understand how CPP contracts can be structured by the energy risk manager. We assume that the structuring desk of the energy risk manager will work with two internal trading desks to synthesise this contract:

1. the physical commodity supply desk, which prefers to receive floating market price for provision of commodity, optimising this against all their other physical flows; and
2. the options trading desk, which is happy to manage the dynamic hedging associated with non-linear derivative instruments.

In Figure 89 we denote the floating market price by f, and the cap price by K. Note that, in addition to the premium, the structuring desk receives $\min(avg(f), K)$ from the consumer, but must provide $avg(f)$ to the physical desk. Since

$$\min(avg(f), K) = avg(f) - \max(avg(f) - K, 0)$$

this means the structuring desk is long the floating index, and short an Asian call option. The structuring desk must therefore buy an Asian call, to receive $\max(avg(f) - K, 0)$ from the options trading desk. The premium charged to the consumer is the option premium needed for this call option.

We turn now to the examination of *floored-price physical* (or *FloorPP*, to distinguish them from fixed-price physical contracts) contracts, in which an energy producer receives payment for their physical production at a floored price. This transaction may be represented by the diagram in Figure 90.

Figure 89. CPP structuring

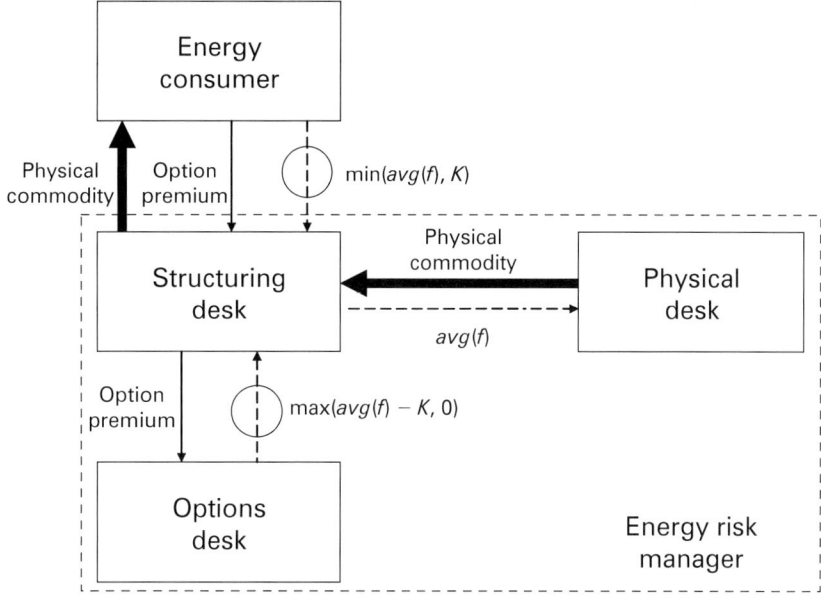

Figure 90. Floored-price physical contract

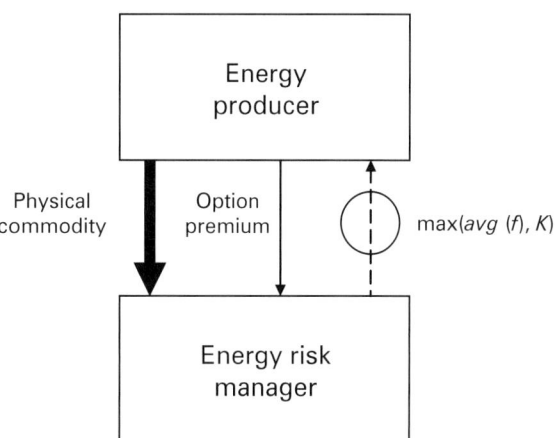

The flows in this diagram are as follows.

- The energy risk manager off-takes physical commodity from the producer.
- The energy producer pays a premium for the protection.
- The producer receives the maximum of the floating market price or the fixed floor, denoted by K, per unit volume of physical commodity.

As the diagram shows, the floored price received by the producer is represented most simply by the mathematical maximum function.

Example: Oil Producer FloorPP

In early October an oil producer, SmartOilCo, is interested in selling forward a portion of next year's firm oil production of 1000 barrels per day with some form of price protection in place. After speaking with its energy risk manager, SmartOilCo decides to investigate the use of a FloorPP contract, since it is feeling bullish on oil prices and does not want to be fully locked into the current market swap price.

Energy Risk Management

Table 39. Oil hedged volumes and market data

Delivery month	Volume (bbl)	Price (US$/bbl)	Risk-free rate (%)	Volatility (%)
January	31000	60.00	5	34
February	28000	60.50	5	33
March	31000	61.00	5	31
April	30000	61.50	5	30
May	31000	62.00	5	29
June	30000	62.25	5	28
July	31000	62.50	5	26
August	31000	62.75	5	25
September	30000	63.00	5	24
October	31000	63.00	5	23
November	30000	63.25	5	22
December	31000	63.25	5	21

Table 40. FloorPP quotations for SmartOilCo

Strike (US$/bbl)	Premium (US$/bbl)
45.00	0.40
50.00	1.10
55.00	2.30
60.00	4.30
62.10 (ATM)	5.35

The energy risk manager advises that the current forward market looks as shown in Table 39, and computes the swap price as US$62.10/bbl.

SmartOilCo's risk managers ask their energy risk manager for quotations on a range of different floor prices, and they receive the prices in Table 40.

After consulting their cashflow forecasts and budgets for the coming year they decide they'd like protection in place in the form of a floor at US$50/bbl. They enter into the FloorPP and pay the premium of US$401500 up front.

---

1. How can the payoff $\max(avg(f), K)$ be synthesised in terms of the floating index and some form of Asian option?
2. How can the energy risk manager synthesise a FloorPP contract?

To understand how the energy risk manager will synthesise the FloorPP contract we assume again that the structuring desk will work with:

- the physical commodity supply desk, which prefers to pay floating market price for commodity; and
- the options trading desk.

In Figure 91 we denote again the floating market price by f, and the floor price by K. In exchange for the physical commodity and the upfront premium the structuring desk pays $\max(avg(f), K)$ to the consumer; it also receives $avg(f)$ from the physical desk. Since

$$\max(avg(f), K) = avg(f) + \max(K - avg(f), 0)$$

this means the structuring desk is short the floating index, and short an Asian put option. The structuring desk must therefore buy an Asian put to receive $\max(avg(f), 0)$ from the options trading desk. The premium charged to the consumer is the option premium needed for this put option.

American Options

Strictly speaking the term "American" refers to a style of exercise, not a style of payoff.

American options can be exercised any time from inception up to expiry, in contrast with European options, which can be exercised only on the expiration date. American options are especially useful to those who monitor market prices, or have a view on future market price movements, since the holder of an American option needs to ask the question "Should I hold, or exercise now?" as each day passes. An American option timeline diagram is shown in Figure 92.

> Would you expect American options to be worth more than, less than or the same as their European equivalents?

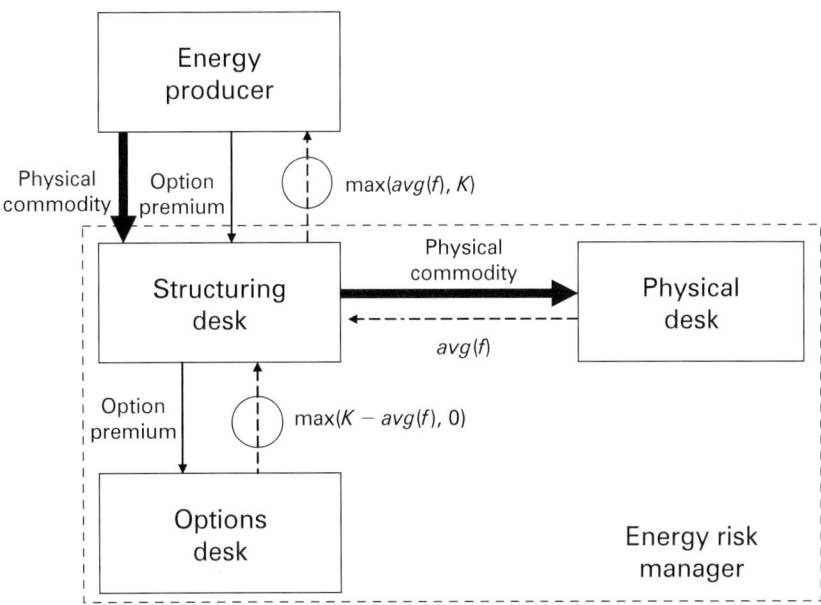

Figure 91. FloorPP structuring

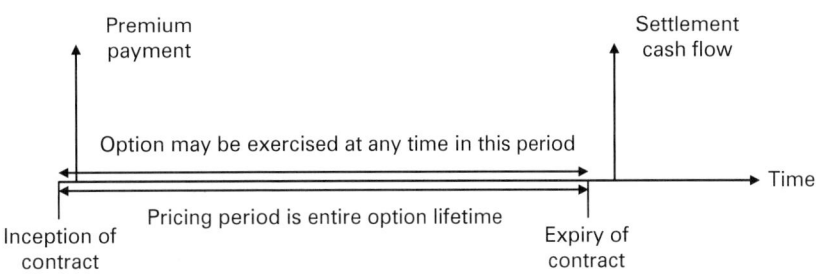

Figure 92. American option timeline with settlement after expiry of underlying

Such options are usually worth more than their European counterparts since they offer greater flexibility to their holder. With European options the holder is left hoping that if the option has moved into the money, then it will continue to remain in the money until expiry. American options can be used to ensure that if some trigger level is achieved, the holder can lock in that price there and then.

Most hedgers first encounter such options as American options on futures, the common option type traded on futures exchanges. Exchange-traded options on futures expire a few days before the underlying futures contract, and if an option is exercised it is delivered as underlying futures contracts. Of course the futures contracts themselves can be liquidated immediately, realising the difference between the futures and strike prices as cash; in this case option "settlement" will have occurred before expiry of the underlying.

The amount of optionality one holds and when it may be exercised are useful ways to categorise energy options. The difference between vanilla American and European options is summarised in Table 41.

As we consider other option types, including real options, we may extend Table 41 to show clearly the distinction between different American and European styles of exercise.

> Suppose a natural-gas consumer is long a cap, which is to say they are long a strip of European exercise-style Asian monthly call options. Since they may exercise on any month during the strip, does this mean that a strip of European options is equivalent to an American option?

No. This is a common confusion, and one that is even more common when considering real options. A strip of European options is exactly that – a series of independent European options, each of which may be exercised, or not, independently of all the others.

In Table 42 I have included now a quarterly strip of European options to show the distinction between strips of Europeans and American options.

American options are the first type of option we've encountered with *contingent optionality* – an exercise decision made at one moment affects one's exercise decisions at later dates. In the case of an American option on a futures contract exercising early removes one's right to exercise later. We can see that a strip of European options has no contingent optionality at all.

Table 41. Categorising European and American options

Consider the holder of an option ...		
Option categorisation	European	American
How many "units of optionality" available to spend?	1	1
How many "units of optionality" must be spent?	0	0
When may the units of optionality be spent?	At expiry only	Any time up to expiry

Table 42. Categorising European and American options, and strips of Europeans

Consider the holder of an option ...			
Option categorisation	Single European	Quarter-length strip of Europeans	American
How many "units of optionality" available to spend?	1	3	1
How many "units of optionality" must be spent?	0	0	0
When may the units of optionality be spent?	At expiry only	At monthly expiry of each European option in strip only	Any time up to expiry

Other option types exist that readers may encounter from time to time:

- *Bermudan options* allow exercise on some specified number of dates between inception and expiry. Bermudan options are so named because their exercise characteristics are somewhere between European and American. They are contingent exercise options.
- *Asian American options* allow their holders to exercise early on the realised average so far of the underlying.
- *Take-or-pay options*, or *swing options*, have contingent optionality. Such options arise in commodity supply or off-take agreements in which the holder of the option can vary the volume of commodity they exercise on any given date, subject to some overall constraints. Swing options have contingent optionality since choosing to exercise a greater volume of commodity at one time, will mean there are fewer "units of exercise" left to exercise at later dates.

More examples of contingent or American-style optionality arise in the field of real options and asset-backed trading.

Swaptions

Options on swaps, *swap options*, or *swaptions* give their holders the right, but not the obligation, to enter a swap contract on exercise. Swaptions are often European in nature, and are distinct from the options contracts we have seen above, which delivered either a futures contract or a cash settlement on expiry. The swap delivered on exercise will give a series of fixed-for-floating cashflow exchanges in the usual manner for such swaps.

The swaption strike price is the price to be used for the fixed leg of the underlying swap contract. A call swaption of strike K gives its holder the right, but not the obligation, to go long a swap with strike price K. Should the call swaption be exercised, the holder will then be long a swap in which they pay the fixed price, and receive floating, in the usual manner. This transaction is represented in Figure 93, where a premium is paid for the right (but not obligation) to receive the fixed-for-floating differences, which on exercise becomes a commitment to do so.

Figure 93. Call swaption

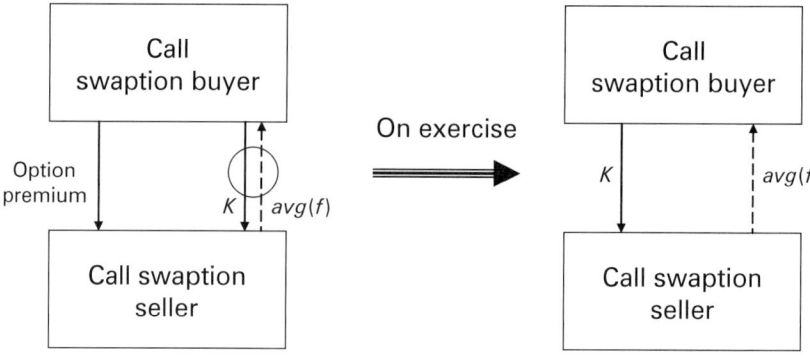

Figure 94. Put swaption

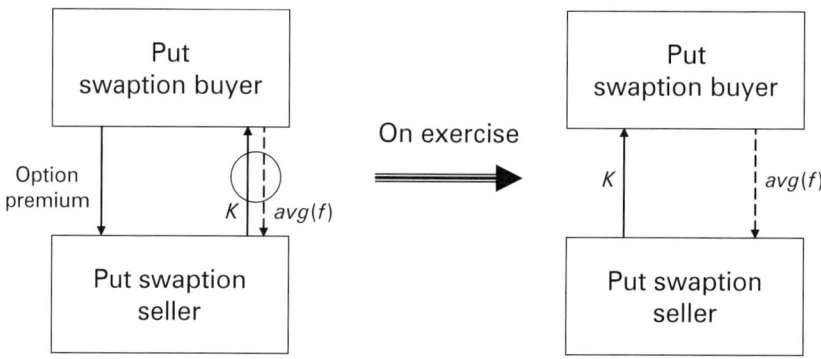

A put swaption gives its holder the right but not the obligation to go short a swap contract on exercise; in this case they will pay floating and receive fixed. A put swaption contract block diagram is shown in Figure 94.

Since swaps, Asian options and swaptions have payoffs dependent on realised prices, it is important to understand the distinction between these instruments.

◆ Swaps contracts place an obligation on their holders to exchange fixed-for-floating cashflows.
◆ Asian options give their holders the right, but not the obligation, to receive the difference between an average price and a strike price once the average price is known.
◆ With swaptions the exercise decision is made before any averaging starts, and swaptions confer on their holders the option to enter a swap contract with a pre-agreed strike price at the market prevailing at exercise time.

Readers should consult the diagrams in Figures 95 and 96 to clarify the distinction between the two types of option instrument.

Swaptions may be used by hedgers who want to fix prices, but feel there is great uncertainty about the direction of the market. Rather than lock in commodity prices with a swap immediately, they buy a swaption, allowing them to delay the locking-in decision. As the swaption approaches its expiry date the hedger will review the market.

Figure 95. Asian option timeline

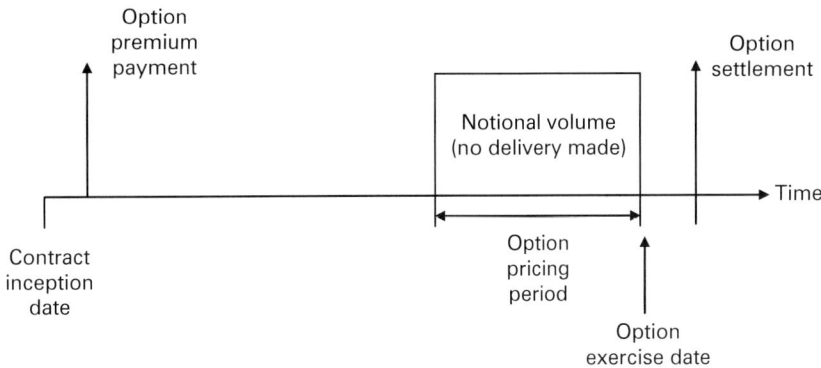

Figure 96. Swaption timeline

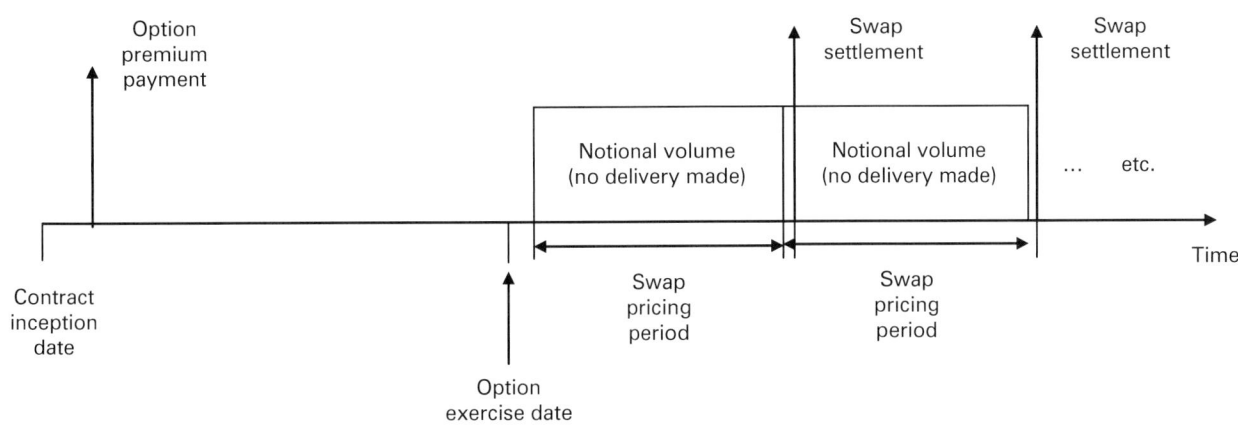

♦ If the swaption is ITM at the expiry date, the holder exercises the swaption and enters a swap, effectively locking in commodity prices at the swaption strike price.
♦ If swaption is OTM, they don't exercise the swaption. Instead they enter a new swap at the prevailing market swap price, allowing them to lock in a more favourable price.

Example: Natural Gas Swaption

In early July, a large US consumer of natural gas are considering their hedging for the next calendar year. Their usual policy is to lock in prices through the use of NYMEX lookalike natural-gas swaps. Recent high natural-gas price volatility means that they are concerned about where prices may move in the coming months. They feel it is too early to lock in the next calendar year with a swap, but are concerned that if they wait too long then prices may climb significantly. After consulting with their energy risk manager they decide to investigate the use of swaptions.

Their energy risk manager advises them that a call swaption on the next calendar year will mean they can enter a swap contract at a level to be fixed today, if they wish, near year end. It would be favourable for them to do so if market prices climb between now and the end of the year. If prices drop, they simply let the swaption expire unexercised, and enter a swap contract at the prevailing market price.

Table 43. Call swaption quotations

Call swaption strike price, US$/MMBtu	Premium, US$/MMBtu
7.00	1.17
7.50	0.90
8.00	0.63
8.50	0.45
9.00	0.30
9.50	0.20
10.00	0.13

The current swap price for the following calendar year is US$8.00/MMBtu, and the energy risk manager offers them the quotations for call swaptions shown in Table 43.

The consumer decides that, while they can bear prices above the current swap price, they'd be uncomfortable with natural gas prices above US$9.00/MMBtu. They feel that the premium of US$0.30/MMBtu is affordable protection and enter into a US$9.00/MMBtu call swaption, as indicated in Figure 97.

At the end of the year, if the swap price for the next year's natural gas is at or above US$9.00/MMBtu, then the gas consumer will exercise their swaption, and lock in prices at this level. If the market is lower than US$9.00/MMBtu, they will let the option expire unexercised, and lock in at the current lower price.

> Draw the block diagram for a producer of crude oil interested in the right, but not the obligation, to lock in WTI crude prices at US$55/bbl. (Assume that they sell their crude into the market at a monthly average index.) What kind of instrument is the producer using?

Swaptions are also extremely important for their role in constructing packages of risk management products such as extendables, cancellables and so on. See the chapter "Derivatives Packages" for more details.

The Cost of Hedging with Options

In this chapter we have looked at a number of examples of how options may be used to hedge physical energy positions, and have also considered the factors that impact the cost of such protection. In all the cases examined so far the hedger pays an option premium for the protection offered.

> What can a hedger do if they feel that the option premium is too expensive?

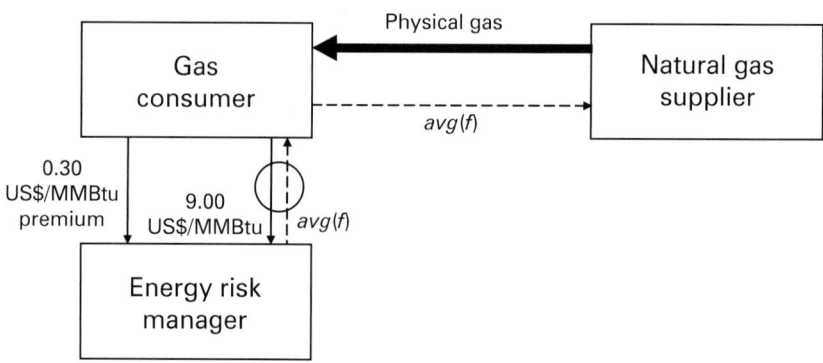

Figure 97. Natural gas consumer call swaption

Fundamental Option Concepts

In all cases the level of premium charged is appropriate for the protection offered. Since there is no such thing as a free lunch, the only way to lower the premium is to forego some of the protection. With the examples we have seen so far, the possibilities we might consider are:

- change option strike price; and
- don't hedge the full physical volume.

> With a call option, does raising the strike price make the option cheaper or more expensive? What about with a put option?

For call options, raising the strike price makes the option cheaper, since the option holder will not see any benefit until they feel more "pain" from the market. For put options the converse is true. In Figure 98 we can see the change in call option premium for a US$50/bbl call as the strike price changes, while in Figure 99 we see the corresponding graph for a US$50/bbl put option.

Since the total premium paid is the product of premium per unit volume and the total volume hedged:

$$\text{total premium} = \text{premium per unit volume} \times \text{volume}$$

another way of lowering the total payment is to hedge less than the full volume. Derivatives where only a portion of the exposure is hedged in order to reduce premium are called *participating options* or *participations*. The P&L

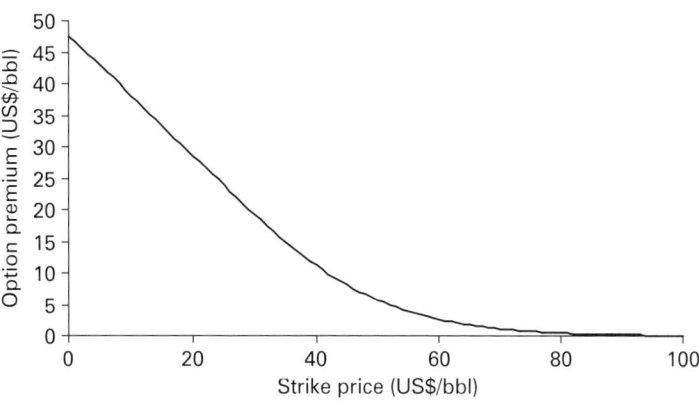

Figure 98. Call option dependence on strike price

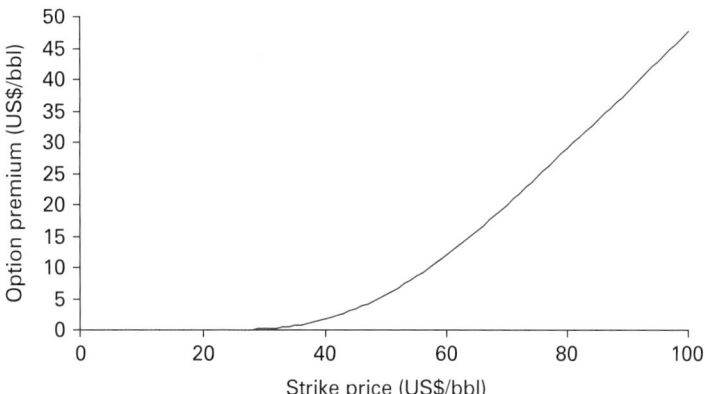

Figure 99. Put option dependence on strike price

Figure 100. Call option and 50% participating call option

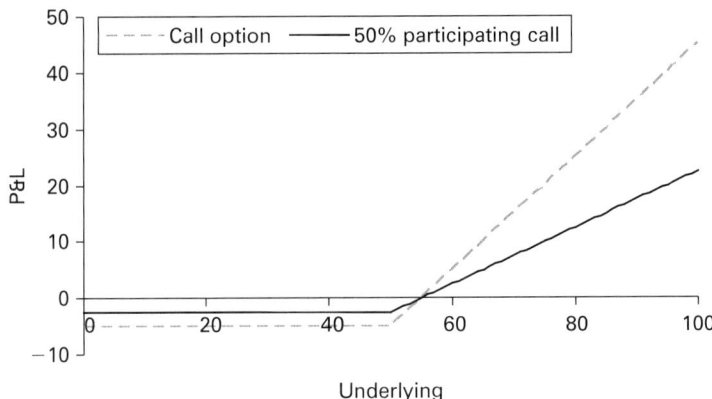

diagram for a full 50 strike call option, and a 50% participating 50 strike call option, is shown in Figure 100. Note that:

- the slope of the 50% participating call is only half that of the full call option; and
- the premium is only half the size.

Example: Oil Producer Reduces Option Premium by Sacrificing Some Protection

An oil producer is considering the use of put options to hedge 1000 barrels per day of production throughout the coming year. The oil swap price for the next production year is around US$62.00/bbl, and while the producer would like to buy a floor close to this price level they are concerned about the cost of the hedge programme. The producer asks their energy risk manager for a range of quotations for:

- different floor strikes; and
- different participation levels.

The producer's risk management budget for the coming production year is around US$1 million, and they would like to understand what kind of protection they could receive for this much premium.

The energy risk manager responds with the prices in Table 44.

Table 44. Different floor strikes vs different put participation levels

Full-volume put hedge		Participation, strike = US$60/bbl	
Strike (US$/bbl)	Total premium (US$)	Participation level (%)	Total premium (US$)
60.00	1409574.00	100	1409574.00
59.00	1246463.00	95	1339095.30
58.00	1095088.00	90	1268616.60
57.00	955479.60	85	1198137.90
56.00	827577.60	80	1127659.20
55.00	711233.30	75	1057180.50
54.00	606205.20	70	986701.80
53.00	512160.60	65	916223.10
52.00	428678.40	60	845744.40
51.00	355254.90	55	775265.70
50.00	291312.00	50	704787.00

The oil producer can see that their budget of US$1 million will buy them either a floor for their total volume of US$57.00/bbl, or a participating floor of US$60/bbl on 70% of their volume.

> How do option traders make their money?
>
> Option traders engage in a wide range of trading activities that reflect the broad categories of trading defined in the Break-out Box "Types of energy trading" in the chapter "Risk in Energy Markets". This may include writing options and hedging these positions dynamically in the market, speculative trading through treating volatility itself as an asset, buying options when they expect volatility to increase and selling when they expect it to decrease, or selling flexibility from asset operations in order to monetise optionality. All forms of option trading involve running theoretical option pricing models, then making adjustments to these prices based upon market liquidity, volume and market lot sizes to arrive at a practical price or hedging strategy.

Chapter Review and Look Ahead

In this chapter we started our investigation of options through the use of European options. After learning the basic language associated with these instruments, we learned that there is a distinction between payoff and P&L diagrams, since options have a premium associated with them. After a basic look at how hedgers may use options to protect themselves against downside market movements, we moved on to an examination of what factors impact option premiums. This necessitated an examination of volatility, its term structure and what assumptions must be made for models to arrive at theoretical option values.

After leaving these theoretical issues behind, we moved on to the most common option types used by energy hedgers, namely OTC Asian or average-price options, and exchange-traded American options. We examined how Asian options can be used by integrated energy risk managers to offer managed-price physical contracts to their clients, and learned a way of categorising options according to when they may be exercised, and whether exercising affects later exercise opportunities. Then, a look at swaption contracts gave us the opportunity to understand how a hedger may buy the right to lock in prices at some later date.

We finally moved on to look at some simple premium-reduction strategies for hedgers, in which they sacrifice some of their protection in exchange for a cheaper option premium payment. In the next chapter we take this subject further, looking at how combinations of multiple derivatives, or *derivative packages*, may offer hedgers cheaper protection through sacrificing price upside in very specific price ranges. Derivatives packages may allow for a better matching of a hedger's risk management needs to the level of premium they are prepared to pay.

> Risk management themes encountered so far:
>
> - locking in;
> - tying costs to revenues;
> - switching one price exposure for another;
> - joint hedging of combined currency and commodity exposures;
> - protecting against downside;
> - delaying a locking in decision;
> - sharing the pain using participation; and
> - managed price physical.

Technical Appendix: Black–Scholes Option Valuation

In this section we reproduce the Black 1976 formula for pricing an option on a futures contract. The Black 1976 formula is a special case of the Black–Scholes formula, and is the most widely used basic option pricing formula in energy derivatives. The prevalence of Black 1976 is due to the fact that the bulk of energy derivative trading and hedging is conducted using the futures and swaps markets, rather than by buying spot physical, holding, then selling at a later stage.

Suppose the current market futures price is F, the strike price for the option is K, the risk-free interest rate is r, the time to expiry of the option (and assumed cash liquidation) is T and the implied volatility is σ. With these parameters the price for a call option is

$$prem_{call} = e^{-rT}(FN(d_1) - KN(d_2))$$

and for a put option is

$$prem_{put} = e^{-rT}(KN(-d_2) - FN(-d_1))$$

In both these expressions $N(x)$ is the cumulative standard normal distribution function,

$$d_1 = \frac{\ln(F/K) + \frac{1}{2}\sigma^2 T}{\sigma\sqrt{T}}$$

and

$$d_2 = d_1 - \sigma\sqrt{T}$$

Notes

1 For simplicity's sake we assume that the futures price on which the option pays off, and the index on which the consumer is purchasing their physical heating oil, match precisely – that is, we ignore the proxy risk.
2 We assume for the examples in this section that prices are lognormally distributed.
3 The most common Asian options still have a European exercise style – that is to say they can be exercised only at a single date. The terminology of Asian, European, American and so forth is somewhat arbitrary but is completely standard. The adjective *Asian* refers to a style of payoff, while the adjective *European* refers to at what point the holder of an option may exercise.

6 Derivatives Packages

Act with earnestness

Combining Derivatives into a Package

There are times when a single derivative instrument cannot meet the risk management needs of an energy market participant, or where the protection offered by such an instrument is prohibitively expensive. In these cases the player may wish to consider *derivatives packages*, which are a combination of a number of more basic swap and option contracts. Packages allow energy players to:

- receive a tailored solution to their risk management needs;
- minimise their premium by sacrificing some upside potential;
- benefit from a view they may have on market price movements; and
- build in flexibility.

Before we look in more detail at how and why such structures may be used, let's examine the mechanics of constructing some simple packages.

Example: Call Spread

A *(bull) call spread* structure consists of a long call option, with a short call option at a higher strike price. In this example we construct a call spread with strikes at 50 and 70. To construct the package we simply tabulate the values for the long and short options, then add their values, as shown in Table 45.

Table 45. Bull call spread

Underlying	Long-call payoff	Short-call payoff	Call spread payoff
...	...	...	...
10	0	0	0
20	0	0	0
30	0	0	0
40	0	0	0
50	0	0	0
60	10	0	10
70	20	0	20
80	30	−10	20
90	40	−20	20
100	50	−30	20
...	...	...	...

Figure 101. Bull call spread payoff at expiry diagram

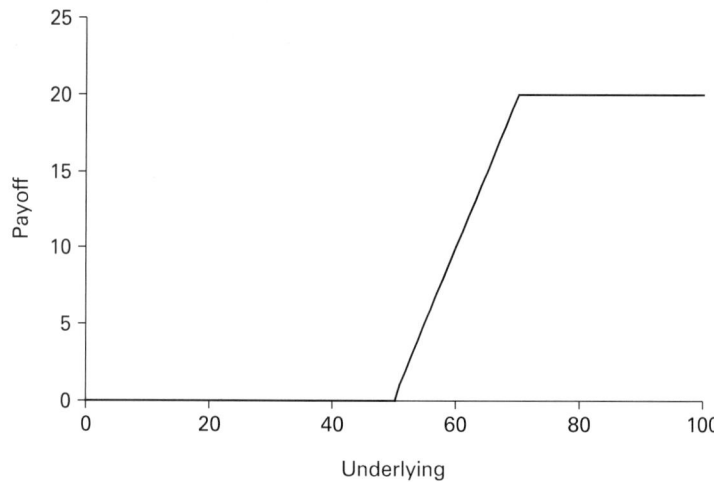

Figure 102. Bull call spread block diagram

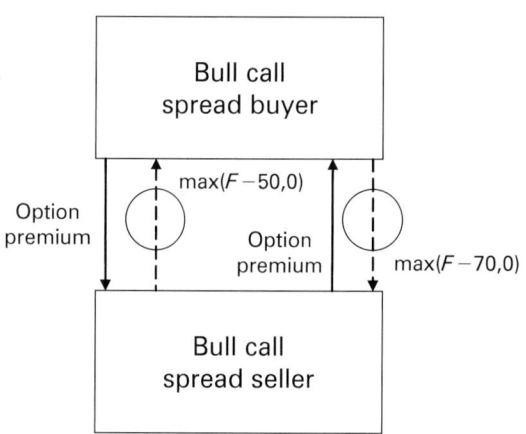

Figure 103. Bull call spread P&L before expiry

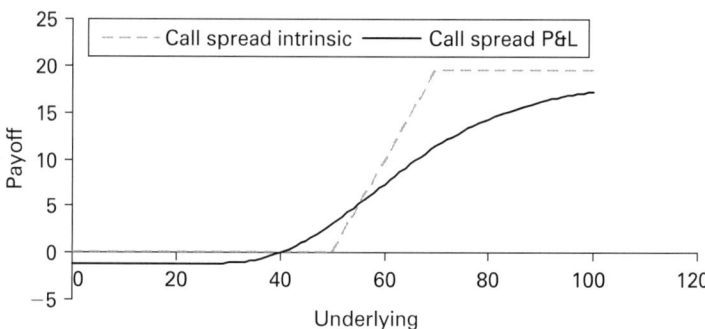

The results of Table 45 are plotted as a payoff diagram in Figure 101.

As a financial block diagram the transactions leading to a bull call spread are those shown in Figure 102.

As the figure shows, each counterparty pays some premium to the other for the option they are buying; in practice, the larger premium is lowered by netting off against the smaller premium.[1] The P&L diagram before expiry is shown in Figure 103, which assumes the current market is at 40.

This first derivative package introduces us to some of the most important concepts needed to understand packages:

- adding multiple payoffs at expiry; and
- netting of premiums.

Since such spreads are useful building blocks for other derivatives packages, we conduct here a brief examination of the different types of simple spread that may be constructed. *Bull spreads* are generically those packages that pay off an increasing amount as the underlying at expiry increases; it is from the bullish fact that they make greater profit in a rising market that they derive their "bull" name. In contrast, *bear spreads* are those that pay an increasing amount as the underlying market decreases, taking a "bearish" view.

Package: Bull call spread.

Construction: Constructed from a long call at strike K_1 with a short call at a higher strike price K_2.[2] See Figure 104.

Payoff characteristics: Pays off zero, or an amount increasing between the two strike prices, up to a maximum of $K_2 - K_1$.

Cost: Since call option premiums decrease with increasing strike price (see Figure 98) the long call costs more than is earned back from the short call. Therefore, a bull call spread requires an upfront investment, and pays back an amount that is either zero or positive.

Package: Bear call spread.

Construction: Constructed from a short call at strike K_1 with a long call at a higher strike price K_2. See Figure 105.

Figure 104. Bull call spread construction

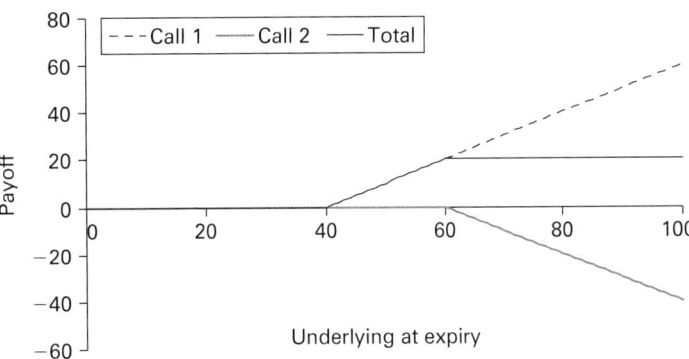

Figure 105. Bear call spread construction

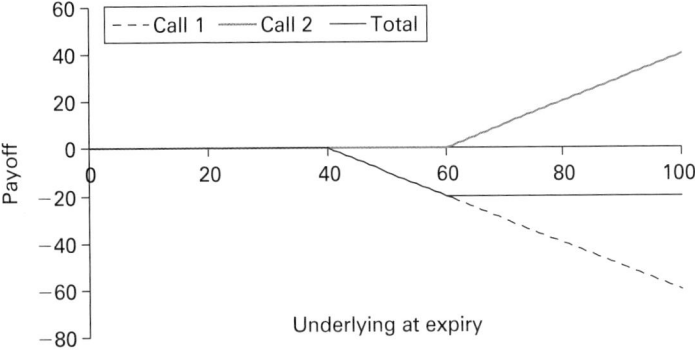

Figure 106. Bull put spread construction

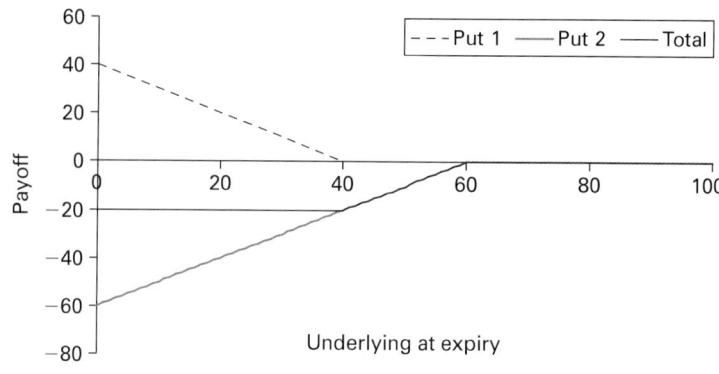

Figure 107. Bear put spread construction

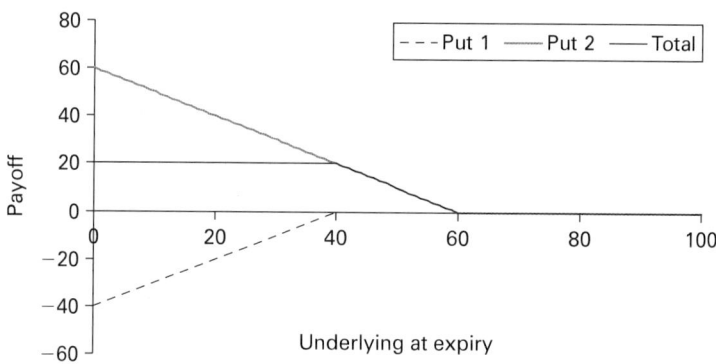

Payoff characteristics: Pays off zero, or an amount increasingly negative between the two strike prices, to a maximum negative amount of $K_1 - K_2$.

Cost: Since call option premiums decrease with increasing strike price (see Figure 98) the long call costs less than is earned from the short call. Therefore, a bear call spread earns money upfront, and pays out an amount that is either zero or negative, requiring that the structure holder pays either zero or a positive amount.

Package: Bull put spread.

Construction: Constructed from a long put at strike K_1 with a short put at a higher strike price K_2. See Figure 106.

Payoff characteristics: Pays off a negative amount ($K_1 - K_2$ at its most negative), or an amount increasing between the two strike prices, up to a maximum of zero.

Cost: Since put option premiums increase with increasing strike price (see Figure 99) the long put costs less than is earned from the short put. Therefore a bull put spread earns money upfront, and pays out an amount that is either zero or negative, requiring that the structure holder pays either zero or a positive amount.

Package: Bear put spread.

Construction: Constructed from a short put at strike K_1 with a long put at a higher strike price K_2. See Figure 107.

Figure 108. Swap-call P&L diagram

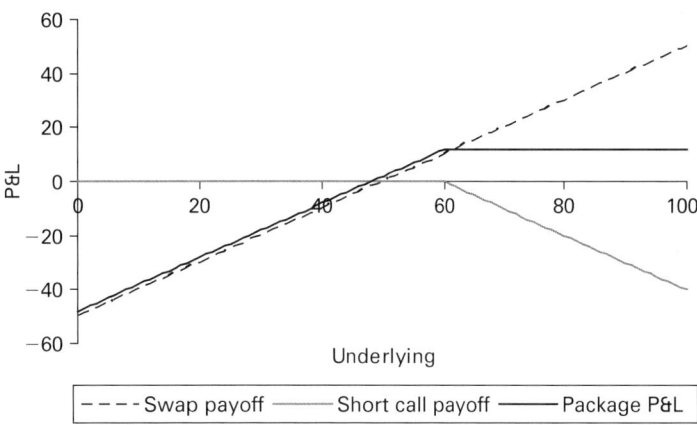

Payoff characteristics: Pays off a positive amount (a maximum of $K_2 - K_1$), or an amount decreasing between the two strike prices, down to a minimum of zero.

> The bear put spread pays an amount that is positive or zero. Do you think the holder of such a structure must pay upfront, or do they receive premium upfront?

Common sense dictates that if the structure provides a non-negative return the holder must pay money to enter the position. We can therefore complete our categorisation of the bear put spread:

Cost: Since put option premiums increase with increasing strike price (see Figure 99) the long put costs more than is earned back from the short put. Therefore, a bear put spread requires an upfront investment, and pays back an amount that is either zero or positive.

> Swap-call package
> Suppose a market participant enters into a derivative package in which they are long a swap (assuming the market to be at 50), and short a 60 strike call option.
>
> ♦ Draw the P&L-at-expiry diagram. Assume the premium of the call option is 2.
> ♦ Draw the block diagram for this transaction.

Since the market participant is short the call option they receive the premium of 2. The P&L-at-expiry diagram is shown in Figure 108.

The block diagram corresponding to this transaction is shown in Figure 109.

If we compare the flows of fixed and floating quantities, it is clear that, on netting:

♦ the structure buyer makes a fixed payment of 48 each month; and
♦ the structure buyer receives a floating payment only up to 60, above which they sacrifice any potential upside.

Figure 109. Swap-call block diagram

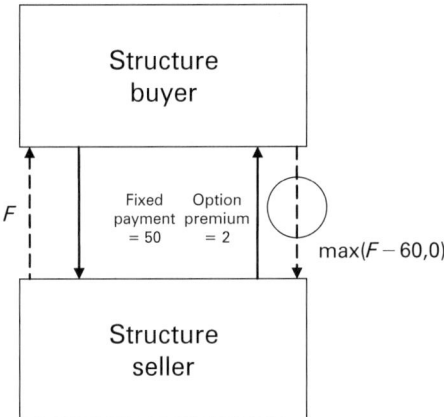

> Does the form of the package P&L resemble any single instrument you have encountered? (You need to ignore the axes and look only at the shape of the payoff.)

The package P&L resembles the payoff of a short put option. This is not a coincidence, as the next section shows.

Relationship Between Put and Call Option Values

Put–call parity is the relationship obeyed between call and put options with the same strike, and relates their prices to MTM value of the underlying futures or swap contract.

> Suppose the current swap price for a commodity is 50. Can you construct the swap payoff-at-expiry diagram using a package of calls and puts? (Clue: You'll need to use ATM calls and puts.)

A 50 strike swap payoff diagram may be formed by using a long 50 strike call option and a short 50 strike put option. This is demonstrated in Figure 110.

This same behaviour can be confirmed by consulting the payoff table in Table 46.

Figure 110. Put–call parity diagram

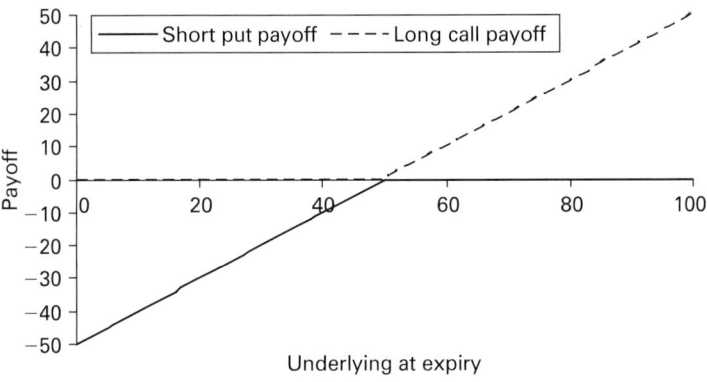

Table 46. Put–call parity payoff table

Underlying value	Long call payoff	Short put payoff	Package payoff
...	...	...	...
10	0	40	−40
20	0	30	−30
30	0	20	−20
40	0	10	−10
50	0	0	0
60	10	0	10
70	20	0	20
80	30	0	30
90	40	0	40
...	...	...	...

> What types of call and put option did you use in constructing your put–call parity relationship?

Since you were replicating a swap payoff you needed to use Asian calls and puts in your derivative package. Swap payoffs are based upon realised commodity prices, and so are those of Asian options. If you were replicating the payoff for a futures contract you'd have needed European options on futures contracts.

The put–call parity relationship is:

$$\text{Call payoff} - \text{Put payoff} = \text{Swap payoff}$$

This may be rearranged algebraically to give:

$$\text{Call payoff} = \text{Swap payoff} + \text{Put payoff}$$
$$\text{Put payoff} = \text{Call payoff} - \text{Swap payoff}$$

It is possible to develop an intuition for put–call parity by a number of methods, where the most obvious one is to draw payoff tables and corresponding diagrams, then convince yourself of the result.[3] These put–call parity results hold for all times up to expiry (not only *at* expiry), and so we can refine our put–call parity relationship to say:

$$\text{Call premium} - \text{Put premium} = \text{Swap MTM}$$

> Show that for ATM options: call premium = put premium.

When ATM, the MTM of a swap is zero. Since

$$\text{ATM call premium} - \text{ATM put premium} = \text{ATM swap MTM}$$

we must have

$$\text{ATM call premium} - \text{ATM put premium} = 0$$

or

$$\text{ATM call premium} = \text{ATM put premium}$$

This relationship demonstrates that when one goes long an ATM call and short an ATM put the premiums of the two transactions cancel perfectly, replicating a swap (which is of course costless to enter). If the strike prices don't match perfectly, then:

- a premium may be due; and
- the net payoff may resemble a familiar derivative, but shifted above or below the x axis.

These points are what we observed in the question above, where we considered going long a swap and short a call. The net result looked like a short put option, but shifted above the x axis.

> More on option delta
>
> Following on from the box "Moneyness and option delta" in the chapter "Fundamental Option Concepts", we now look in a little more detail at the notion of option delta. Option delta is formally defined as the slope of the option premium in an option payoff diagram; for an OTM call or put the payoff is almost horizontal, and the delta is near zero. For an ITM call the payoff slopes at almost 45 degrees to the x axis, and the delta is near one since the gradient is near one at this point. Similar considerations apply for put options, though the slope of an ITM put is close to minus one, since each penny *increase* in the price of the underlying leads to a near-penny *decrease* in the option value. As the option payoff passes the strike price its slope passes close to plus or minus one half, and so we can say that ATM call options have delta near $+0.5$, and ATM put options have delta near -0.5. As always, these facts may be better summarised on a graph, and so the deltas for call (Figure 111) and put (Figure 112) options are illustrated.

Figure 111. Vanilla call option delta

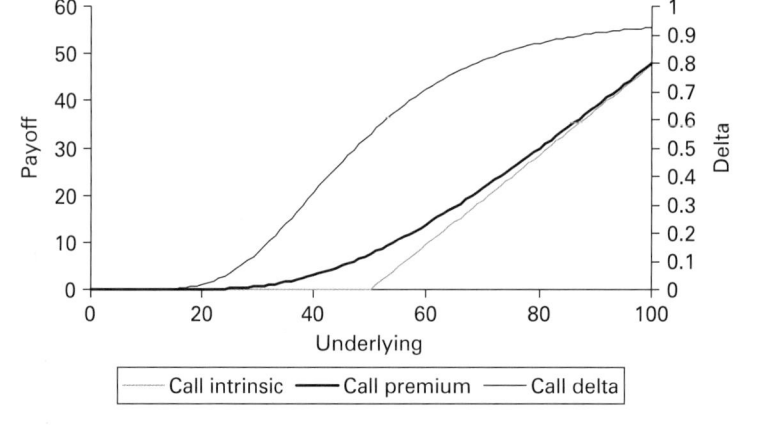

(continued)

Figure 112. Vanilla put option delta

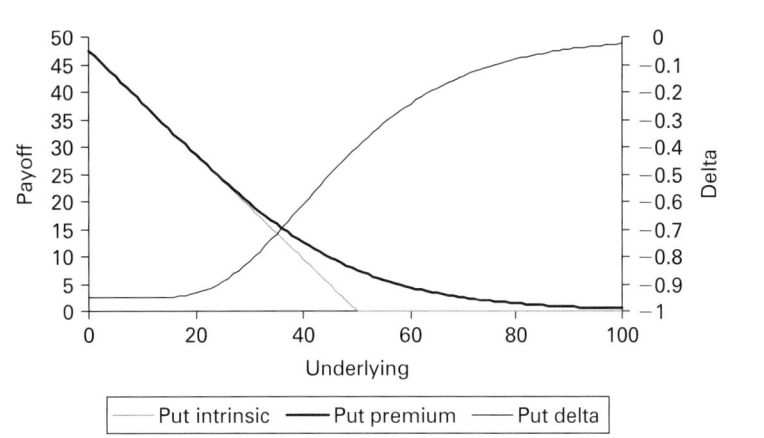

To understand the delta of an options package one needs to know the following:

- the delta of a short option is the negative of the delta of the long option position;
- the delta of a volume of option position is the volume multiplied by the delta of a single unit of the option; and
- to find the delta of an options package one needs only add the deltas of its component parts.

To illustrate some of these points, in Figure 113 is shown the delta of a bull call spread.

Figure 113. Delta of bull call spread

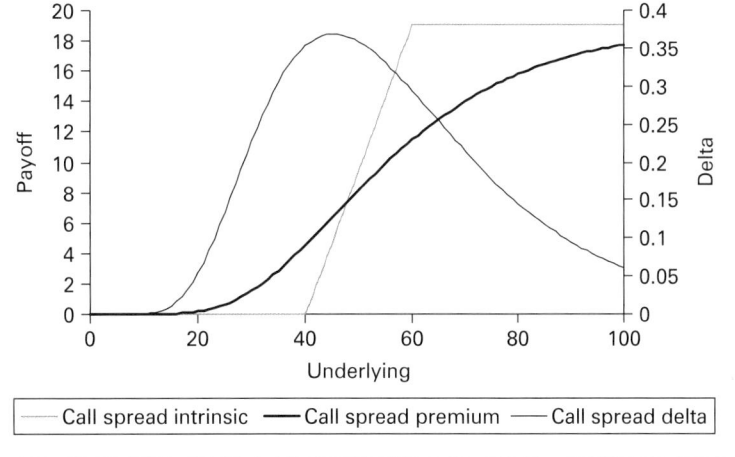

Collars and Premium Reduction

The *collar* instrument is a simple derivatives package designed to offer producers or end-users price protection at an affordable level of premium. This is achieved by buying protection against downside price movements using a floor or cap in the usual way, and reducing the premium by giving up some of their upside also.

A *consumer collar* involves the consumer purchasing a call option (for downside protection) and selling a put option of a lower strike. Suppose a consumer is buying physical commodity at some floating price F, and is concerned about prices moving above 60. They enter into a consumer collar

Figure 114. Consumer collar transaction

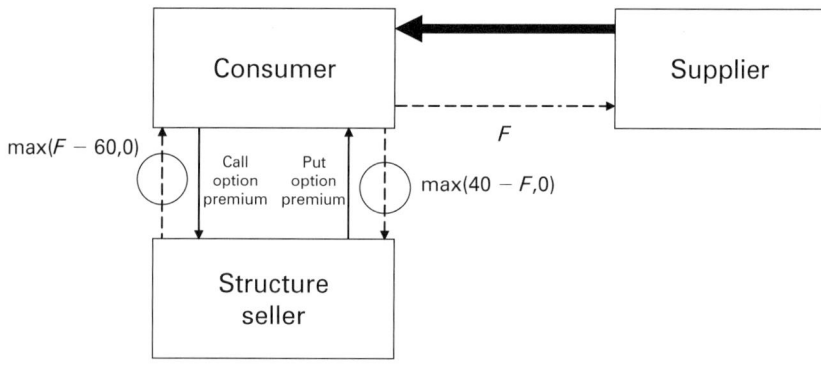

Figure 115. Consumer collar payoff diagram

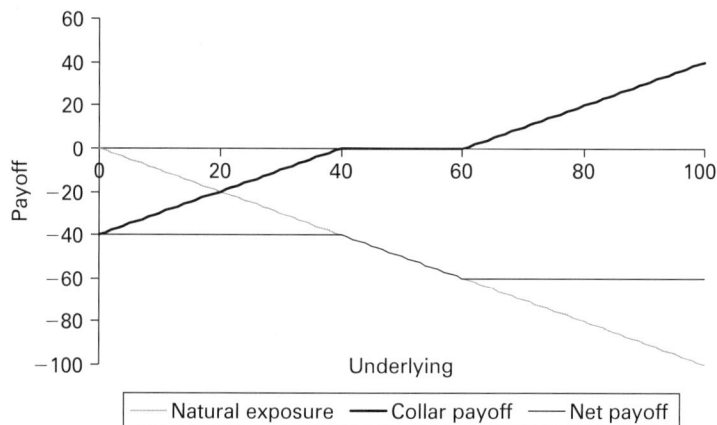

transaction in which they buy a cap at 60, but sell a floor at 40. (In practice only the net of the two premiums needs to be paid.) The transaction is shown in Figure 114, together with the exposure they are assumed to be hedging.

Selling the put option means the consumer doesn't enjoy the full benefit of falling market prices, but the premium earned from selling the derivative does reduce the cost of the downside protection. The payoff diagram at expiry is shown in Figure 115.

Example: Gasoline Consumer Collar

Consider a motor vehicle manufacturer who is a large consumer of gasoline, because they fuel all new cars on sale. They buy their gasoline in differing specifications on various wholesale price indexes around the country, and after considering the liquidity of various underlyings decide to hedge some portion of their fuel purchases using the NYMEX front-line gasoline index. On contacting their energy risk manager they first ask for a quotation for a cap. With the swap market at 160 USc/gal a cap with strike 170 USc/gal would cost 8.63 USc/gal, but their budget will allow a spend of no more than 2.50 USc/gal. Since the motor manufacturer considers this cap to be too expensive, they ask their energy risk manager for a range of collar quotations with this same cap. The quotations they receive are shown in Table 47.

Given the gasoline consumer's risk management budget of 2.50 USc/gal, they realise they must forgo any upside for prices dropping below 143 USc/gal. They therefore choose to enter into a 143/170 consumer collar.

Table 47. Gasoline collar quotations

Call strike (USc/gal)	Put strike (USc/gal)	Collar cost (USc/gal)
170	145	1.49
170	144	1.85
170	143	2.20
170	142	2.53
170	141	2.85
170	140	3.17

> Can you work out what kind of structure a producer collar would be?

Suppose a producer is concerned about falling market prices, and they wish to protect themselves against these downside movements. They could simply buy a floor, but for the volumes they are hedging the premium may be prohibitively expensive. As with the consumer collar above, it is possible to construct a corresponding *producer collar*, in which the cost of purchasing a floor is offset by the sale of a cap. Consider the case of a producer who is concerned about market prices dropping below 40. They may purchase a floor at 40, and offset the cost of this protection by selling a cap at 60. The net effect of this is to ensure they receive no less than 40 for their production, they enjoy market prices between 40 and 60, but that they enjoy no further benefit if the market goes above 60; this transaction is shown in Figure 116, with the corresponding payoff diagram in Figure 117.

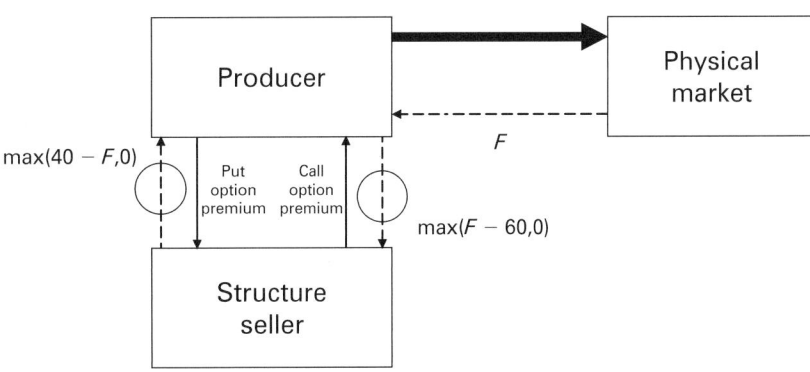

Figure 116. Producer collar block diagram

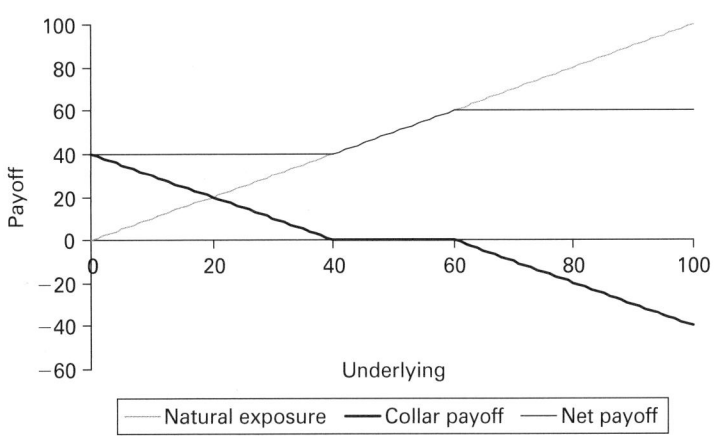

Figure 117. Producer collar payoff diagram

Table 48. Crude oil collar quotations

Put strike (US$/bbl)	Call strike (US$/bbl)	Collar cost (US$/bbl)
48	54.00	0.43
48	55.00	0.63
48	56.00	0.91
48	57.00	1.16
48	58.00	1.29
48	59.00	1.50
48	60.00	1.61
48	52.40	ZCC

Example: Crude Oil Producer Seeks Price Protection with a Collar

A crude oil producer is seeking protection against declining oil prices. The current market swap price for crude oil is around US$50/bbl, and they wish to protect their revenues against any significant decrease in prices. The producer would like to ensure they receive no less than US$48/bbl for their production, and since this level is only just out-of-the-money they cannot afford the use of a simple floor at a premium of over US$3/bbl. They therefore ask their energy risk manager for a range of quotations for collars, showing the cost of protection where upside is sacrificed beyond various upper strike prices above US$53/bbl. The energy risk manager responds with the numbers in Table 48.

The oil producer must decide beyond which price level they are prepared to sacrifice upside. For reference purposes, the energy risk manager has also provided a quotation for a 48.00/52.40 producer collar, which is available at zero cost; the producer would need to give up all upside beyond a near-the-money US$52.40/bbl, but need pay nothing upfront for this protection.

A *zero-cost collar* (ZCC) is a special case of a collar where the strike prices are chosen to ensure the premiums cancel exactly. While this may sound like the dream derivative, readers should note that zero-cost collars are only zero cost in terms of their *upfront cost*. Selling upside to fund downside protection may lead to too large a sacrifice of upside, while one's competitors are enjoying the favourable market conditions. It is useful therefore to consider one's budget levels, risk management aims and the competitive landscape before entering into a hedging instrument in which large amounts of potential upside are sacrificed to reduce premiums. The only true protection against downside price movements that offer full upside benefit is offered by caps or floors, which of course cost money.

> From a "package-building" perspective what kind of ZCC is a swap?

A swap is special case of a ZCC, where the strike prices coincide. Since swaps, by definition, are always struck at the money, an ATM ZCC is equivalent to a swap. This is our friend, put–call parity, revealing itself yet again.

Three-Way Options

Simple collar structures strictly limit the buyer's potential to enjoy upside benefit, and so variations on this theme have evolved[4] to offer some upside participation. The package we'll consider in this section is known variously as the *three-way option*, *three-way collar* or *enhanced collar*. Three-ways are related to collars, but the holder starts to benefit again from sufficiently large upside market movements. Three-ways take their name from the fact that they are packages of three underlying options instruments.

Figure 118. Consumer three-way payoff at expiry

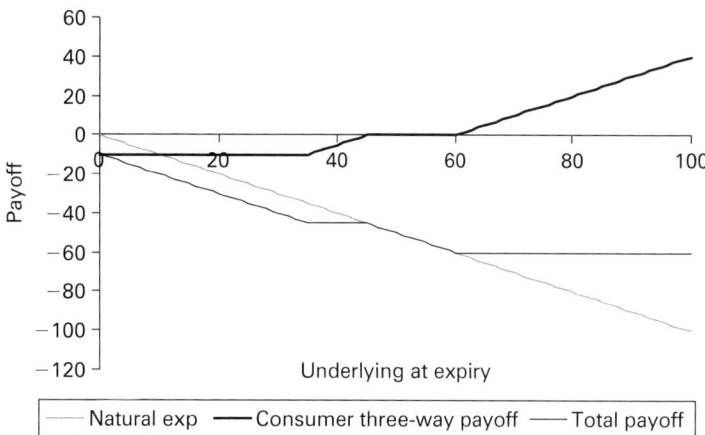

Can you engineer a combination of a consumer collar, and another put, to ensure the holder enjoys sufficiently large upside movements?

A consumer three-way can be constructed from a consumer collar (long a call, short a put of lower strike) together with a further long put at an even lower strike. This has the effect of ensuring that sufficiently large price movements to the consumer's upside (ie, decreasing prices) lead to a decreasing net exposure for the consumer. How does this work? A regular consumer collar ensures that for all prices below the put strike the consumer receives a fixed price. This is because every dollar decrease in the underlying is balanced dollar for dollar by the sold put. Buying another put means that for sufficiently large price drops the "effect" of the first put is cancelled out. Since a picture is worth a thousand words, see Figure 118.

Example: Natural Gas Consumer

Suppose a consumer of natural gas buys at the Henry Hub front-line index, and is interested in receiving protection against price increases; the market is currently at US$8/MMBtu. While they could enter into a cap, they are concerned about the potentially large upfront premium required. Collars and three-ways appear attractive, and they decide to look most seriously into three-ways since they are concerned that dropping market prices could advantage their competitors too much. Their energy risk manager gives them the quotations in Table 49, where the structure of the three-way is defined in terms of its strike prices for (respectively) the long put, short put and long call.

After examining the figures, the consumer decides they are particularly interested in the second quotation; they are completely protected if prices rise

Table 49. Consumer three-way quotations

Strike 1 (US$/MMBtu)	Strike 2 (US$/MMBtu)	Strike 3 (US$/MMBtu)	Cost (US$/MMBtu)
6.00	7.00	9.00	0.29
6.00	7.00	9.50	0.16
6.00	7.00	10.00	0.07
6.00	7.00	10.50	0.00
6.00	8.00	8.00	0.18
6.00	7.00	8.00	0.65
5.00	7.00	8.00	0.48

Figure 119. Gas consumer three-way structure

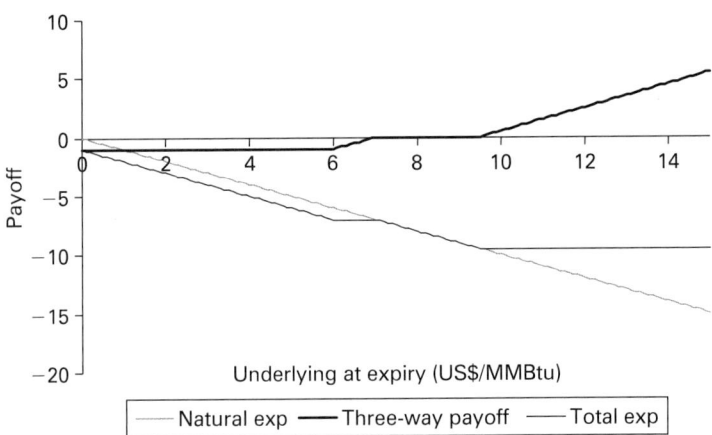

above US$9.50/MMBtu; they start to benefit again if prices drop below US$6/MMBtu, and they consider the premium of US$0.16/MMBtu to be reasonable. The payoff diagram for their chosen structure is shown in Figure 119.

Note that three-way options can, like collars, be constructed to be zero-cost packages. In the example we've just seen the zero-cost three-way was a 6.00/7.00/10.50 package, which the consumer found gave downside protection at too high a market level.

A consumer three-way can be understood in a different way than "consumer collar with an extra put". It is in fact a cap that is funded by another structure: a bull put spread. Obviously the purchase of a cap costs money, while readers may recall that going long a bull put spread earns upfront premium, in exchange for making payment on expiry. Three-way options are the first case we'll see of a *contingent premium structure*. A contingent premium structure is one with zero or much-reduced upfront cost, where the protection (in the consumer case, a cap) is purchased or discounted with the proceeds earned from the sale of another structure. The holder of the structure effectively pays back the premium by giving up a portion of their upside. The advantage to the holder of such a structure is that there is less of a draw on their working capital, that is, reduced need to make an upfront premium payment.

The structure the buyer has sold to fund their protection must claw back the premium they should have paid upfront. Since there is no certainty that this structure will pay the full premium for the downside protection required it must claw back more than the certain upfront premium would have been; this ensures that the seller of the structure is compensated in a fair market sense for this uncertainty.

As with all things such protection comes at a price; in this example the cap alone would have cost approximately US$0.40/MMBtu if the gas consumer had paid the premium upfront. Instead they have reduced their upfront premium to US$0.16/MMBtu, but had to give up US$1/MMBtu of upside should market prices fall below US$6/MMBtu. The gas consumer has agreed to pay up to US$1.16/MMBtu of premium on a price-contingent basis, rather than pay US$0.40/MMBtu upfront.

The transactions leading to a consumer three-way are illustrated in Figure 120.

Figure 120. Consumer three-way option diagram

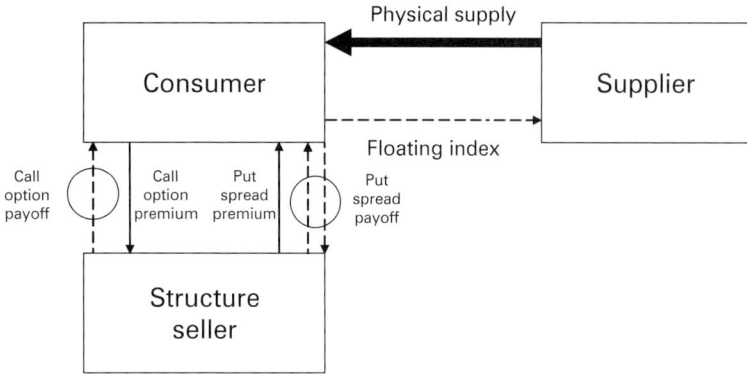

Figure 121. Zero-cost consumer three-way option

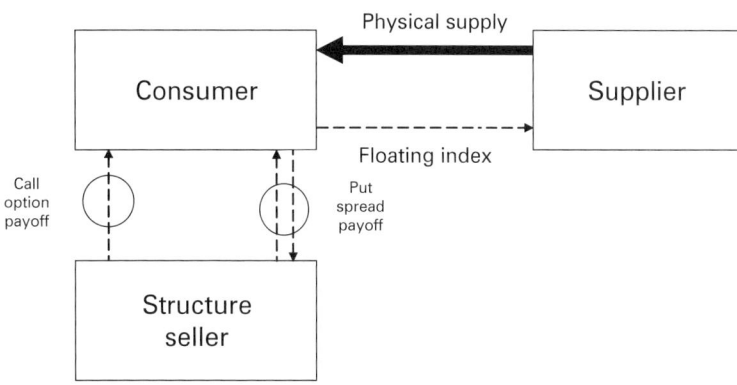

Figure 122. Producer three-way payoff at expiry

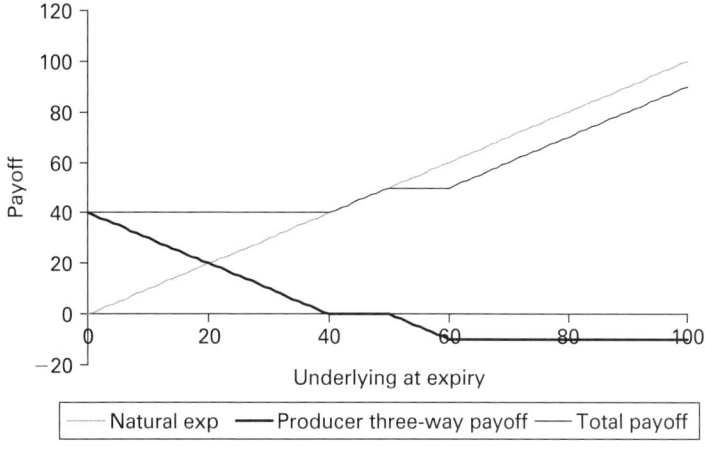

Note how the put spread option transaction is represented, due to its joint long and short nature. The call option premium is effectively reduced, or even eliminated, by the sale of the put spread. In the case of a zero-cost consumer three-way option the block diagram may be simplified further, as shown in Figure 121.

A producer three-way option is a floor funded by the sale of a call spread. The floor ensures that the producer enjoys a certain minimum level for their commodity sales, while the call spread will claw back some or all of the premium of this floor on a price-contingent basis. The payoff at expiry for a 40/50/60 producer three-way is shown in Figure 122.

Note in this example how the producer is guaranteed to receive no less than US$40 for their commodity, but that should prices rise above US$50 (the price contingent level) the premium will start to be clawed back, costing up to US$10 of price-contingent premium.

Example: Crude Oil Producer Three-Way

A crude oil producer wishes to put some protection in place to ensure they never receive less than US$40/bbl for their crude oil; the market is currently at US$50/bbl. After speaking with their energy risk manager they decide on a zero-cost producer three-way option. The strike prices agreed for the call spread (which will fund the US$40/bbl strike put option) are US$53.50/bbl and US$68/bbl respectively. The effect of this structure is to ensure that:

- the producer will never receive less than US$40/bbl for their production;
- between US$40/bbl and US$53.50/bbl, the producer enjoys all the upside of oil price movements;
- if prices exceed US$53.50/bbl, the energy risk manager will take this additional upside to fund the floor protection; and
- should prices move significantly higher, then above US$68/bbl the producer will again enjoy dollar-for-dollar increases in the oil price.

The payoff/P&L diagram to illustrate this zero-cost structure is shown in Figure 123.

Draw the block diagram for a producer three-way option.

The block diagram for a producer three-way option is shown in Figure 124.
Once again we may simplify this diagram in the case where the premium earned from the call spread balances the premium due for the put option. The block diagram for a zero-cost producer three-way option is shown in Figure 125.

With this examination of three-way structures it is worth emphasising that we're now firmly in the world of risk management themes again; funding protection through the sales of other structures is a common theme found throughout derivatives structuring, and the names get less standardised as the payoff diagrams become more complex.

Figure 123. Producer three-way example

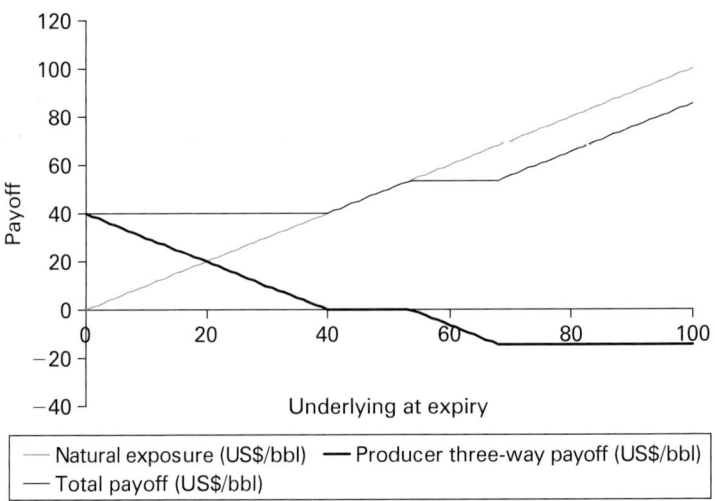

Figure 124. Producer three-way option block diagram

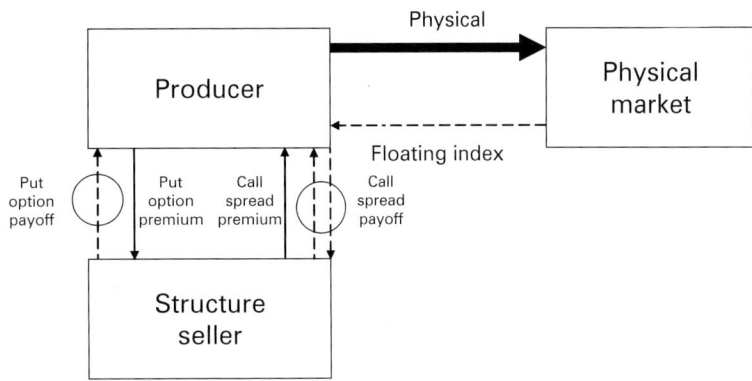

Figure 125. Zero-cost producer three-way option

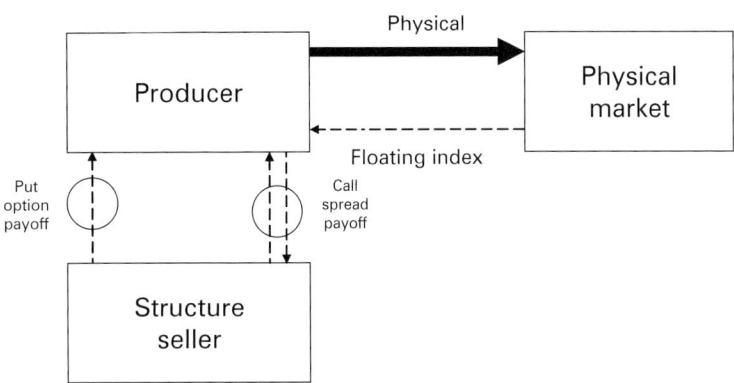

> Can you make up other examples of price-contingent structures? What would a five-way option payoff look like, for example?

Buy-Downs and Participations

The theme of "buying down" or "premium reduction" is one that we've already seen in the cases of collars and three-ways: the price of the option protection a producer or consumer wants is discounted through the sale of another option structure. The term *buy down* is used most often for derivative packages in which the protection afforded by a swap is discounted through the sale of one or more derivatives. Since swaps are zero-cost instruments in their own right, selling derivatives to raise premium has the effect of making the swap fixed-price payment cheaper, but at the price of sacrificing some of the swap's protection.

We have already seen an example of a *bought-down swap* in the section "Combining derivatives into a package" earlier in this chapter, in which a swap and a short call were assembled into a package. Let's examine how this might be used in practice.

Example: Power Consumer Bought-Down Swap

Consider a large European consumer of baseload power who is interested in locking in the next calendar year's power prices. They usually buy their power at the floating market index, for which the next year's swap price is currently at €50/MWh. While they could lock in €50/MWh as the price for their power consumption they feel that baseload prices are unlikely to climb too high. The consumer therefore decides to buy a swap, but sell a call option with a €90 MWh strike price; this has the effect of creating a bought-down swap.

Figure 126. Bought-down swap P&L diagram

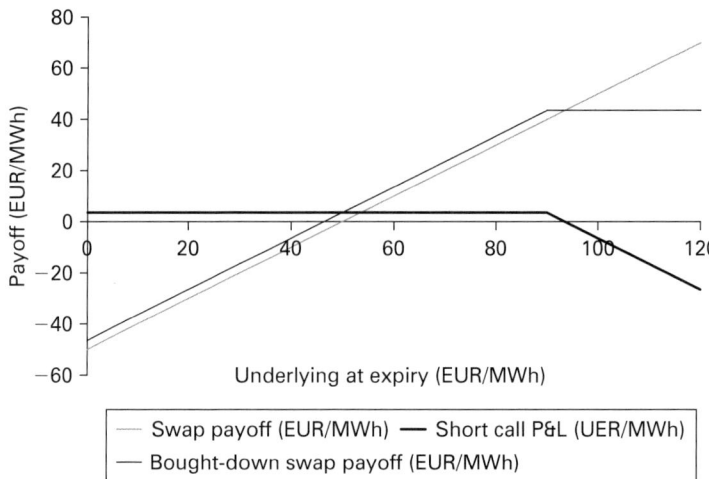

Figure 127. Bought-down swap P&L diagram around current market strike

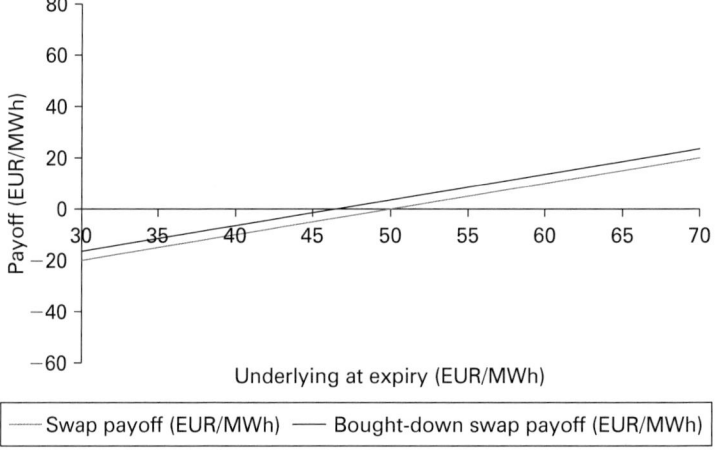

After contacting their energy risk manager they are advised that buying down the swap with a €90/MWh strike call option will yield them just over €3.50/MWh. The P&L diagram for the transaction is shown in Figure 126.

If power prices really do remain below €90/MWh, the power consumer has achieved their aim of hedging power on the cheap. A consumer with such a strong view on the market has a blinkered view of the payoff diagram, seeing only the section around the current market strike price, as shown in Figure 127.

Clearly, if market prices move up significantly then the call option the consumer has sold will be exercised by the energy risk manager. This will give the consumer a euro-for-euro exposure to rising prices above €90/MWh. The full picture can be understood only by consulting the full-exposure P&L diagram, which shows the effect of netting the bought-down swap P&L with the consumer's exposure to the market index. This is shown in Figure 128.

Bought-down swaps are useful to those hedgers with a strong view on market prices (and the licence to take that view in the market), or a diverse portfolio of hedges and/or physical supply contracts. In some cases natural offsets may be identified in the portfolio, allowing such protection to be purchased – in these cases hedgers are merely buying the most appropriate protection, and are avoiding overhedging.

Figure 128. Consumer bought-down swap full-exposure P&L

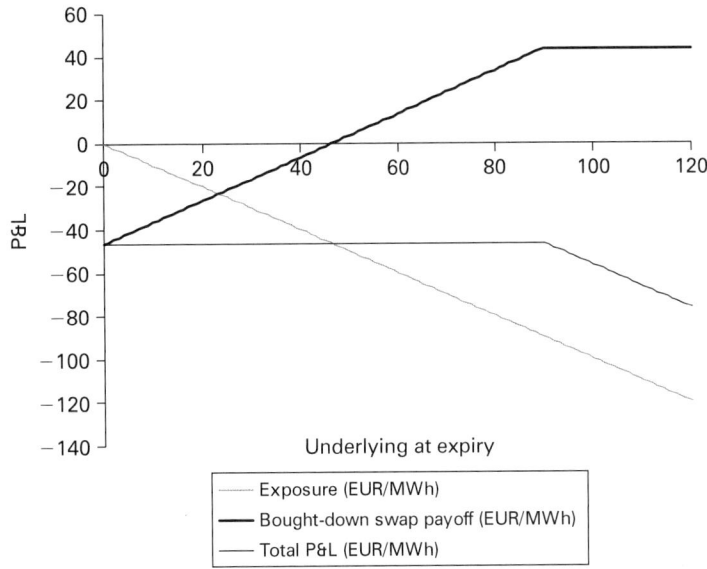

> What sort of natural offsets might the power consumer of the last example have to ensure that the bought-down swap is an appropriate and cost-effective hedge?

Suppose the power consumer has some flexibility in their physical supply contract, and that they have some inefficient oil-fired on-site power generation able to generate power for €90/MWh. In this case their own power plant (if it's reliable) is effectively a €90/MWh strike call option on power, and so they don't need to be protected beyond this level.

Some consumers with very strong markets views (or very diverse portfolios) buy down their swaps using both puts and calls.

Example: Refiner Crude Purchasing Consumer Hedge

Suppose the current market price for crude oil is US$50/bbl, and a refiner is interested in hedging some of their crude oil purchases using bought-down swaps. Given their portfolio of contracts and hedges, and their market view, they elect to enter into an aggressively bought-down swap, funding the buy down with both caps and floors.

After consulting with their energy risk manager they decide to buy a swap, and sell caps and floors at both US$25/bbl and US$80/bbl respectively. The sale of the puts will yield them US$1.50/bbl in premium and the sale of the calls US$2/bbl. The structure they are buying is shown in Figure 129.

The P&L diagram shows the "double down" feature of this structure in which even low market prices "hurt" the consumer. The result of netting this structure with their natural exposure is shown in Figure 130.

Trading regulations often mean that energy risk managers will offer bought-down structures only if the hedged volumes are significantly lower than the customer's physical exposure, and they are satisfied that the hedger understands the nature of the structure they are buying.

We have already seen in the previous chapter that *participation* allows purchasers of risk management products to share upside market price

Figure 129. Consumer double bought-down swap

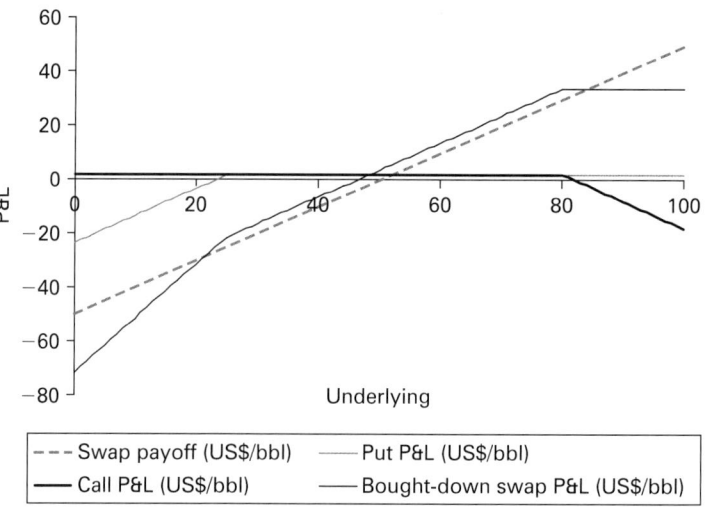

Figure 130. Consumer double-down exposure

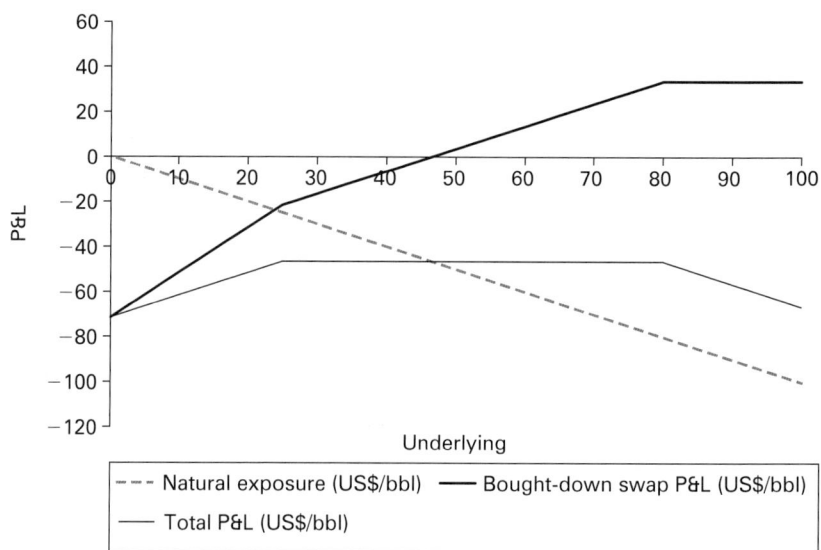

movements with their energy risk manager, thus reducing the premium due for the protection. As a theme, participation can be incorporated into almost any package we're likely to see, and we will examine a few examples here to understand the principle.

Example: Producer Put with Upside Sharing

Suppose an oil producer is interested in buying a put to protect themselves against downside movements in crude-oil prices, and that the current market swap level for the next calendar year is US$50/bbl. They would like to place a floor of US$45/bbl on their production costs, and on contacting their energy risk manager they find that the cost of a 45 strike floor would be US$3.60/bbl, which they consider to be too expensive.

After considering the various possibilities available to them, they decide they would be happy to share some portion of their upside, and ask for quotations for different participation levels above US$45/bbl. The energy risk manager responds with the figures in Table 50 for a *put with upside participation*.

Table 50. Producer put with upside participation quotations

Participation level (%)	Premium (US$/bbl)
0 (Simple floor)	3.61
5	3.19
10	2.77
15	2.35
20	1.92
25	1.50
30	1.08
35	0.66
40	0.23
45	−0.19
50	−0.61

Figure 131. Producer put with upside participation transaction

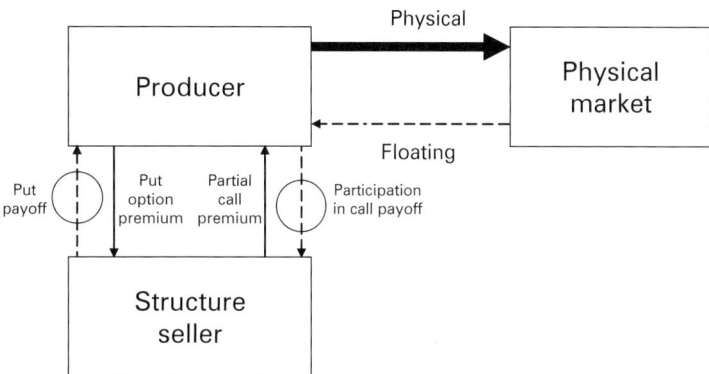

This participation in the upside is achieved by the producer selling some portion of a US$45/bbl strike call option to the energy risk manager. The transaction may be represented by the block diagram in Figure 131.

Note that:

- since the floor being requested is *out of* the money, the cap being sold with the same strike must therefore be *in* the money;
- since the market swap price is currently US$50/bbl the 45 strike call is immediately worth money to the energy risk manager; and
- for sufficiently high participation levels the energy risk manager will actually pay a premium to the producer to enter this structure; participation levels of 45% or more on the US$45/bbl call is as good as money in the bank for the seller of the structure.

After considering the amount of upside participation they are prepared to offer the energy risk manager, the producer decides to opt for a 25% participation level, paying US$1.50/bbl for the package. The P&L diagram for the structure they choose to enter is illustrated in Figure 132.

> What would the structure in this example be equivalent to if a 100% upside participation were requested?

Figure 132. Producer put with 25% upside participation

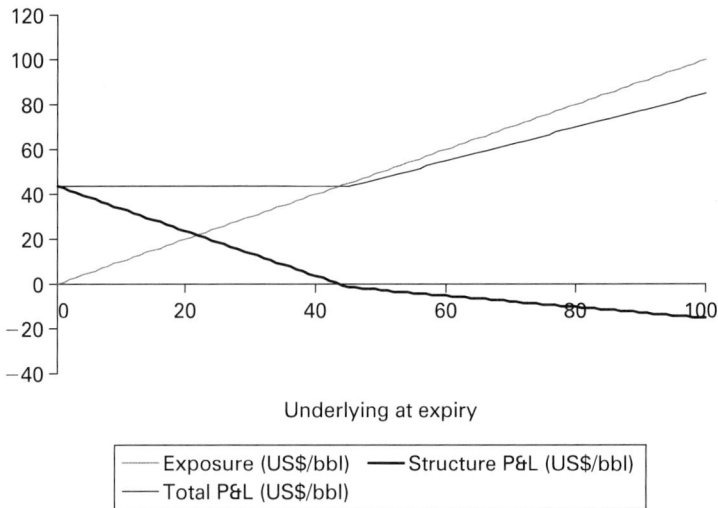

The payoff diagram would resemble that of a swap, but where the swap strike price is US$45/bbl, rather than the current market level of US$50/bbl. This structure is yet another example of put–call parity at work, and the resulting structure is called an *off-market swap*. While swaps are costless to enter, off-market swaps will cost money for one party to the trade. The price of an off-market swap is equivalent to the amount by which the structure deviates from ATM, discounted appropriately for the time value of money.

Participations needn't be constructed where the strike price of the upside participation option matches that of the downside protection option, as shown in the next example.

Example: Gas Consumer Participating Collar

A large industrial consumer of UK natural gas wishes to buy protection against rising market prices. They wish to reduce the premium due for a cap by selling some of their upside, and have considered various possibilities. They feel that entering into a collar would be too large a sacrifice of potential drops in market prices, and are veering towards either three-ways or some sort of participation package. Their energy risk manager proposes a *participating collar* since it has very easy-to-understand characteristics:

- complete protection against downside risk; and
- a sharing of some fixed proportion of upside.

The participating collar may be described by three key numbers:

1. the strike price beyond which they want complete price protection to be in force;
2. the strike price below which they are prepared to share their upside; and
3. the proportion of upside they are prepared to share, or participation level.

With the NBP natural gas swap currently priced at 30 ppth the consumer decides they'd like complete protection to start at 32 ppth, necessitating the

Table 51. Participating collar quotations

Put strike 27 ppth		Put strike 25 ppth	
Participation level (%)	Cost (ppth)	Participation level (%)	Cost (ppth)
0	1.94	0	1.94
10	1.77	10	1.80
20	1.60	20	1.67
30	1.42	30	1.54
40	1.25	40	1.41
50	1.08	50	1.28
60	0.91	60	1.14
70	0.74	70	1.01
80	0.57	80	0.88
90	0.40	90	0.75
100	0.23	100	0.61
55	1.00	71	1.00

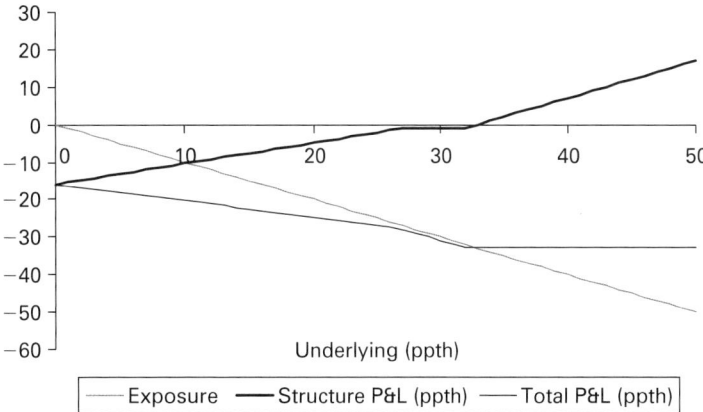

Figure 133. Participating consumer collar P&L diagram

purchase of a 32 ppth strike cap. The gas consumer requests that the energy risk manager produce quotations for put strikes at 25 ppth and 27 ppth for different participation levels. They expect that they can budget around 1 ppth for protection, and ask for specific structures tailored to this guide price. The energy risk manager responds with Table 51.

The gas consumer is reluctant to give up over 70% of their upside, and so they elect to give up 55% of the upside for all market prices below 27 ppth. They therefore decide to buy the structure illustrated in Figure 133 for 1 ppth.

The amount of upside participation doesn't need to be fixed for all levels of the underlying market: packages can be structured to "phase in" the participation for larger market movements, as shown in the next example.

Option package nomenclature

In this chapter a number of new risk management themes are introduced, many of which will be unfamiliar even to readers who understand basic derivatives. The themes are summarised here for ease of reference. *Funding* refers to the concept of decreasing, or even eliminating, the cost of downside protection through the sale of some upside that reaps back the premium for the writer of the protection. Fully funded protection leads to *zero-cost* structures, while *participation*

(continued)

> refers to the act of sharing some market upside, in order to decrease the cost of protection. *Buying down* is a strategy used by swaps buyers who may be prepared to sacrifice all downside protection beyond a certain point in order to decrease their fixed payments, while *selling up* refers to a similar strategy, increasing the fixed payments received by swaps sellers.

Example: Oil Producer Put with Phased Upside Participation

An oil producer is concerned about declining oil prices: the current market swap price is US$50/bbl, and they want to ensure they earn no less than US$48/bbl. They are looking for innovative ways to fund some of the premium for this floor, since they need to earn more upside for modest upside market moves, but they are prepared to give away more upside for larger market movements. They ask their energy risk manager for suggestions, who proposes they tailor a *put with phased upside participation* appropriate to the producer's needs.

While the floor alone would cost the producer US$5/bbl, a phased upside participation appropriate to the producer's requirements can more than halve this premium. The structure agreed works as follows:

- The producer will go long a floor with a strike of US$48/bbl.
- For oil prices above US$48/bbl, the producer will share 10% of this upside with the energy risk manager.
- Above US$55/bbl, the producer will share an additional 15% of their upside, a total of 25% of upside and so on.
- The complete phasing is summarised in Table 52.

The phasing is achieved by the producer selling back a call for each phase, with the specified strike and at the extra participation level. The P&L diagram for the structure is shown in Figure 134.

The structure proposed will cost the producer US$2.40/bbl.

Participation, or *phasing*,[5] may also be used to determine the speed at which contingent premiums are clawed back in three-way and similar structures. In the three-ways we've seen so far the call or put options are funded through the use of put or call spreads – these spreads were transacted for exactly the same volume as the main call or put. Modifying the strikes and volume of the spread gives a range of different possibilities for energy hedgers, allowing better tailoring of the amount of upside to be sacrificed and in which price ranges.

Table 52. Phasing for producer put with phased participation

Phase	Strike (US$/bbl)	Extra participation (%)	Cumulative participation (%)
1	48	10	10
2	55	15	25
3	65	25	50
4	80	25	75

Figure 134. Producer put with phased participation

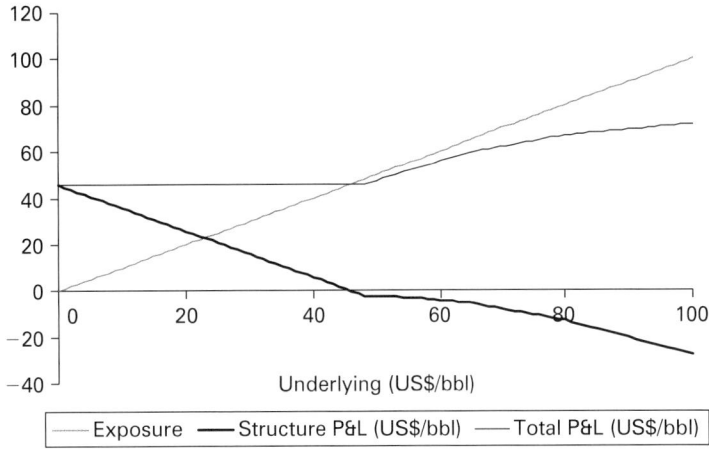

Example: Consumer Phased Three-Way

A consumer buys heating oil indexed to the NYMEX front-line contract, and is interested in buying downside protection. They're interested to understand the range of *phased three-way* call options available, and ask their energy risk manager for advice. With the swap market currently at US$1.70/gal, and the consumer needing to prevent prices rising above US$/1.75 gal, the energy risk manager suggests the following arrangements:

- a zero-cost three-way structure;
- the clawing back of the premium starts at US$1.75/gal;
- if market prices drop sufficiently quickly, the clawing back will be complete, and all remaining upside is the consumer's;
- that there are a range of structures corresponding to differing "speeds" of claw-back;
- that these structures differ by the range of heating oil market prices over which the premium is clawed back; and
- that if premium is clawed back over a smaller range of prices, the phasing must be higher to ensure all premium is clawed back quickly enough.

The interrelationship between market prices and the clawing back is shown in Figure 135.

Having set the cap strike price (US$1.75/gal in this case), the zero-premium structure can be defined by only two parameters:

1. lower strike price by which claw-back is finished; and
2. the phasing parameter that determines the speed of claw-back to guarantee a zero premium.

The whole structure may be described by the lower strike, the upper strike and the phasing parameter.

The energy risk manager shows the consumer two examples of phased three-way option P&L diagrams to help them understand the structures'

Figure 135. Consumer phased three-way strike prices and "claw-back zone"

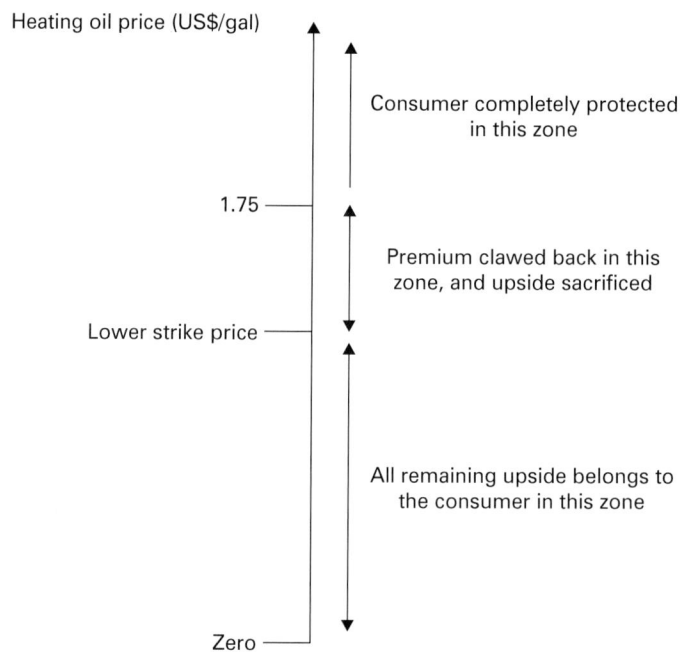

Figure 136. 1.40/1.75/170% consumer phased three-way

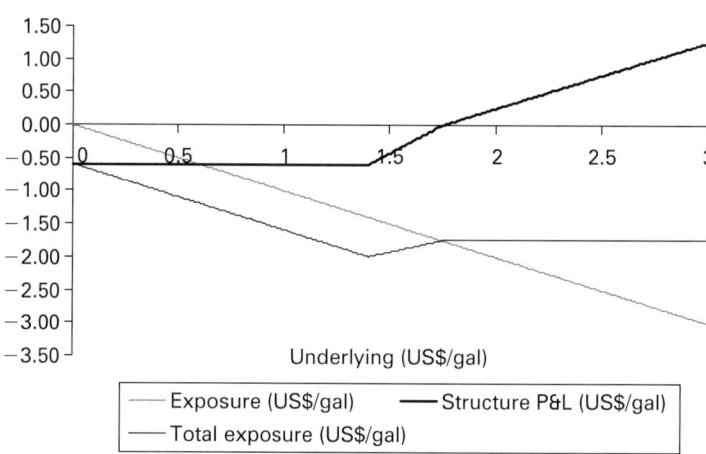

Figure 137. 1.70/1.75/510% consumer phased three-way

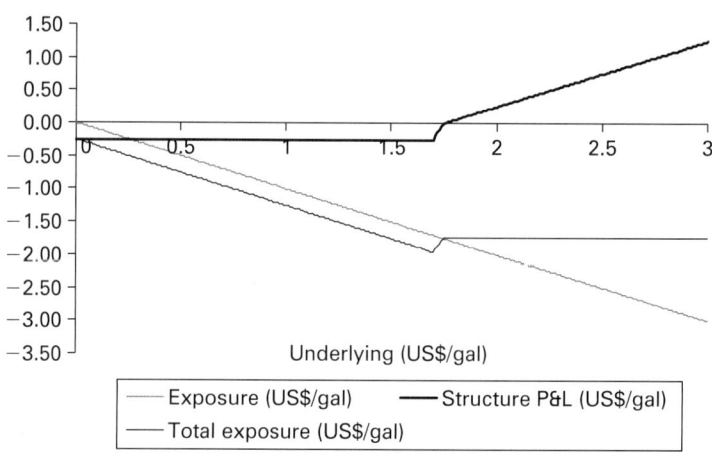

characteristics: a 1.40/1.75/170% structure (Figure 136), and a 1.70/1.75/510% structure (Figure 137).

Note that the maximum amount of upside sacrificed differs significantly between the two structures:

Table 53. Zero-premium phased consumer three-way quotations

Lower strike (US$/gal)	1.20	1.40	1.50	1.60	1.70
Upper strike (US$/gal)	1.75	1.75	1.75	1.75	1.75
Phasing (%)	150	170	230	290	510
Maximum premium clawed back (USc/gal)	83	60	58	44	26

- for the 1.40/1.75/170% structure the maximum sacrifice of upside is 60 USc/gal; and
- for the 1.70/1.75/510% structure the maximum sacrifice of upside is 26 USc/gal.

The smaller the range of prices over which the premium may be clawed back, the more likely is the energy risk manager to recover their entire premium; quite simply the market is more likely to move a smaller amount than a larger amount.

The energy risk manager shows the heating-oil consumer the range of zero-premium structures in Table 53, and asks them to decide which of these they'd prefer to enter.

The consumer considers the various structures and decides that, given the high volatility in the product markets, they'd rather sacrifice their upside more quickly, with a lower overall premium being clawed back. They therefore elect to enter into the 1.70/1.75/510% structure.

In all cases it is interesting to compare the contingent premium (the maximum amount clawed back) with the upfront cost of just buying a call: 19.7 USc/gal. This difference between the contingent premium and the call premium alone is because there is no certainty that the market will move enough to ensure all the premium can be clawed back.

> Can you imagine what a 1.75/1.75/p% consumer phased three-way structure would look like? What would the phasing be for such a structure?

The answer to this question will be supplied in the section "Digital options" in the next chapter.

> **Constructing consumer and producer packages**
>
> At various places in this chapter we refer to consumer collars, producer three-ways and so on. In most cases the consumer or producer is looking for absolute downside protection, and is prepared to sacrifice some part of their upside in order to fund this. Constructing protection for these players will therefore involve assembling the appropriate derivative for the absolute downside protection, and adding one or more other instruments to provide the funding. Rather than commit a wide variety of structures to memory, readers need only remember to start with the appropriate downside protection, and fund it from there. The instrument needed as a starting point can be easily remembered from the initial letters of the type of market player and the derivative needed for downside protection:
>
> Consumers need Calls, Producers need Puts.

Structures with Volume and Term Flexibility

Many physical supply or offtake agreements have volumetric flexibility, and if hedgers wish to lock in prices it is necessary to enter into a derivative package that offers corresponding volumetric flexibility. Volumetric flexibility while locking in may be achieved by:

- entering into a swap contract to lock in prices for any firm portion of the physical volumes to be hedged, and
- buying an appropriate option on any flexible volumes.

Note that such a derivative structure assumes that the decision to flex volumes will be based on market price movements only, and not on any other sources of uncertainty. When structures are built using this principle we say that the package writer is assuming *ruthless exercise*, ie, that the counterparty will exercise with respect to market signals and nothing else.

To understand how flexible volume packages may be hedged it is most useful, as always, to start by examining the hedger's natural exposure to the underlying commodity. Suppose a large consumer of heating oil has a supply contract in which they pay a floating market index for their supply, and have the right but not the obligation to double the volume of commodity they take (an example of a *double-up* right). If we assume that they will be entering a 150 USc/gal swap contract to hedge their firm volumes, and that if market prices rise above this level they will choose to double up, then their natural exposure is as shown in Figure 138.

Example: Natural Gas Consumer with Volumetric Flexibility

Consider a large US consumer of natural gas, with a physical supply contract in place that provides 60000 MMBtu per month, with the flexibility to increase this quantity by 50%. The gas consumer wishes to lock in the price of their supply, whether they take the nominal 60000 MMBtu or the flexed volume of 90000 MMBtu. They contact their energy risk manager who suggests a *flex-up swap*; with the natural gas market currently at US$7/ MMBtu ruthless exercise suggests that:

- if market prices are at or below US$7/MMBtu the consumer will use their firm volume of 60000 MMBtu/month, paying US$7/MMBtu; and that

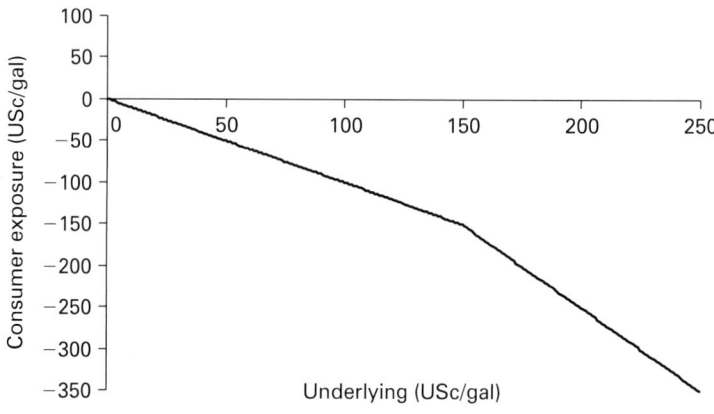

Figure 138. Heating-oil consumer double up exposure

Figure 139. Gas consumer flexible volume contract and flex-up swap hedge

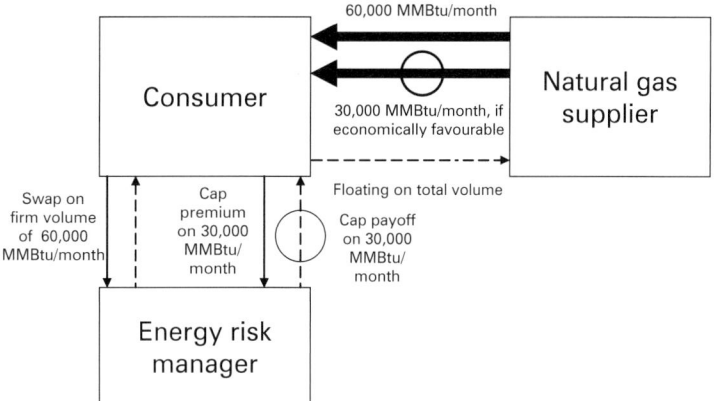

- if market prices are above US$7/MMBtu the consumer will exercise their flex rights and consume a total of 90000 MMBtu/month, paying US$7/MMBtu.

A flex-up swap is a package of a swap for the firm volume plus an ATM cap for the flex volume, which fulfils the consumer's ruthless exercise requirements with respect to the market. The physical and hedge positions are illustrated in Figure 139.

The premium for the embedded cap may be deferred and paid as part of the fixed leg of the swap; the gas consumer will therefore be paying slightly above market for the swap on the firm volume in order to have the right, but not obligation, to take the extra volumes.

> Draw the P&L diagram for the flex-up swap in the previous example. Assume that the premium paid is US$0.75/MMBtu. Include the hedger's natural exposure (assuming ruthless exercise), and show how the flex-up swap fixes prices.

The P&L diagram for the combination of a long swap and a long ATM cap is shown in Figure 140.

Figure 140. Flex-up swap P&L diagram

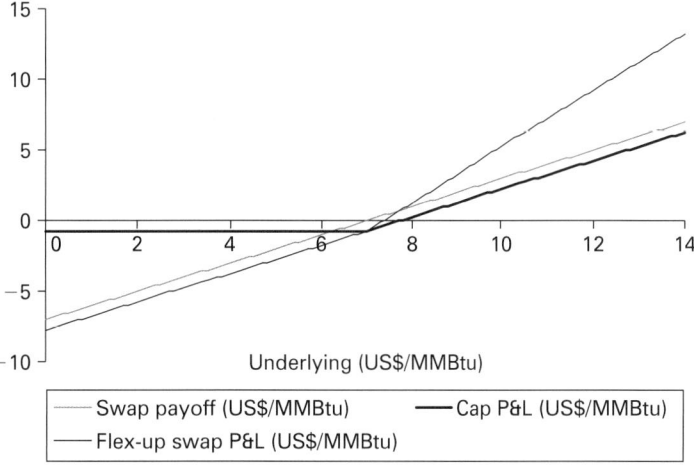

Figure 141. Flex-up swap hedging flexible volumes

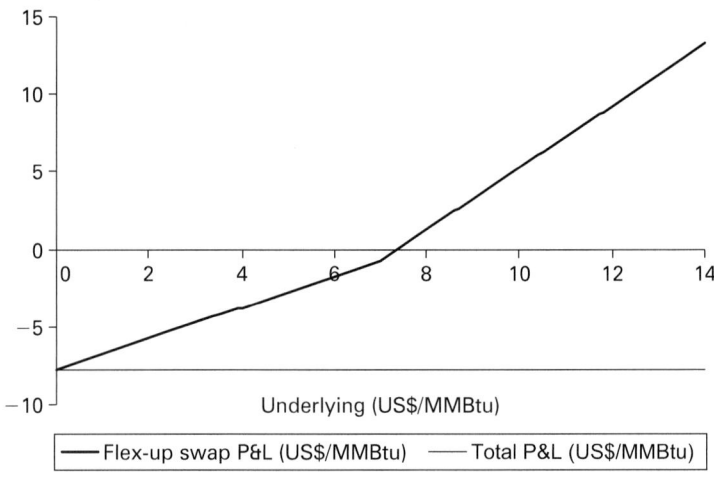

Figure 142. Oil producer flex down exposure

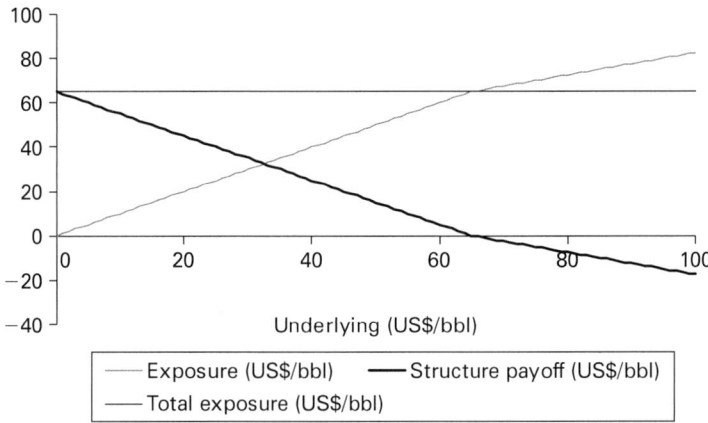

The flex-up swap P&L may be added to the consumer's natural exposure to stabilise completely the cashflows, as shown in Figure 141.

Naturally, the usual proxy risk considerations enter into hedging with swaps and Asian options, and if the consumer doesn't take a similar volume of commodity each delivery day in a month they may find that the hedge is not very effective.[6]

Example: Producer Requires Flex Down Hedge

A small crude oil producer expects demand for their oil production to decrease by 50% if crude prices climb above US$65/bbl. They contact their energy risk manager and ask for an appropriate fixed-price hedge accounting for this expected drop in demand. Their expected exposure to market prices is shown in Figure 142, together with the hedge required to fix prices.

The hedge required may be formed in two equivalent ways:

1. a short off-market swap with a strike of US$65/bbl on the full volume, together with a long US$65/bbl cap on half the volume; and
2. a long US$65/bbl floor on half the volume together with a short off-market swap with a strike of US$65/bbl on half the volume.

In both cases, the hedger will be going long an option for half the volume, and short some volume of swap.

Derivatives Packages

> Why are these two structures equivalent?

These two structures are equivalent due to put–call parity. Since

$$\text{Call} - \text{Put} = \text{Swap}$$

we must have

$$1/2 \times \text{Call} - 1/2 \times \text{Put} = 1/2 \times \text{Swap}$$

leading to

$$1/2 \times \text{Call} - \text{Swap} = 1/2 \times \text{Put} - 1/2 \times \text{Swap}$$

Volumetric flexibility is most often embedded into a combined physical and financial package, and may include rights to cancel or reduce volumes (also formed from swaps and options), or other types of flexibility. Volume flex deals are a form of *swing optionality*, though for swing options there is usually a global limit on the number of flex rights, which must be distributed optimally across the term of the deal, rather than booked as a complete strip. We shan't discuss such deals in greater detail here, and instead refer readers to their own energy risk manager.

Term flexibility refers to the right, but not obligation to extend or shorten the term of a hedge. Swaps can be assembled into packages with swaptions to construct either *extendable swaps* or *cancellable swaps*.

Example: Natural Gas Consumer Extendable Swap

A large consumer of natural gas is reviewing their rolling hedging programme for the coming years. They intend to lock in their next calendar year's consumption, and, fearing increasing natural gas prices, would like the option to extend their hedge for a further year at the same level. They speak to their energy risk manager, who recommends an extendable swap.

Entering the next year's swap is, of course, costless, while the consumer needs to pay a premium for the extension option. With the next calendar year trading at US$7.50/MMBtu, the energy risk manager computes that a premium of US$0.90/MMBtu is due for the extension option, which will be added to the fixed leg of the first year's swap. The package bought by the consumer is therefore a long swap and a long call swaption, as shown in Figure 143.

Figure 143. Consumer extendable swap

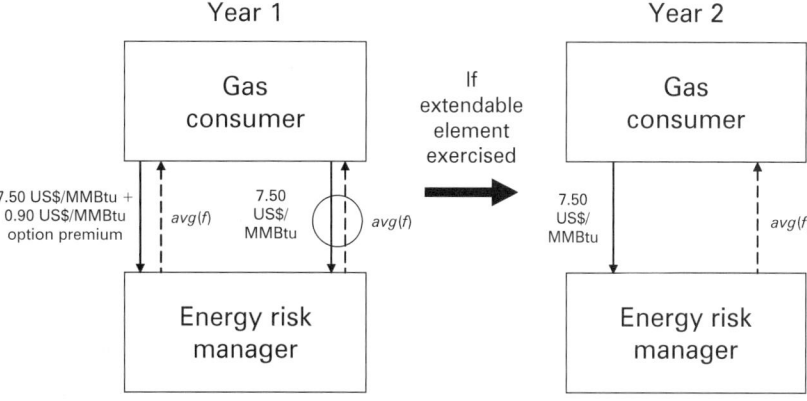

Figure 144. Extendable swap time line

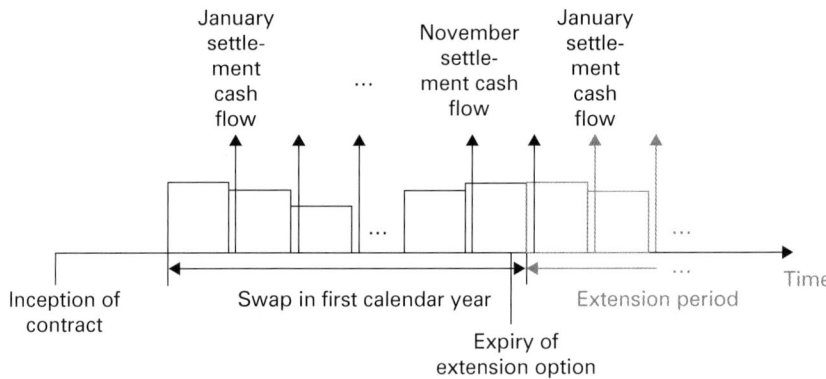

The option to extend the swap with the same strike as the initial year expires at the end of the first year of the hedge. The contractual timeline is illustrated in Figure 144.

In the example of an extendable swap we've just seen, the consumer will exercise their extension right if the call swaption is in the money at expiry – that is to say that, if the calendar swap is above the US$7.50/MMBtu strike price, they will exercise their right to lock in the next year's prices at that level. Needless to say, a corresponding producer extendable swap can be created in which the producer buys a put swaption together with selling a swap, in order to achieve a similar effect.

We turn now to another use of swaptions in term flexible packages, in which a producer "sells up" their swap by selling cancellation rights to their energy risk manager.[7]

Example: Oil Producer Sells up a Swap Using Cancellation Optionality

An oil producer is happy with the current high level of the crude-oil markets, and decides to sell a swap to lock in some portion of their production. They contact their energy risk manager and elect to enter into a two-year swap, which they *sell up* by selling their energy risk manager the right to cancel the second year's swap position. Since the energy risk manager has the optionality, they pay a premium to the oil producer, who thus augments their first year's income.

The transaction the producer enters into is shown in Figure 145.

The oil producer has sold a two-year swap, and has also sold a put swaption on the second year of their production. The energy risk manager will exercise their optionality if their swaption is in the money at the end of the first year, meaning that the forward market is below the strike price. Exercising the option means that the swap in the extension period will cancel the second year of the original swap, leaving the producer unhedged. This action would "hurt" the producer, who will be receiving only the market floating price at precisely the time when they'd like to have retained the protection of a swap. It is for this reason that they received additional premium as compensation in the first year of the hedge.

Flex options and extendable/cancellation options differ only by the time at which the exercise decision must be made, since both are concerned with whether and when to vary volumes.

Figure 145. Oil producer cancellable swap

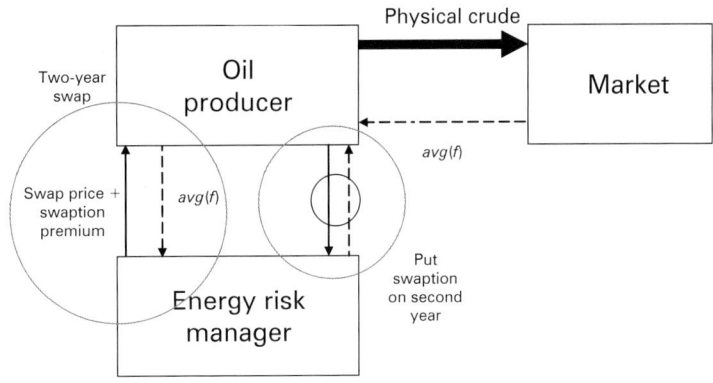

- In the case of flex options the decision to exercise is retrospective, based upon realised prices; the rationale being that, if the market conditions are being met, the holder of physical flexibility will flex their volumes anyway, and will seek appropriate fixed-price protection on these volumes. These packages are built from swaps and Asian options.
- In the case of extendable and cancellation options, the decision of whether or not to exercise is based upon the forward market, and the exercise decision results in a long or short swap position. These packages are built from swaps and swaptions.

Further block diagram notation

In this and the previous chapter we have made extensive use of block diagrams to illustrate how derivatives transactions may be constructed. Through following the text and examples readers will have become familiar with the elements of these diagrams, and the main points are summarised in this box for reference purposes.

Optional flows are represented by circles placed on arrows, and the circle should literally be taken to mean that conditions are placed upon the flow. Single call or put option payoffs are represented by a single arrow, with circle, and two- or three-option packages by the appropriate number of arrows sharing a circle, while swaptions are represented by a fixed-for-floating pair of arrows sharing a circle. The arrows flow in the direction of the party receiving the cash, that is, in the direction of the party long the option (see Figure 146).

Figure 146. Further block diagram notation

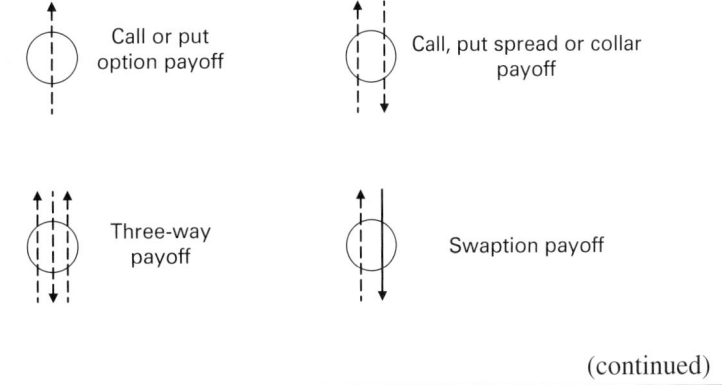

(continued)

Figure 147. Physical volumetric flexibility

Figure 148. Fixed quantity, flowing only if market conditions are met

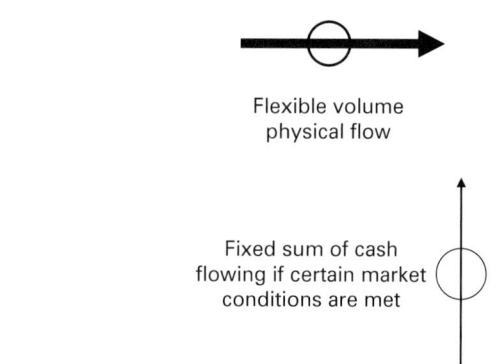

The notion of an optional flow can also be extended to physical flows subject to conditions, as we can see in the flex swap examples, and illustrated in Figure 147.

Finally a fixed amount of money, fixed independently of the market, which only flows if certain market conditions are met, may be represented by a solid arrow carrying a circle (Figure 148). This is applicable both for extendable fixed-price physical contracts (in which the condition is one of whether the holder wishes to extend the option) and for digital options, which are encountered in the next chapter.

Integrated Physical and Financial Structures

All examples presented so far in this chapter have assumed that the producers or consumers have a physical supply or offtake agreement in place with a physical player, and that they are looking to enter into a separate risk management position with their energy risk manager. Any derivative payoff structure can, in principle, be embedded in a physical supply or offtake agreement, and in previous chapters we have seen a few simple examples of managed-price physical, or MPP, contracts in the shape of:

- fixed-price physicals (FPPs);
- capped-price physicals (CPPs); and
- floored-price physicals (FloorPPs).

MPPs may, of course, encompass the full range of structures seen in this chapter, and more. Since, by now, readers will be gaining a reasonable insight into the way in which such contracts can be synthesised, I will limit myself to just a couple of illustrative examples of MPPs in this section.

Example: Oil Producer ZCC Physical Offtake

Suppose an oil producer is interested in entering into a physical offtake agreement in which they are guaranteed to receive no less than some floor amount. Since they are unwilling to pay upfront for this protection, they elect to sacrifice some of their upside by entering into a *collared priced physical* (or *CollarPP*) physical offtake agreement with their integrated energy risk manager. The energy risk manager proposes to construct a zero-cost collar embedded within a physical offtake agreement, with a floor price of US$40/bbl, and a cap price of US$60/bbl. This means that the producer receives no less than US$40/bbl, and can receive no more than US$60/bbl. The payoff diagram for this agreement is shown in Figure 149.

Figure 149. Producer collared-price physical payoff diagram

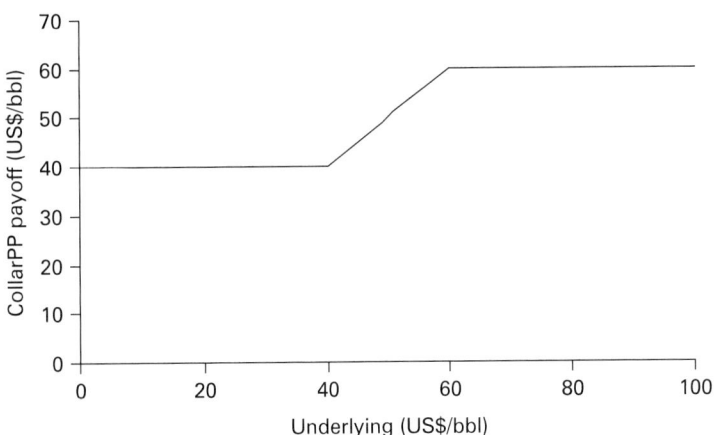

Symbolically, the producer's payoff from this contract is

$$\min(\max(avg(f), floor), cap)$$

> How can the energy risk manager synthesise this structure?

This structure may be synthesised by the energy risk manager's structuring desk by entering into the following series of transactions:

- physical offtake with the physical crude desk, receiving the floating market price;
- buying a floor from the options trading desk; and
- selling a cap to the options trading desk.

These are illustrated in Figure 150.

Figure 150. Block diagram to show how producer CollarPP may be synthesised by energy risk manager

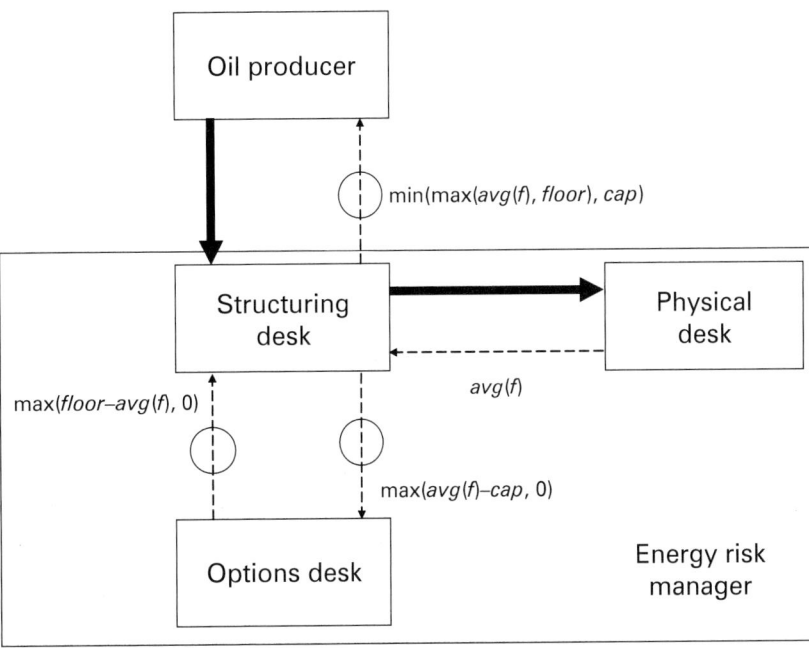

Table 54. Producer CollarPP calculations

Market (US$/bbl)	Producer receives from energy risk manager (US$/bbl)	Structuring desk receives from physical desk (US$/bbl)	Structuring desk receives from options desk (US$/bbl)	Structuring desk pays to options desk (US$/bbl)	Structuring desk receives net from physical and options desks (US$/bbl)
...	...	...	...	...	...
36	40	36	4	0	40
37	40	37	3	0	40
38	40	38	2	0	40
39	40	39	1	0	40
40	40	40	0	0	40
41	41	41	0	0	41
42	42	42	0	0	42
43	43	43	0	0	43
44	44	44	0	0	44
45	45	45	0	0	45
...	...	...	...	...	...
57	57	57	0	0	57
58	58	58	0	0	58
59	59	59	0	0	59
60	60	60	0	0	60
61	60	61	0	1	60
62	60	62	0	2	60
63	60	63	0	3	60
64	60	64	0	4	60
...	...	...	...	...	...

Readers may confirm that this series of transactions *does* actually synthesise the correct payoff to the producer by comparing the flows between the different entities within the diagram. The calculations are shown in Table 54.

Formulating MPP contracts requires rigorous risk analysis, with appropriate treatment of variations in commodity volume or quality as part of the combined physical and financial package. Readers are referred to their energy risk manager to discuss ways in which such packages can be formulated.

Example: Gas Supply Contract with Embedded Lock-in Optionality

A large industrial consumer of natural gas wishes to enter a fixed-price physical supply agreement with their energy risk manager for a two-year term. It is concerned that, with new sources of gas coming on line in the medium term, gas prices may decline by the time the second year of the contract starts. Being locked into these higher prices may put it at a disadvantage to its competitors in the market. Equally, delays in these new sources of gas could lead to a rise in market prices, and so consumer doesn't want to find itself needing to lock in at a higher market price in a year's time.

On speaking with its energy risk manager, it elects to enter a fixed-price physical supply contract for the natural gas, with an embedded lock-in option for the second year. If prices have fallen by the end of the first year, it will choose not to exercise its lock-in option, but will enter a new swap at the prevailing lower market rate. If prices have climbed, its embedded option will be in the money, and it will exercise its option to extend the original terms of

Figure 151. Extendable fixed-price physical contract

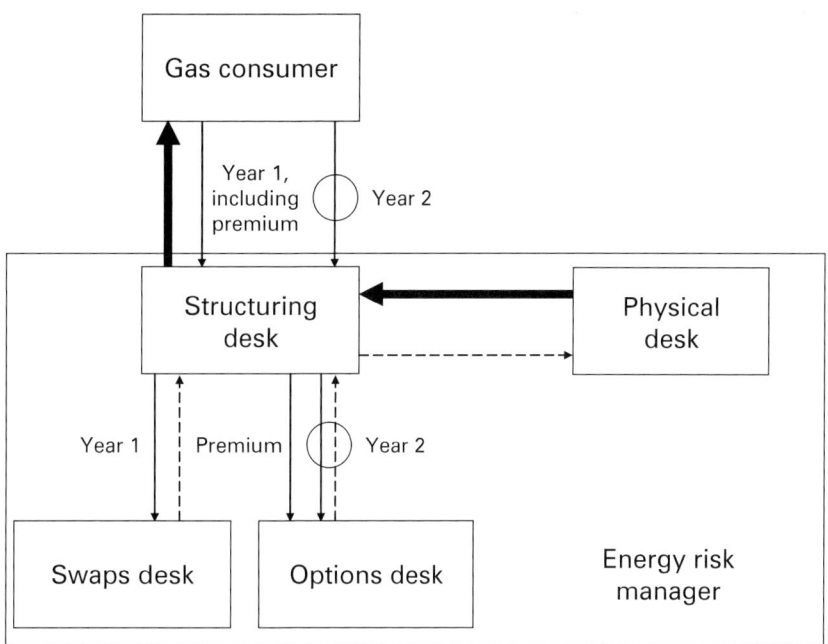

the first year's fixed-price contract for a further year. This optionality will cost the consumer a premium in the first year of the contract.

The transactions to synthesise this *extendable fixed-price physical* (or *extendable FPP*) contract are shown in Figure 151.

Chapter Review and Look Ahead

In this chapter we have taken the basic derivatives instruments examined in the previous two chapters, and seen how they can be combined packages to suit the practical needs of energy producers and consumers. These requirements may include matching a very specific price risk exposure, decreasing the premium that must be paid for protection, or acquiring (or even offering) volume or term flexibility.

On the way to understanding how such packages can be constructed we uncovered a fundamental parity relationship between the values of call and put options, and examined a range of well-known option packages including collars, three-ways, buy-downs, extendable and cancellable swaps, and so on.

By this stage in the report, readers will be equipped with a good understanding of how and why such structures may be assembled, and through the examples in this chapter should be developing an intuition of how to step away from specific packages towards the construction of transactions to address a variety of themes. These themes may be addressed either as part of a pure paper transaction, or embedded within a physical supply or offtake agreement.

As we've moved into the latter part of this chapter we have moved away from the specific numerical examples of previous sections, into the area of how these transactions may be structured. Readers will understand that various levels of premium can be achieved by the smart use of participation, and the range of packages that may be constructed is as wide as the range of producers' and consumers' risk management requirements.

Chapter Review and Look Ahead

Common to all the discussions in this chapter is that we have been concerned only with single-commodity price exposures, and options that pay off penny for penny beyond strike prices, in a single currency only. In the next chapter we take a brief tour through some further topics in commodity derivatives and structuring, building on the intuition we have built so far.

> Risk management themes encountered so far:
>
> - locking in;
> - tying costs to revenues;
> - switching one price exposure for another;
> - joint hedging of combined currency and commodity exposures;
> - protecting against downside;
> - delaying a locking in decision;
> - sharing the pain using participation;
> - sacrificing upside;
> - contingent premium payment;
> - buying down;
> - selling up;
> - volume flexibility;
> - extendability;
> - cancellability; and
> - embedding derivatives within physical agreements.

Notes

1. As an option trade in its own right a bull call spread may be entered into by a player who believes that market prices and/or volatility may rise, but doesn't feel it's worth paying the full premium for a 50 call. By capping the payoff they may receive at US$20, they reduce their potential upside, but make the cost of entering the position lower.
2. For the purposes of this categorisation we will choose the strike prices to be 40 and 60 respectively.
3. Aspiring traders and quants can use no arbitrage arguments to show that any other relationship would lead to a risk-free profit, which we assume isn't possible in liquid markets.
4. And of course numerous others may be constructed on demand.
5. "Phasing" is used for its greater generality than participation. Participation usually refers to structures with less than 100% of the volume of the main hedge instrument or physical exposure. Phasing may be used to refer to "participation" levels of greater than 100%.
6. If the consumer actually has daily double-up flexibility then a strip of daily exercise options may be a better bet for their exposure.
7. In any derivative package, who holds the optionality determines whether the hedger pays a premium for the extra flexibility, or receives a discount because the flexibility is with their energy risk manager.

7 Further Topics in Derivatives Structuring

Strengthen the will

Exotic Options and Tailored Structures

In this section we will review some of the most important concepts needed to understand the wider world of exotic and tailored derivatives. The style in this report has so far been highly pedagogical, introducing concepts carefully through simple numerical examples and block diagrams. Now that the language and nature of energy derivatives has been established, we shall pick up the pace somewhat and look at a wider selection of risk management, derivatives and structuring topics. Given the sheer size and complexity of this subject (demanding of several reports of similar size to the present volume), I will present a sample of issues, rather than attempt a methodical exposition of the entire subject.

The first generalisation we make is away from options whose payoffs depend on a single commodity, and look at spread and basket options that pay off on a number of commodity underlyings. These instruments may be used to hedge energy transformer risk exposures. We then look at digital options that pay a fixed lump sum if the market passes some trigger price, and see how these rebate-style derivatives can be used, including their role in constructing zero-premium structures. Our next generalisation is to consider how cross-currency payoffs can be incorporated into options, before finally surveying a miscellaneous range of other important and interesting option structures. By this time it is hoped that readers will be well placed to understand the ways in which risk management themes are reflected in derivatives structures, and start to think of their own generalisations of derivatives and how they might be employed in their own companies.

With the risk management themes well understood, we then proceed to look at two important topics in the world of physical trading and asset financing: *real options* and *hedge-linked financing*. We restrict ourselves to assets and projects that are tied to traded commodity markets, and consider the limits of fair-market pricing in the valuation of physical assets.

Spread and Basket Options

We start our tour of more specific options with a look at spread and basket options. These derivatives have a payoff depending not on a single commodity price, but on a set of such prices. *Spread options*' payoffs depend upon the difference between two risk factors, while *basket option* is a generic term for an option whose payoff depends upon two or more risk factors.

> Underlyings and Risk Factors
> The term *underlying* usually refers to the physical commodity being traded, whose price forms the basis for the payoff of a derivative instrument. Those underlyings with forward markets trade at various maturities and we can speak of, eg, 3rd nearby Brent or August natural gas. For the purposes of this guide we use the term *risk factor* to denote a specific underlying at a specific maturity. Thus September and October baseload power is one underlying, but two risk factors.

Spread and basket options, in common with their more vanilla Asian call and put version above, allow their holders to protect against downside price movements, though in the case where "downside" doesn't refer to a *single price* being high (for consumers) or low (for producers), but on whether some *combination of prices* is high or low. Some examples are:

- spark spread options, whose payoffs depend upon the difference between power and gas prices for the same maturity;
- crack spread options, whose payoffs depend upon the difference between a refined product and crude oil price for the same maturity;
- calendar spread options, whose payoffs depend upon the difference between different months' prices for the same underlying;
- locational spread/transmission/transportation options, whose payoffs depend upon the difference between the same physical commodity at two different geographical locations; and
- refinery basket options, whose payoffs depend upon the difference between a weighted average of refined product prices and crude oil.

Multi-underlying options such as spreads and baskets arise naturally from the hedging of physical transformative processes such as power generation and oil refining, physical transportation optionality or from timing optionality, for example in choosing when to load a physical cargo. While energy transformers may choose to lock in their margins using basket swaps, those seeking price upside will naturally look for options on these margins. In this section we consider Asian basket options, and their two-asset special cases, Asian spread options, which are the simplest forms of multi-underlying derivatives available.

Basket and spread option payoffs are based on a weighted average of underlying prices, where these basket weightings could be relative volumes from a refinery, power plant heat rates or similar. Since a basket option's payoff is a single cashflow, based on multiple input prices, a basket option transaction may be represented in block diagrams as shown in Figure 152.

Figure 152. Basket option transaction block diagram

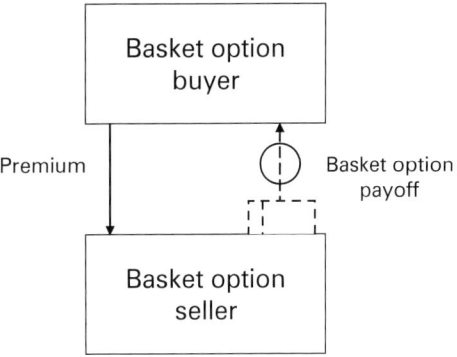

Example: Oil Refiner Seeks Downside Protection

An oil refiner looking to protect its refining margins may purchase a strip of Asian basket put options (or a *basket floor*) to protect its income.[1] Suppose that the refiner chooses to protect its margins using a set of liquid traded products in the form of a 3-2-1 crack, in which each three barrels of crude oil are considered to be transformed into two barrels of gasoline and one barrel of heating oil. The refiner's variable production costs are US$4/bbl, and at present the market has crude at US$60/bbl, gasoline at US$70/bbl and heating oil at US$66/bbl. While the refiner could lock in a margin of

$$1/3 \times ((2 \times \text{gasoline} + 1 \times \text{heating oil}) - 3 \times \text{crude}) - \text{US\$4/bbl}$$
$$= \text{US\$4.67/bbl}$$

using a basket swap, they instead feel that refinery outages and low stock levels could lead to refined products climbing still higher, and so they elect to pay US$1.50/bbl for a strip of Asian basket puts, each with payoff

$$\max(8.6 - \tfrac{1}{3}(2 \times F_{\text{gasoline}} + 1 \times F_{\text{heat}} - 3 \times F_{\text{crude}}), 0)$$

This payoff will, as demonstrated in Table 55 for various market-price scenarios, ensure that no less than US$4.6/bbl is received in exchange for the US$1.50/bbl premium.

While a refiner or power generator could protect the various "legs" of their exposure with a series of independent options on each underlying, they may be overpaying for this protection since:

Table 55. Refinery hedge using basket put option

Monthly price averages (US$/bbl)				Other cashflows (US$/bbl)			
Gasoline	Heating oil	Crude	3-2-1 crack	Variable costs	Refining margin	Basket put payoff	Net cashflow refining margin + option payoff
70.00	66.00	60.00	8.67	4.00	4.67	0.00	4.67
75.00	71.00	62.00	11.67	4.00	7.67	0.00	7.67
65.00	61.00	60.00	3.67	4.00	−0.33	4.93	4.60
65.00	65.00	62.00	3.00	4.00	−1.00	5.60	4.60
82.00	72.00	78.00	0.67	4.00	−3.33	7.93	4.60
78.00	72.00	55.00	21.00	4.00	17.00	0.00	17.00

- The physical player exposed to margins is indifferent to what the individual components of the basket do; only their combination is significant. If the movement of one underlying is perfectly offset by the movement of another, the margin remains the same. Optionality allowing the "picking off" of individual underlyings' movements will go unused if only the margin is being protected.
- Correlation effects mean that there is less variance in a basket of underlyings than the independent variances of the basket components would suggest. Lower variance (or *volatility* in derivatives-speak) means lower-cost protection.

Since readers are now accustomed to reading option payoffs written using the mathematical maximum function, in box "Basket option payoffs" I offer a general definition of basket option payoffs.

Basket option payoffs
Asian basket call options have the generic payoff at expiry

$$\max((a_1 F_1 + a_2 F_2 + \cdots + a_n F_n) - K, 0)$$

while *basket puts* have payoff

$$\max(K - (a_1 F_1 + a_2 F_2 + \cdots + a_n F_n), 0)$$

where the quantities F_i are realised average prices for a set of market commodities, and the coefficients a_i are some appropriate weighting factors chosen to match the physical transformative process, such as efficiencies, relative volumes or similar. The coefficients may be positive or negative according to the exposure being hedged. *Spread options* are the two underlying special cases of basket options, where the coefficients are of opposite sign.

Valuation of multi-underlying options such as spreads and baskets requires the usual Black–Scholes style inputs, namely strike price, forward prices for each underlying, implied volatilities, interest rate and time to expiry, but it also requires something new: the set of correlations between the underlyings. In intuitive terms the higher the correlations between the underlyings, the lower the option premium, since higher correlation means less independence in the way the underlyings may evolve.

Consider a simple ATM two-asset spread option

$$\max(K - (F_1 - F_2), 0)$$

where $K = 10$, $F_1 = 50$ and $F_2 = 40$. Varying the correlation between -100% and $+100\%$ produces the variation in the premium shown in Figure 153.

Option traders may face significant challenges in the practical hedging, and therefore pricing, of basket options since:

Figure 153. Spread option premium dependence on correlation

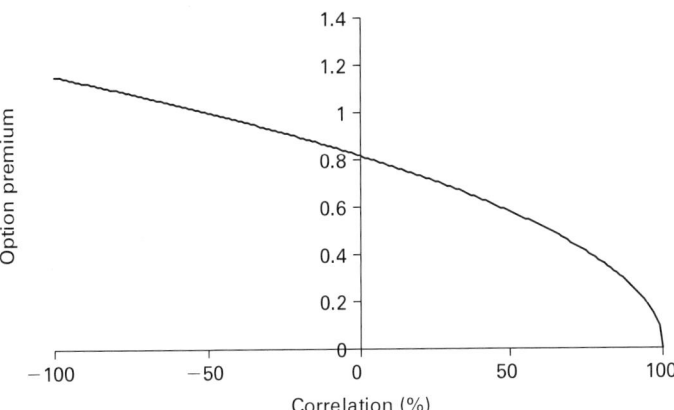

- the larger number of underlyings, and potentially low liquidity of some of them, may result in significant transaction costs as the option is hedged; and
- the market may not offer implied correlations between the underlyings, leading the trader either to try to imply them from history or to take a view.

Some traders try to circumvent the first of these problems by choosing a simpler basket, with fewer, more liquid, components, as a proxy for the full basket, on the grounds that imperfections in this imperfect basket's tracking performance will be more than balanced by the reduced hedging costs.

Option valuation for multi-underlying options

The classic Black–Scholes inputs required to evaluate vanilla options on a single underlying are:

- current market price;
- strike price;
- time to expiry;
- risk-free interest rate; and
- volatility of the underlying.

For options on multiple risk factors (such as spread, basket and quanto options) the option valuation models need:

- current market price (and FX rate, for quanto options) for each risk factor;
- strike price for the option;
- time to expiry;
- risk-free interest rate;
- volatility of each risk factor;
- weightings to apply to each component of the basket; and
- the set of correlations between risk factors.

Readers should note that option traders do not have a completely free choice of correlations between multiple underlyings, and that basic quantitative reasoning places a constraint on the relationships between correlations. In simple terms, if asset A is strongly correlated with asset B, and asset B is strongly correlated with asset C, then asset A must be quite strongly correlated with asset C.

Example: Cargo Load Date Slippage

A refiner has contracted to purchase a cargo of crude from an offshore producer in July, and will pay the producer the monthly average crude oil price for the month in which the cargo loads. The refiner would like to lock in today the price for the oil by entering into a July swap, but the oil producer fears that production problems may lead the cargo loading date to slip into the following month. If the refiner enters into a July swap, and August prices turn out to be higher than July prices, then the crude purchaser will be out of pocket; similar considerations apply if they enter into an August swap. They contact their energy risk manager to see if they can help.

The energy risk manager suggests a July one-month *slippage swap*, which pays out the best of two consecutive months' realised average prices, in this case July and August, in return for a fixed strike price. The refiner will need to pay a premium for this protection, and the suggested transaction is shown in Figure 154.

To help the refiner understand the mechanics of the slippage swap the energy risk manager shows the refiner the figures in Table 56, which assumes that the refiner fixes a price K today.

In all cases the refiner pays no more than the fixed strike price plus the premium for their oil. Since the oil producer is unable to commit to a firm loading month, but the refiner has a production schedule to meet, the fair-market way for the refiner to negotiate would be to *demand a discount* from the monthly price for this inconvenience. The discount demanded should be equal to the premium paid for the slippage swap, ensuring that the refiner is never out of pocket.[2]

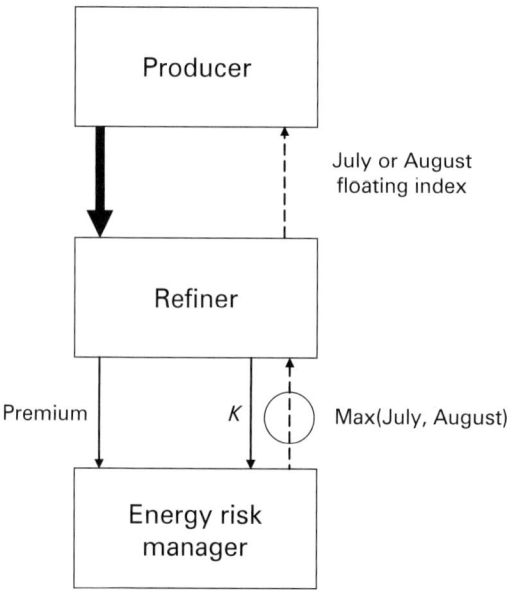

Figure 154. Slippage swap transaction

Table 56. Slippage swap payoff table

Loading month	Purchaser pays for physical	Actual average prices (US$/bbl)	Slippage swap pays (US$/bbl)	Net to purchaser (US$/bbl)
July	Average of July	July = 45 August = 42	45 − (K + prem)	−(K + prem)
		July = 45 August = 46	46 − (K + prem)	1 − (K + prem)
August	Average of August	July = 45 August = 42	45 − (K + prem)	3 − (K + prem)
		July = 45 August = 46	46 − (K + prem)	−(K + prem)

The slippage swap in the previous example can be synthesised using a July swap and an Asian time spread option on the difference between realised August and July prices. This can be achieved since

$$\max(A, B) = A + \max(B - A, 0)$$

leading to the slippage swap payoff being written as

$$\max(F_{July}, F_{August}) - K = (F_{July} - K) + \max(F_{August} - F_{July}, 0)$$
$$= (\text{July swap})$$
$$+ (\text{August} - \text{July time spread option})$$

If the refiner succeeds in negotiating the market-based discount from the producer, then the transaction, including the way in which the energy risk manager synthesises the slippage swap, is shown in Figure 155.

The slippage swap can be extended to multiple slippage months through the use of *Asian calendar multi-spread options*, which are outside the scope of this report.

> Does increasing volatility always lead to increasing option value?

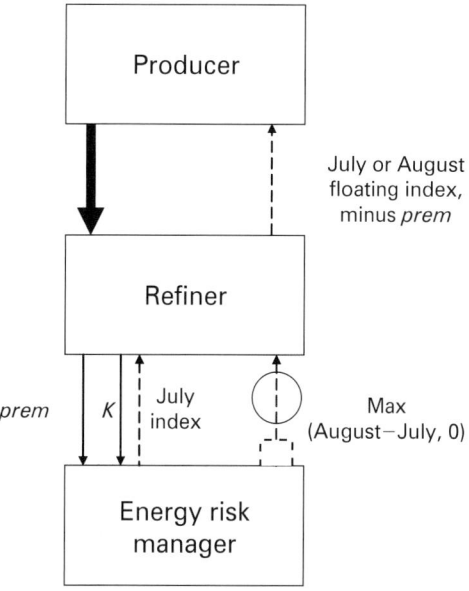

Figure 155. Slippage swap synthesis

I have seen traders bawling out quants and risk managers on the grounds that their spread option models must be wrong since increasing the volatility of an underlying decreases the option premium. In general terms increasing the *total volatility* of a spread or basket will increase the option's value, though increasing the volatility of a *subset* of the underlyings can actually *decrease the overall volatility* of the basket. This counterintuitive behaviour arises from the interplay between volatilities and correlations, and a mildly quantitative explanation for a spread option is given in the technical appendix, "Option value needn't increase with increasing volatility". The bawling trader was a vanilla trader who'd strayed into the world of multi-commodity options, and discovered that his intuition was lacking.

> Option gamma
> Gamma is the second of the so-called *Greeks* or *Greek letters* we encounter in derivative finance (the first being delta). The *gamma* of an option is defined formally as the delta's sensitivity to changes in the underlying market price; this somewhat dense definition may be better understood by thinking of gamma as the slope of the graph of the option's delta.
>
> If delta is a proxy for the moneyness of a vanilla option, then gamma tells option traders how responsive the moneyness of the vanilla option is to changes in the underlying market. For a deep in- or out-of-the-money option the delta is relatively insensitive to changes in the underlying market; deep in- or out-of-the-money options are more likely to remain so than ones that are nearer the money, and so their gamma is near zero. Near-the-money options are highly sensitive to changes in the underlying market, moving in or out of the money with relatively little change in the underlying. The delta and gamma of a call option are illustrated in Figure 156, and readers can confirm that an ATM call option has the highest gamma.
>
> By examining the slopes of the deltas, readers can check that the gamma of a long vanilla option, whether a call or a put, is always positive, whereas the delta is positive for long calls, and negative for long puts.
>
> Gammas, like deltas, are additive, and computing the gamma of a derivative package is achieved by adding the gammas of its component parts.

Figure 156. Call option gamma

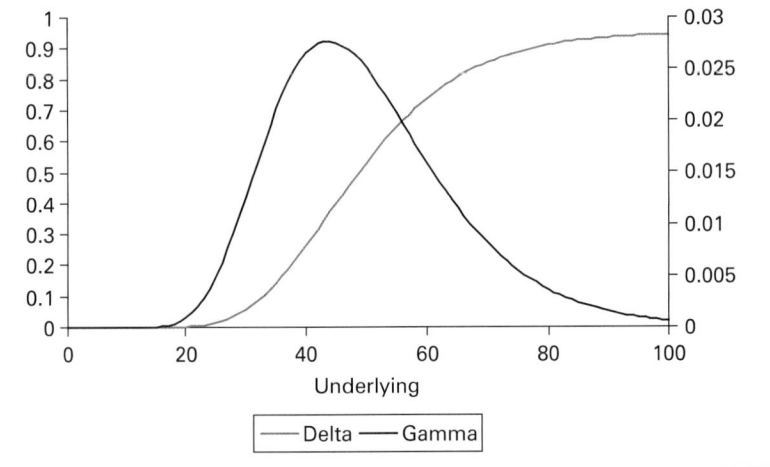

Digital Options

Asian digital options pay a fixed amount if average market prices pass some given threshold, in contrast with the options seen so far, which pay an amount that escalates the further past the strike price the market settles. Digital options are more like a bet or conventional insurance payout than the derivatives seen so far, though their payoff is still dependent on market prices passing some threshold.

An Asian digital call option payoff paying out a unit sum of cash if the average market price, F, meets or exceeds the strike price, K, may be written using a new symbol as

$$1_{F \geq K} = \begin{cases} 1, & \text{if } F \geq K \\ 0, & \text{otherwise} \end{cases}$$

while an option paying out N units of cash would have payoff

$$N 1_{F \geq K}$$

Conversely, a unit Asian digital put option has payoff written as $1_{F \leq K}$

> Draw the payoff diagrams for unit Asian digital call and put options with strike of 50.

The payoff diagrams for Asian digital call and put options are shown in Figures 157 and 158 respectively.

Digital options act as a form of rebate for their holder, and don't have an obvious role in the hedging of the simple market-indexed supply or off-take agreements considered in previous chapters. Digital options usually occur:

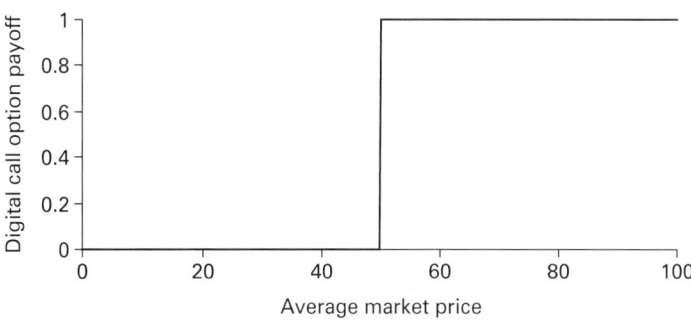

Figure 157. Asian digital call option payoff

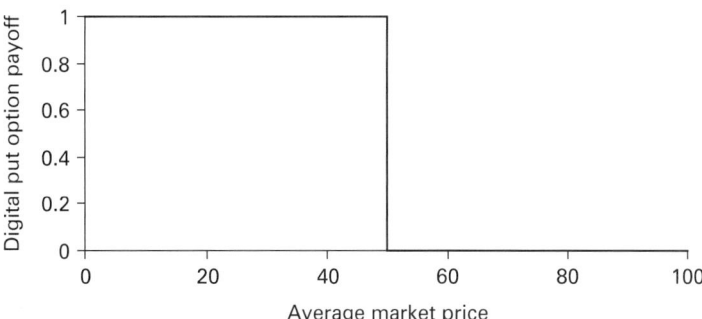

Figure 158. Asian digital put option payoff

- in the precise tailoring of option payoffs to risk exposures containing market-indexed rebates;
- where they are embedded as rebates within physical contracts; and
- as a means to achieve contingent premium options.

Since a digital option payoff is fixed in quantity, but flows only if a specific market condition is met, the transaction may be represented by the block diagram in Figure 159.

Example: Asset Disposal with Market-Contingent Rebate

An oil major is disposing of an oil-producing asset, and is collecting bids from various players. The two most competitive bids are quite different in nature, and the mergers-and-acquisitions group don't know how best to compare the values of the two deals. They turn to the structuring group on the trading floor for assistance in understanding the bids. The bids are as follows:

- Bidder A offers a fixed lump sum of US$50 million for the asset.
- Bidder B offers a smaller lump sum of US$35 million up front for the asset, and lump sums of US$10 million in each of the three following years if oil prices remain above an average of US$40/bbl in the respective years.

These bids are represented using the block diagrams in Figure 160.

Figure 159. Digital option transaction

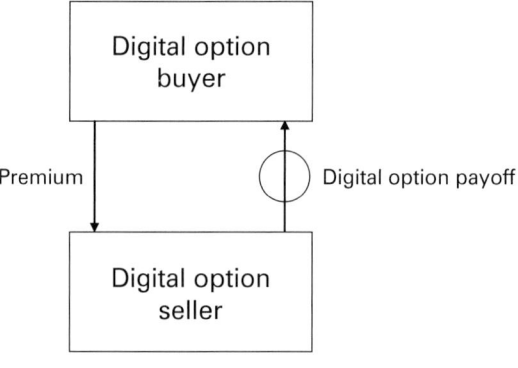

Figure 160. Two bids for the same asset

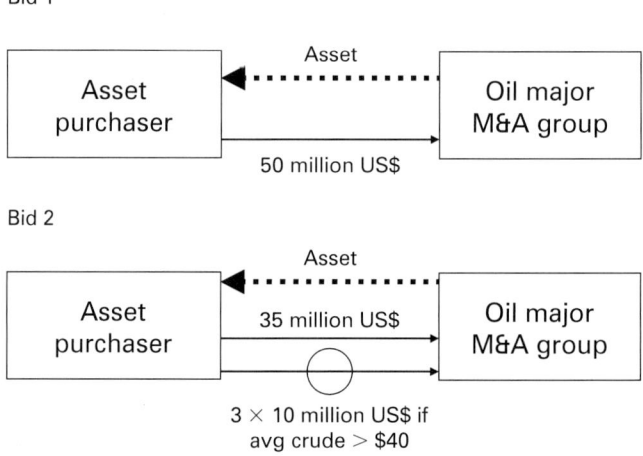

Figure 161. Monetising embedded digital options in asset disposal

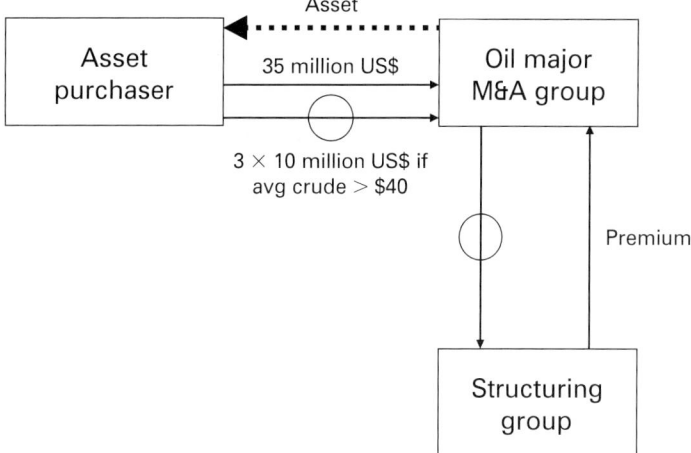

The structuring group recognise the second bid as being equivalent to a lump sum, plus a strip of three Asian digital options, each with a one-year averaging period. Since the M&A group are not interested in receiving market-contingent payments for an asset they've sold some years before, but are required to maximise income for the company, they ask the structuring group if anything can be done.

The structuring group offer to monetise the options. This amounts to buying the options from the M&A group, offering them a firm upfront premium payment, in exchange for the market-contingent future cashflows. The M&A group would therefore receive US$35 million plus the premium for the asset, and the structuring group would be buying a strip of Asian digital options. The proposed transaction is shown in Figure 161.

The strategy for the M&A group is now clear: if the US$35 million lump sum plus the option premium exceeds the alternative US$50 million bid, they should proceed with bid 2. The structuring group quote a premium of US$22 million for the strip of digital options, which together with the lump sum of US$35 million comfortably exceeds the US$50 million bid. The M&A group proceed with bid 2, raising US$7 million of additional value from the asset disposal.

> Can you construct something resembling a digital call option using a package of vanilla options?

A digital call option can be approximated by constructing, eg, a bull call spread with very close strike prices. For very close strikes the volume of the call spread will need to be quite large since a large change in payoff is required from a small change in the underlying market. In the sequence of payoff diagrams in Figures 162, 163 and 164, we see how using closer strikes yields a structure closer to a digital call option. The notion of *phasing* has been used again (as in the discussion of three-way options above) to denote the volume of options needed to ensure a unit payoff from the structure.

A bull call spread with a phasing of 1000% corresponds to 10 units (ie, 1000% of) a long call and 10 units of a short call with strike 0.01 higher. A long digital call option corresponds to a bull call spread in which the strikes coincide, and the phasing is infinite.

Figure 162. Bull call spread, strikes 10 apart

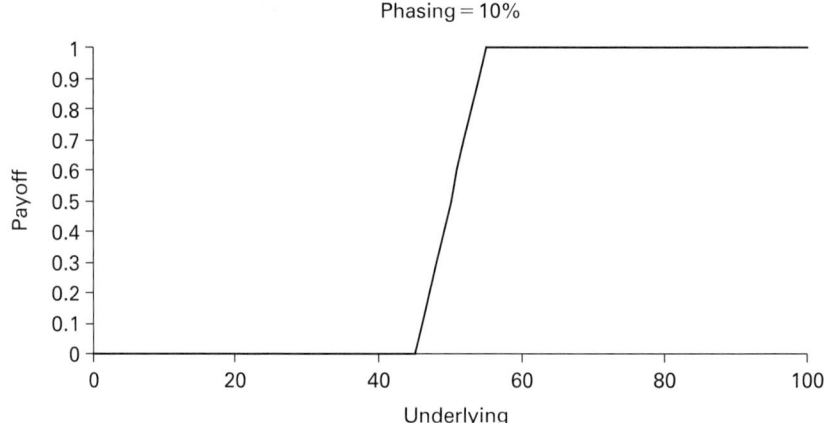

Figure 163. Bull call spread, strikes 1 apart

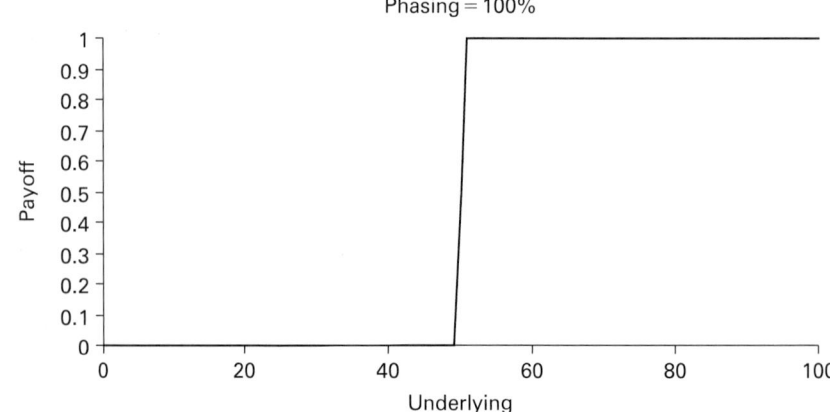

Figure 164. Bull call spread, strikes 0.01 apart

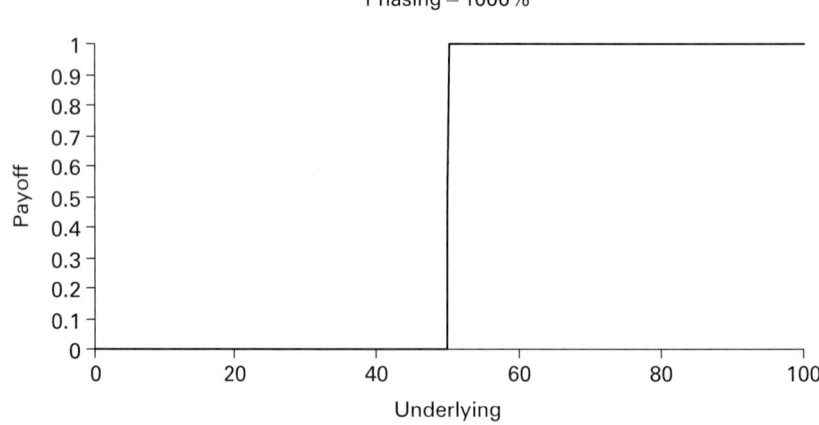

Example: Contingent Premium Structure Using Digital Options

A heating oil distribution company wish to buy an OTM cap on NYMEX front-line heating oil with a strike of 1.90 US$/gal, but:

♦ they don't want to pay an upfront premium, ruling out a straight cap;
♦ they don't want to sacrifice all their upside beyond a certain price, ruling out a collar; and
♦ they are prepared to take a "single hit" if the call option is out-of-the-money, but want full protection beyond the cap.

Figure 165. Contingent premium call option using digital option

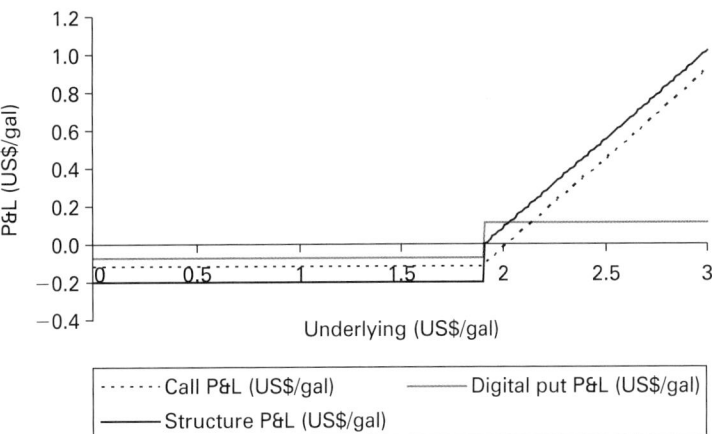

Their energy risk manager responds by offering them a contingent premium cap consisting of a long call option and a short digital put option of the same strike. No upfront premium is due; and the digital option reaps back the premium due immediately, with no "phasing" of the reap-back. The P&L diagram for this structure, and its component parts, is shown in Figure 165.

The cap alone would have cost the distributor an up-front premium of 12.5 USc/gal, but by entering into the contingent premium structure they may end up taking a "hit" from the digital option of 30 USc/gal. The difference between these two premiums is the price the consumer needs to pay for making the premium contingent.

Now we have considered the relationship between vanilla option spreads and digital options, it should be clear that the contingent premium structure in the previous example is essentially a consumer three-way option, in which the contingent premium is reaped back immediately.

> Is the gamma of a long option position always positive?

While the gamma of a long vanilla option position, whether a call or a put, is positive, it isn't necessarily true for other option types. As we have seen, a digital option resembles a call spread, and since the call spread package contains both a long and a short vanilla option, we should expect the digital option to have both positive and negative gammas according to the value of the underlying.

The payoff and delta of a digital option are shown in Figure 166. Note that the delta curves upwards on the way to the strike price, and then downwards after the strike price is passed.

The gamma of the same option may be found by computing the gradient of the graph of the option's delta for different values of the underlying. The gamma is shown in Figure 167.

Quanto Options

Quanto options, like quanto swaps, offer their holders joint protection against both commodity and currency movements. In energy we define a quanto option to be one in which the option payoff is in a different currency from the underlying commodity being traded. Examples might be:

Figure 166. Payoff and delta of a digital call option

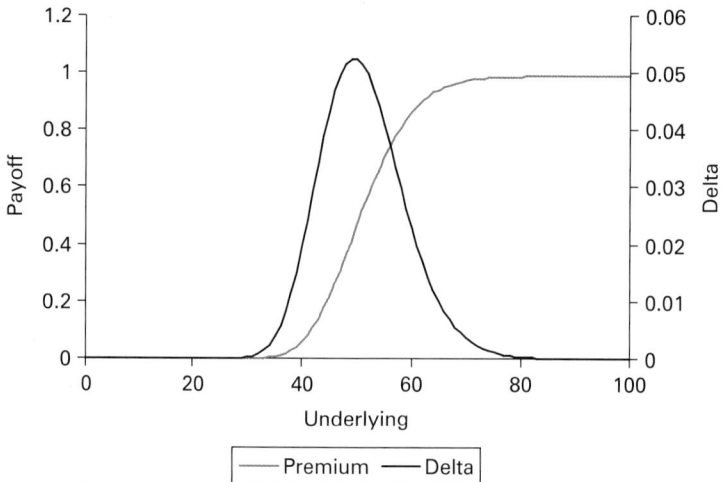

Figure 167. Delta and gamma of a digital call option

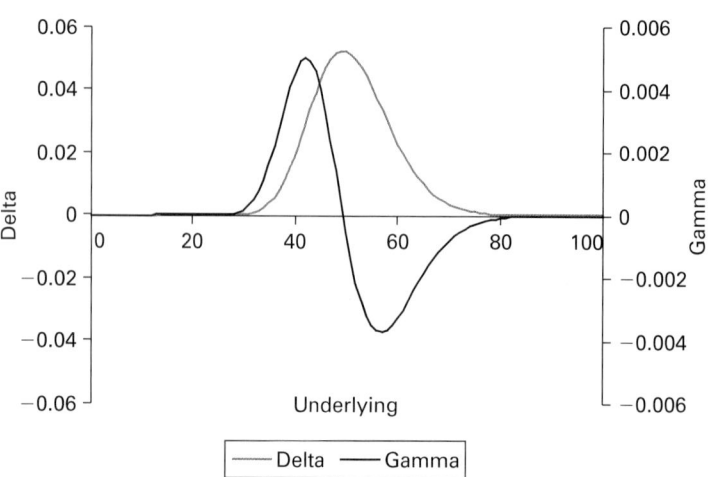

- a put on Brent crude oil, which is traded in US dollars per barrel, with strike price and payoff in pounds per barrel;
- a call on NYMEX heating oil, which is traded in US dollars per gallon, with strike price and payoff in Canadian dollars per gallon; and
- a call on UK NBP natural gas, which is traded in pence per therm, with strike price and payoff in euros per therm.

Just as with vanilla options, consumers may buy quanto caps or producers quanto floors, to allow themselves access to market upside. Only those companies whose costs and revenues are in the same currency as their energy costs can afford to ignore cross-currency effects in their hedging. Typical buyers of Asian quanto options would be:

- Canadian oil producers, buying Canadian dollar crude oil floors;
- European airlines, buying euro jet caps; and
- Australian mining companies, protecting their fuel purchases with Australian dollar fuel oil calls.

Further Topics in Derivatives Structuring

The payoffs for Asian quanto options resemble those of regular, or *native currency*, options, except that the commodity prices are translated in some way by the appropriate FX rate before being used to compute the option payoff. As with quanto swap settlement conventions above, it is necessary to pay attention to the precise way in which the commodity prices are adjusted by the FX rates. Readers are reminded that the simplest conventions are as follows:

- The monthly floating price is computed as the average of each day's spot commodity index adjusted by each same day's spot FX rate. Put another way:

$$\text{floating price} = avg(\text{daily commodity index} \times \text{daily spot FX})$$

- The monthly floating price is computed as the average of each day's spot commodity index, where the overall average is adjusted by the average of each day's spot FX rate. Symbolically:

$$\text{floating price} = avg(\text{daily commodity index}) \times avg(\text{daily spot FX})$$

- The monthly floating price is computed as the average of each day's spot commodity index, where this overall commodity average price is adjusted at the last daily spot FX rate available in the month. This may be summed up mathematically as:

$$\text{floating price} = avg(\text{daily commodity index}) \times \text{last spot FX}$$

As we have seen, a variety of other averaging methods also exist.

Using the first of these conventions for simplicity's sake the payoff of a quanto Asian call option is

$$\max\left(\frac{1}{N}(FX_1 F_1 + FX_2 F_2 + \cdots + FX_N F_N) - K, 0\right)$$

where the payoff depends upon N foreign-exchange fixings, FX_i, and N commodity prices, F_i. Likewise the payoff of a quanto Asian put option is

$$\max\left(K - \frac{1}{N}(FX_1 F_1 + FX_2 F_2 + \cdots + FX_N F_N), 0\right)$$

In both cases the strike price is assumed to be in the foreign currency, and the FX rate is assumed to be quoted in units of foreign currency per unit of native currency.

Example: European Oil Producer Quanto Hedge

A small UK-based oil producer wishes to protect some portion of its crude sales against downside price movements in order to underwrite the budget for next year's capital expenditure. This expenditure will be paid primarily in sterling, and the producer is concerned that entering into a conventional dollar floor may still leave it unable to meet its costs if the dollar weakens against the pound. The oil producer contacts its energy risk manager, who suggests a *quanto floor* for the next year.

With crude oil trading at US$50/bbl, and the dollar–sterling spot FX rate at US$1.70/GBP, the producer elects to buy an OTM floor with strike price £23.50/bbl. As it sells its crude into the spot market it can translate the proceeds straight into sterling for its own accounts. Should monthly revenues from these crude sales fall below the equivalent of £23.50/bbl, the Asian quanto put option will compensate them sterling penny for sterling penny.

Since quanto options are multi-underlying options, their value depends not only upon the current market prices, rates, volatilities and so on, but also upon the correlations between these values. Quanto options share this feature with basket options, and as discussed above for baskets, it may be more cost-effective to purchase a quanto option than to protect the individual currency and commodity legs separately.

All the considerations of the previous chapters regarding the construction of option packages, strategies for reducing, eliminating or making contingent option premiums, apply equally well to quanto options. There is therefore no need to discuss these matters here.

Correlation matrices

Where an option payoff depends upon multiple risk factors, traders must employ a set of correlations between these risk factors. These correlations may be assembled into a matrix known as the *correlation matrix*, and this is conventionally the way the data are presented.

Suppose an option is being valued on a refiner's basket of crude, gasoline and heating oil. The option valuation function needs to be supplied with the correlations between crude and gasoline, crude and heating oil, and gasoline and heating oil. These correlations are of course symmetric, and everything is correlated with itself perfectly. This set of correlations may be assembled into a matrix

$$\begin{pmatrix} 100\% & \rho_{\text{crude, gasoline}} & \rho_{\text{crude, heating oil}} \\ \rho_{\text{gasoline, crude}} & 100\% & \rho_{\text{gasoline, heating oil}} \\ \rho_{\text{heating oil, crude}} & \rho_{\text{heating oil, gasoline}} & 100\% \end{pmatrix}$$

where correlations are conventionally represented by the Greek letter ρ.

The instruments we've examined in the earlier part of this chapter, namely spread options, basket options and digital options, may also be offered in quanto form, thus completing the suite of tools available for hedging out cross-commodity exposures and for constructing contingent premium structures. Quanto Asian basket options, eg, could be used by a Southeast Asian refiner to protect their refining margins against downside movements in their local currency.

Other Option and Structure Types

The world of exotic options is wide and at times bewildering to the uninitiated. Options can be created to match almost any risk exposure, and the challenge for treasurers, CFOs and risk managers is to understand the aggregate of these exposures and to identify the most appropriate hedges. The question of what makes an option "exotic" is a subtle one, and there is no accepted definition of *exoticity*. In the words of my former boss Vincent Kaminski, when he was global head of research for Enron, "Exoticity is in the eye of the beholder." In practical terms exotic options are considered to be those that:

- have payoffs that differ from the conventional vanilla swaps, calls and puts; and
- have payoffs based on unusual or very specific underlyings.

According to the former criterion a basket or digital option is exotic. According to the latter, an hourly option on peak-load electricity is exotic.

In any case we shouldn't consider "exotic" to mean "abstruse" – all options, whether vanilla or exotic, are created to service some real demand: an oil refiner may consider a basket option to be entirely appropriate as a hedge for their exposure, while a large industrial user of power with a highly variable demand pattern may consider hourly power caps to be just the protection they need. So-called exotic options may be the most effective hedge to a specific kind of risk exposure, and may be better able to demonstrate hedge effectiveness to one's auditors. Unfortunately, the word "exotic" is often taken to mean "obscure", and scares hedgers away from what may be more appropriate protection.

Natural "exotic" generalisations of the kind of options we've encountered so far in this guide are the following:

- *Asian American options*: Asian options that can be exercised during the averaging period if the average so far reaches a desirable price level.
- *Compound options*: An option to enter an option, or an option to enter a strip of options. Typically form part of an extendable package, in which a buyer of a derivatives package wishes to have, or to offer, the right to extend the entire package for a further time period.
- *American swaptions*: Offer the holder the right, but not the obligation, to enter into a swap contract, where the decision may be made any time up to expiry. If the swap price reaches a desirable level during the option's life the swaption may be exercised, and the swap price locked in at that time.
- *Swing options*: In which a volume of commodity may be bought or sold during the lifetime of the option, subject to some constraints. For example, the holder of an annual call swing option may choose how much commodity to buy for the strike price in any given month, provided they don't exceed the monthly volume constraint, and provided they don't buy more than the overall annual volume.
- *Quanto swaptions*: Provide the holder with the right, but not the obligation, to enter into a quanto swap.

- *Quanto basket digital options*: Options that pay a fixed amount of cash in a foreign currency if an underlying basket price, when converted into the same currency, passes some threshold.
- *Barrier options*: Calls or puts that either "come alive" (*knock in*) or "die" (*knock out*) if prices move beyond a certain threshold.

Real Options

Real options are flexibilities that occur in the operation of physical assets or in the planning and operation of projects, and the practice of real-option theory is the attempt to use option-style thinking in these projects or asset operations. *Real optionality* arises from the possession, and exercise, of flexibility in the face of uncertainty.

Given my bias towards derivatives, I prefer to use the term *option* only where there is a traded market underpinning the valuation; anything else is a *choice* or a *flexibility* in my preferred terminology. Through this more careful use of language I distinguish between *optionality*, which derives from hedgeable, fair-market valuations, and *choices*, which do not. Through introducing a trading mindset into the valuation of optionality we have all the technology of energy derivatives at our disposal, which give us defensible fair-market valuations.

As readers will know *discounted cashflow* (*DCF*) analysis is the most traditional way to evaluate a project's net present value (NPV), and it involves discounting back each forecast cashflow along the project's timeline at some discount rate reflecting the riskiness of the venture. This style of analysis in its simplest form doesn't incorporate uncertainty into its valuations, nor does it incorporate flexibility. Figure 168 shows a sample project time line with forecast cashflows at various stages.

This most basic approach to valuation doesn't incorporate uncertainty into its forecasts in any way, and so some practitioners will extend their DCF analysis to consider various scenarios, perhaps each with associated probabilities, as illustrated in Figure 169.

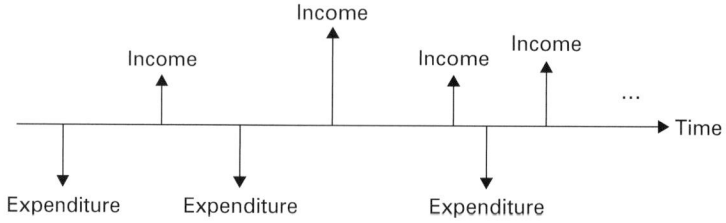

Figure 168. DCF analysis based on forecast cashflows (the project is considered to be economically viable if the NPV is positive at the given level of discounting used to reflect the project's riskiness)

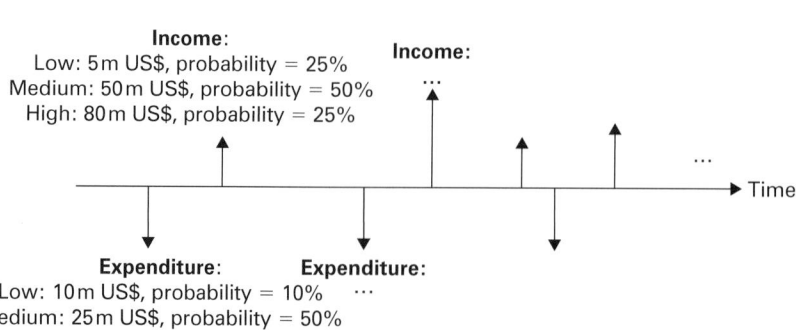

Figure 169. DCF analysis extended to include scenarios

In this case the NPV will be based on probabilistically weighted, or *expected*, incomes and expenditures, rather than a single forecast.[3] The decision about whether the project is considered to be viable will now be based on this range of possibilities. The decision to proceed is being made based on the averages of outcomes; there is still only one decision point at the beginning, about whether to proceed with the entire project or not. In this approach there are no dynamic decisions made as a result of price uncertainty *within* the timeline of the project, and so other approaches have evolved to deal with this need.

Decision analysis, or decision trees, extend DCF to allow their users to consider the impact of making decisions within the project timeline. Decision trees are used to model flexibility in the face of uncertainty, and as such are used to evaluate real "optionality" in the broadest sense of the term. Decision trees recognise that at different points in time one may make decisions based on the path followed so far, and also recognise that uncertainty can lead to the creation of new paths. Let's look at a very simple example.

Example: Decision Analysis Using Decision Trees

Suppose WidgeCorp are considering starting production of their new Gizmo. Gizmo production would involve building expensive new plant, so WidgeCorp's management need to decide whether it is optimal to test-market the Gizmo first. Test-marketing would take one year, and cost US$500000, at the end of which it is expected that the test-marketing will prove successful with a probability of 60%. This is a point of uncertainty, with two outcomes, represented by a circle in the decision tree.

If the test is deemed to have failed, no further investment will be made and the project will be scrapped at that point (this is a decision point, denoted by square nodes in the decision tree). However, if the test succeeds, management need to decide whether to build the new plant (an outlay with a present value of US$10 million) and start production, or not. Successful test-marketing would lead management to expect that the factory will produce a positive cashflow of US$1.5 million every year, at a discount rate of 12%, equivalent to a present value of US$12 million over the project lifetime.

The decision tree representing this simple case is shown in Figure 170.

Decision trees of this form allow decisions to be made only on the basis of *expected* cashflows, a little like DCF above, and do not allow a different decision for each possible cashflow. As with DCF above, decision trees[4] can also be extended to include Monte Carlo generation of scenarios to incorporate market, or other, uncertainties.

Figure 170. WidgeCorp's decision analysis

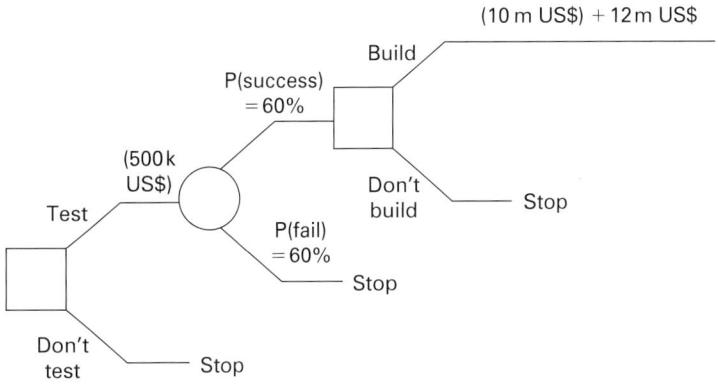

Beware that decisions made on the basis of a Monte Carlo simulation can overvalue projects seriously due to the error of assuming *perfect foresight*. This error arises from simulating prices scenarios through time, then computing the optimal decisions for each given path. The decisions will have been made given a perfect (generated) knowledge of the future, which in practice one doesn't have.

In the absence of traded markets, the techniques described above are the standard ones to employ, and through years of experience management have learned to employ the techniques, and challenge their results, to great effect. Where a traded market does exist, and does impact the project significantly, then other more derivatives-based forms of thinking may be employed.[5] The most derivatives-like forms of real-option valuation consider the "cone of possibilities", which opens up around expected prices in the future, exploiting or "carving off" the favourable prices, while choosing to avoid unfavourable prices. This is precisely what all the options studied above achieve, and approaches to real-option valuation based on this idea are closest to the spirit of this report.

Choice based on averages, or average of choices

Naïve or inflexible approaches to DCF and decision analysis base their decision of whether to proceed on examination of the average of all outcomes. Where one has genuine flexibility, one needn't be exposed to the *average* of all outcomes: one can choose *only the good outcomes*, and choose not to be exposed to the bad ones. The difference between the two approaches can be summed up symbolically as:

- *Naïve or inflexible approach to valuation*:

$$\text{Value} = \max(\text{average outcome}, 0)$$

where the average outcome may be negative, and the decision to proceed is based purely on whether this average is greater than 0.

- *Option-style approach to valuation*:

$$\text{Value} = avg(\max(\text{outcome}, 0))$$

where max(outcome, 0) can never be negative for each individual outcome, and thus the average of these choices can never be negative. This approach corresponds to flexible operation, allowing management to "carve off" the good outcomes only.

When this option-style approach is used, the payoffs from the project are forced to be positive (like options), and management can decide whether the average of these positive payoffs justifies the cost of proceeding with the project, the equivalent of paying the option premium.

Further Topics in Derivatives Structuring

The characteristics of market-traded options are well known: the holder of the option has a right, but not an obligation, to receive or make delivery of some underlying at or by some future time, and the value of such optionality arises from the fact that market prices are uncertain (ie, there is volatility). In real option analysis of energy projects physical assets are often modelled as portfolios of traded instruments. When we talk of the "optionality" of a physical asset we are referring to:

- the asset's operational flexibility; and
- our ability to operate this asset in such a way that we are able to exploit market price movements.

Such flexibility resembles the optionality offered by instruments in traded financial and commodity markets, and so we naturally look to these markets for appropriate techniques to value these instruments. Examples are:

- flexible refinery output as a strip of basket options on the forward refinery cracks;
- merchant power plant considered as a strip of spark spread options between power and gas prices; and
- gas storage facility considered as a set of interacting calendar spread options on gas.

Let's examine an example of this thinking to see where it takes us.

Example: Refinery Upgrade Investment Decision

Suppose a refiner is considering investing in an upgrade to its refinery; its discounted cashflow approach to evaluating the forward crack spreads show that the project is unlikely to break even, which would require an expected crack spread of US$3/bbl for the next five years. Figure 171 shows how the forward market cracks decrease, which in DCF terms makes the refinery attractive only in the first two years of operation, which is not enough to break even.

Figure 171. Refinery valuation based solely upon forward curve and break-even price

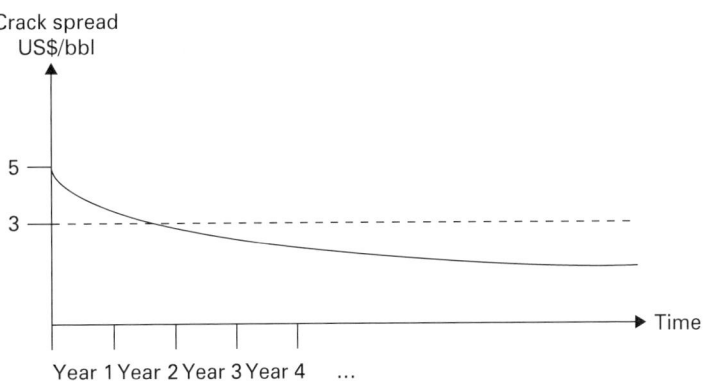

Figure 172. Refinery investment decision based on the forward curve and the "cone of possibilities"

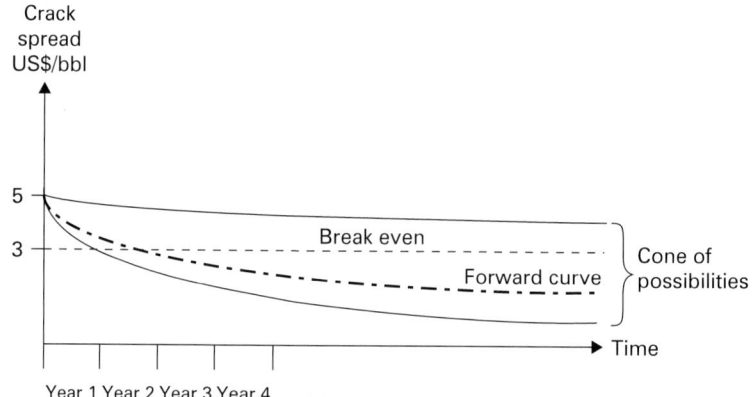

DCF evaluation, even if based on market forward curves rather than planning assumptions, doesn't account for the volatility in the forward market. Incorporating volatility shows a "cone of possibilities" opening around the forward curve, as illustrated in Figure 172. If a crack should occur in a given month that is above the break-even line, then one would choose to run the new equipment earning the crack in that month.

The refinery's ability to respond to volatile market prices shows that one needn't be exposed only to the market's current view of the average price, but may carve off favourable prices, while ignoring unfavourable prices. If there is an expectation that enough of these favourable price scenarios could occur to make running the new plant break even, then the plant's time value will justify the investment, even if the intrinsic value doesn't.

Realising real option value in a market-based investment involves *monetising the optionality*, or selling the right to call upon the flexibility to a counterparty, perhaps in exchange for an upfront payment that can be used to invest in the new plant. Failure to monetise the optionality means that there is no guarantee that the real option value will be realised, and proceeding with the project would still be little better than a gamble. In the next section, "Risk analysis example: hedge-based financing", a risk analysis is conducted for a simplified hedge-based financing transaction, showing how the ideas of derivatives, real options and mapping using the risk matrix may be combined.

Example: Monetising Real Optionality

- *Oil or gas storage owners*: May offer traders access to their storage facility. The price they charge should be based on the (quite subtle) calendar spread optionality their asset offers. Selling this optionality means the storage owner has lost the capacity for its own use – it has sold its optionality, but has received payment for giving up this right to a party better able to exploit its flexibility in the traded markets.
- *Peak-power generation*: Asset owners may sell peak options to clients. If peak power passes a certain threshold, or strike price, the clients may call upon the asset owner to generate power for them.

> The owner of a peak-power-generation asset is able to generate power at a cost of €90/MWh.
>
> (continued)

Further Topics in Derivatives Structuring

> - What kind of option does this resemble?
> - Why would selling a peak option to a counterparty with strike price €110/MWh be attractive?
> - What is the resulting derivatives package if this optionality is monetised in this way?
> - What could go wrong?

The owner of the asset is long a strip of hourly call options, with strike price €90/MWh. If it switches its asset on and off in response to market prices it is left hoping that enough price spikes occur to justify the cost of maintaining and running the asset. Selling strike €110/MWh peak options to a counterparty monetises some of this optionality, earning premium that can be used to pay for maintenance and running costs. The resulting derivatives package is a bull call spread:

- should market price rise above €90/MWh, the asset owner will generate power, and benefit from rising prices above this level; and
- for market prices above €110/MWh they have given up further upside to their counterparty.

While the asset owner has sold a paper derivative, its own option is very much a real option. Sometimes physical plant doesn't work as expected. If the counterparty exercises its €110/MWh strike call, but the asset fails to run properly, the asset owner will have to go to the physical market to source the power to supply to its counterparty. Its potential downside is unlimited, since it will be short a call option. The subject of physical risk management is raised in the next chapter, "Wider Risk Management Questions".

While a rich source of inspiration, and a good form of discipline, option theory has only limited applicability to asset and project valuation. The first objection to the naïve application of the theory is that major projects can involve significant volumes of commodity, which if laid off into the market could adversely affect margins. Simple "mid-market" forward curves should not be used for large-project, real-option valuations, and liquidity adjustments must be made; this objection applies also to traded market derivatives, and is not unique to real options.

A second, and more serious, warning about the use of naïve financial-option methods is the existence of physical operational constraints. Physical plant cannot be switched on and off, or ramped up and down, arbitrarily quickly, and the mode of operation of the equipment can have reliability, maintenance, environmental and safety implications. The existence of such constraints acts to decrease the simple "financial"-style value of an asset, and often dictates how the asset's optionality may be exercised. Physical plant tends to involve "contingent optionality", where an exercise decision made at one time dictates which exercise decisions may be made at later times.[6]

The next major pitfall of the naïve use of option theory is the presence of non-market risk, as mentioned in the decision-tree example above (success of test marketing) and in the unreliable peak-power plant of the last question point. Only hedgeable market risks may be valued using risk-free discounting and the fair-market valuation of traded derivatives. All other sources of uncertainty lead to the need for risk adjustment.

Example: Risk Adjustment

You are invited to play a gambling game in which you are required to offer your house as the stake. A fair coin is tossed, and if the coin comes up heads, you win a house worth twice as much. If the coin comes up tails, you lose your house.

> Will you stake your house on this bet?

Everyone I've ever asked answers "no" to this, which is obviously the correct answer. The coin is a fair coin in an empirical sense, and the "P50 scenario" is that you would keep your house. As a rational player you would require some form of risk adjustment to entice you to play the game; I asked you to stake your house since, presumably you are more attached to this than you would be to, eg, a 10-dollar bill.

The risk adjustment you may require is that the coin be tossed a large number of times; a similar situation would be if you were the lucky owner of one thousand similar houses, and were asked to stake only one of them. The P50 scenario is of no real interest in the undiversified case of staking your one house on one coin toss, since you'll never realise the theoretical-average case. Believing in the relevance of P50 scenarios in an undiversified world is to believe that having your head in the oven and your feet in the deep freeze means that on average you're just fine.

The process of "mapping" refers to turning a project, asset, term sheet or contract into a financially sound quantitative model that encompasses the full range of market and unhedgeable risks, accounting for diversification effects and risk adjustments. Simple market-based option values are derived from:

- access to markets; and
- operational flexibility,

but this "pure" option value is decreased due to the asset's:

- operational constraints; and
- non-hedgeable risks.

The process of incorrect mapping is a business risk, which is present in my risk matrix. Constraints, risk appetite and liquidity must be considered since physical assets cannot be bought and sold as easily as their financial equivalents. Correct real-option valuation involves bringing together the disciplines of derivatives pricing, operational research and optimisation, insurance and portfolio analysis, engineering and physical modelling and many other specialities. In the face of such subtleties it is little wonder that simple theories can be abused by enthusiastic, but unqualified, practitioners!

Given the practical difficulties of truly incorporating all factors into a real-option valuation, I claim that one of the main values of the real-option approach lies in the disciplined thinking involved in *framing the valuation* in the first place. Framing a real-option valuation involves:

- thinking through the full range of flexibilities;
- understanding which ones have a fair-market value;
- attempting to quantify the diversification effects of one's portfolio;
- considering monetisation and financing possibilities; and
- assessing the impact of liquidity, constraints and unhedgeable risks.

These will if nothing else lead to a more rigorous view of a project's NPV, even if a super-sophisticated derivatives/insurance/optimisation model is never built.

The difficulty of expressing derivatives-style valuations on decision trees led me to create a *diagrammatic real option notation* back in 2000, which allows management, structurers and quants to frame their valuation problems in a simple way. The diagrammatic notation may be used with equal ease to express and value DCFs, decision-analysis examples, financial options or real options. See the technical appendix, "Diagrammatic notation", for a further explanation and reference.

Risk-Analysis Example: Hedge-Based Financing

Hedge-based energy financing may be used by those looking to raise funds to invest in energy production or transformation projects. The main principle is that the borrower secures the funds they've raised against future cashflows from their asset or project once it is running. Since the future cashflows from energy-market sales are uncertain, then some portion of them must be stabilised using risk management instruments to ensure the borrower will be able to service their debt to the lender. The theme here is one of locking in, or putting a floor under, future energy-market sales for a producer or transformer, and so the typical derivatives employed would be swaps, or put-based instruments such as producer collars, three-ways and so on.

This section doesn't attempt to teach the principles of hedge-based financing, which is worthy of a report in its own right, but instead attempts to demonstrate the notions of monetising forward production, mapping and risk analysis. The example we'll consider is hedge-linked loan financing, in which a market player wishes to acquire an asset from a seller, as shown in Figure 173.

The asset purchaser wishes to take on a loan to raise the funds needed for the purchase, and so enters into a firm supply commitment with an offtaker (Figure 174). An offtaker with a solid credit rating will be chosen, and their

Figure 173. Hedge-linked loan financing: buyer and seller

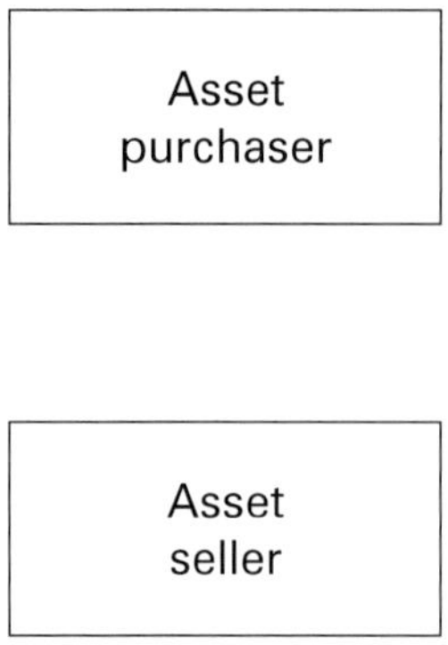

Figure 174. Hedge-linked loan financing: offtaker signs firm agreement to lift physical

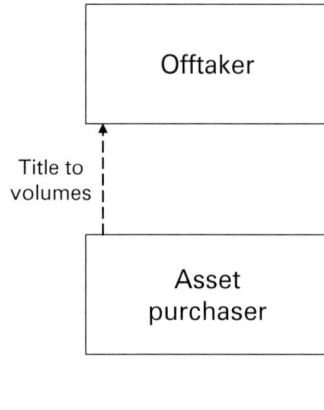

commitment to pay for these future flows of commodity maybe sufficient security to raise a loan.

The asset purchaser can take this offtake agreement as security to the capital markets, and on the back of their agreement can raise funds to purchase the asset (Figure 175). The lenders may insist that the asset purchaser enter into some form of risk management to stabilise the future cashflows from the asset's production.

The asset purchaser enters into a hedging agreement – for the purposes of this example a fixed-for-floating swap – that will allow the uncertain cashflows from the offtaker to be exchanged for a stable revenue stream. Each month the offtaker pays the floating market price for the volumes they've received, the asset purchase swaps these for a fixed cash amount, and uses this to service their loan (see Figure 176).

A summary of the various steps of this transaction is shown in Figure 177.

If we are structuring this deal, perhaps from the perspective of the asset purchaser, perhaps from the lender's viewpoint, we need to consider what might go wrong. The mapping process is best conducted by holding this simplified picture of the transaction up against the risk matrix, and trying to identify what could threaten the various flows of cash and commodity, which contractual arrangements might be put in place to mitigate these risks, how they could affect the credit position and how ultimately they can be used to price the risks and structure the risk management instruments or the loan.

Figure 175. Hedge-linked loan financing: purchaser raises funds on the back of physical agreement

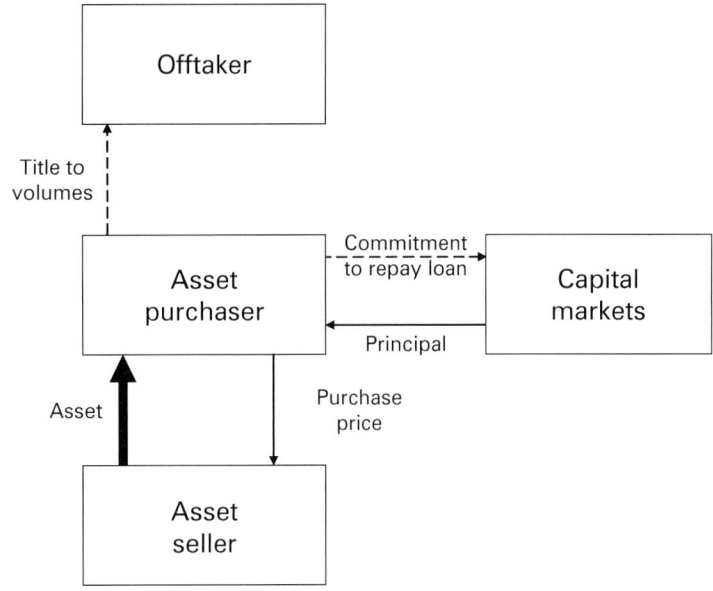

Figure 176. Hedge-linked loan financing – operational phase: offtaker provides revenue stream in exchange for volumes, exchanged for fixed payments with energy risk manager

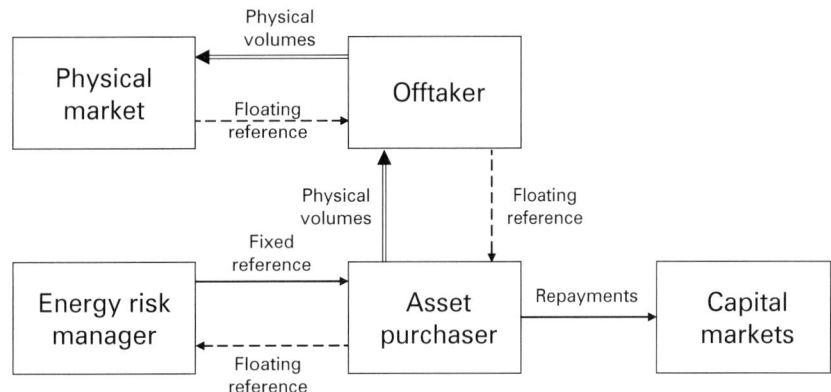

Figure 177. Hedge-linked loan financing: summary

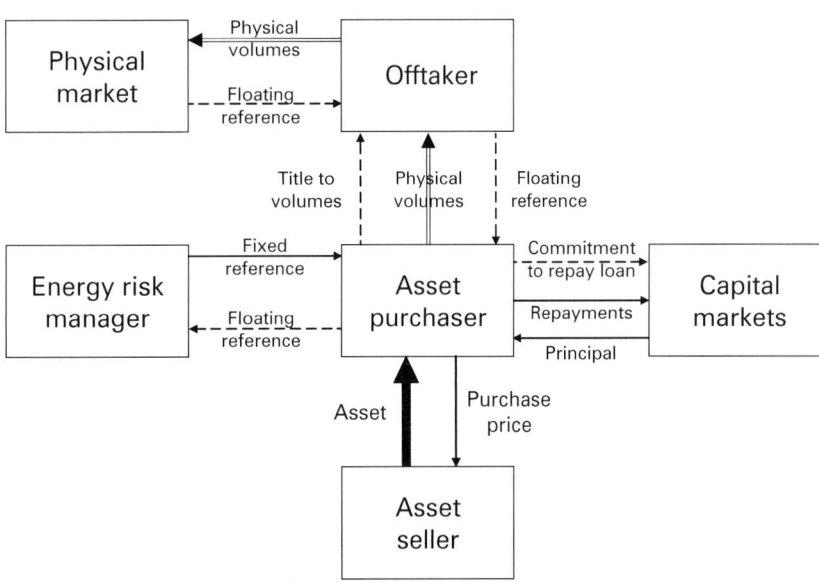

Let's take the list of core risks from the Risk Matrix, hold them up against the operational phase of the hedge-linked financing deal (see Figure 175), and examine some questions intended to provoke a rigorous analysis of the risks.

Core derivatives-based risks from the risk matrix:

- commodity-market risk;
- currency-market risk;
- interest-rate risk;
- proxy risk;
- technical and *force majeure* risks; and
- volumetric risk

Commodity Market Questions (see Figure 178)

- Is the market index traded forward?
- What is the term of the deal?
- What is the volume of the deal?
- Would a ZCC rather than a swap lead to fewer margin calls between the energy risk manager and the asset purchaser, and would this have a favourable credit impact?
- Is there any discount to the fixed swap price for cargo slippage risk?

Currency Market Risk Questions (see Figure 179)

- In which currency was the asset bought?
- In which currency were the funds advanced?
- In which currency are the repayments due?
- In which currency does the swap pay out?

Interest Rate Risk Questions (see Figure 180)

- What interest rate is used? What is it referenced to?
- Does it float? Is it capped?
- Is it, or should it, be tied to commodity market prices?

Figure 178. Hedge-linked loan financing: commodity market questions

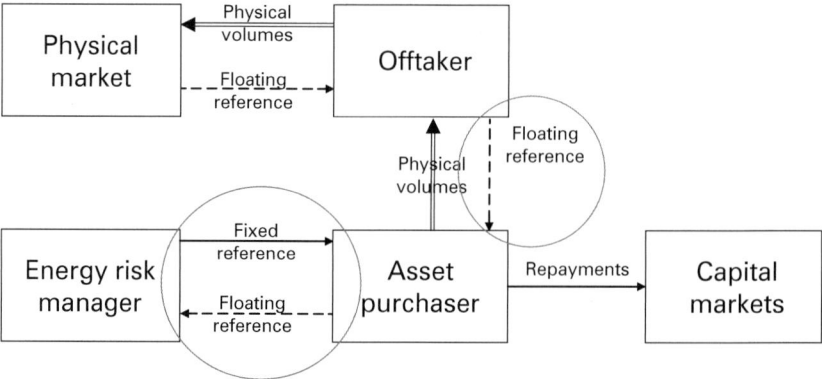

Further Topics in Derivatives Structuring

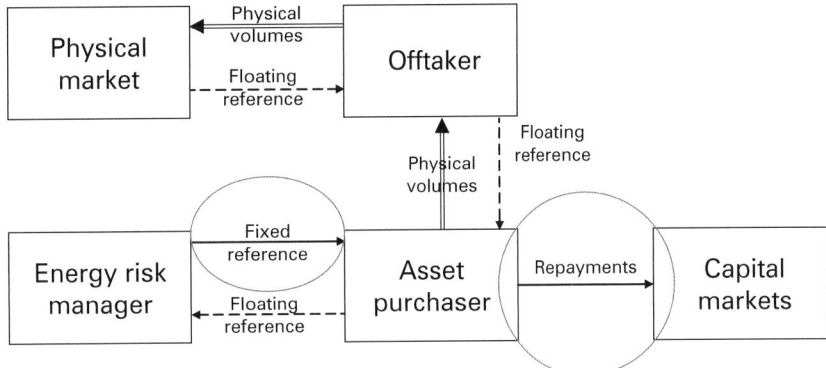

Figure 179. Hedge-linked loan financing: currency market questions

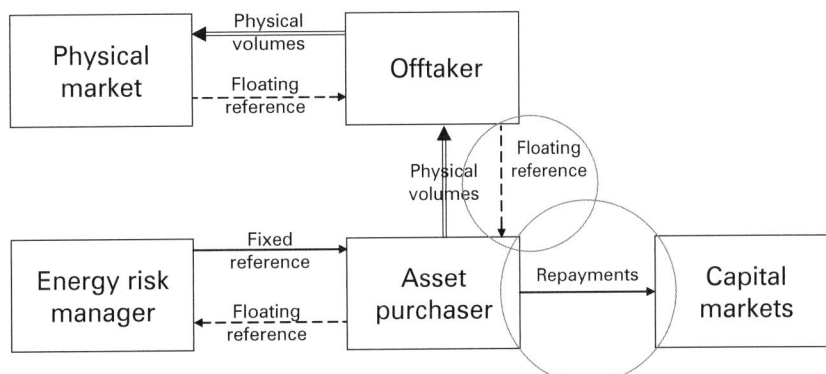

Figure 180. Hedge-linked loan financing: interest rate risk questions

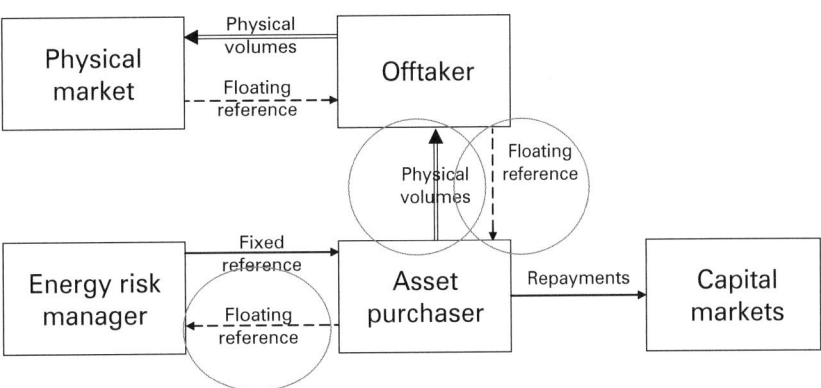

Figure 181. Hedge-linked loan financing: proxy-risk questions

Proxy-Risk Questions (see Figure 181)

- Is the floating reference traded forward?
- If not, can the index be replicated cost effectively?
- If not, what level of proxy risk will there be in using a more liquid underlying as the basis for the hedge?
- What happens if the quality of the commodity being delivered changes through time?

Technical/Force majeure Risk Questions (see Figure 182)

- How are outages built into the physical off-take agreement?
- Can *force majeure* risk be passed on to the capital markets?

Figure 182. Hedge-linked loan financing: technical/*force majeure* risk questions

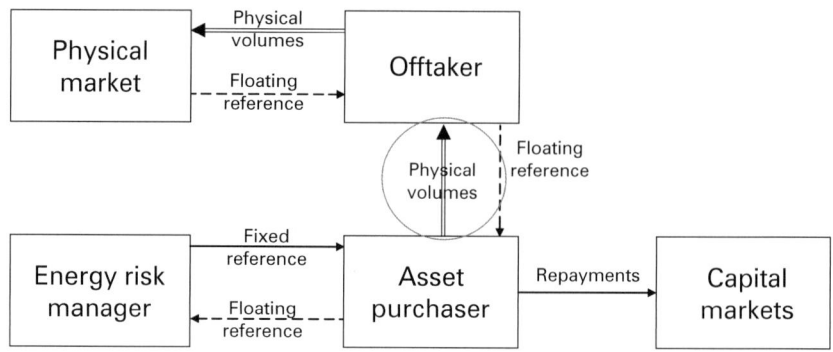

Figure 183. Hedge-linked loan financing: volumetric-risk questions

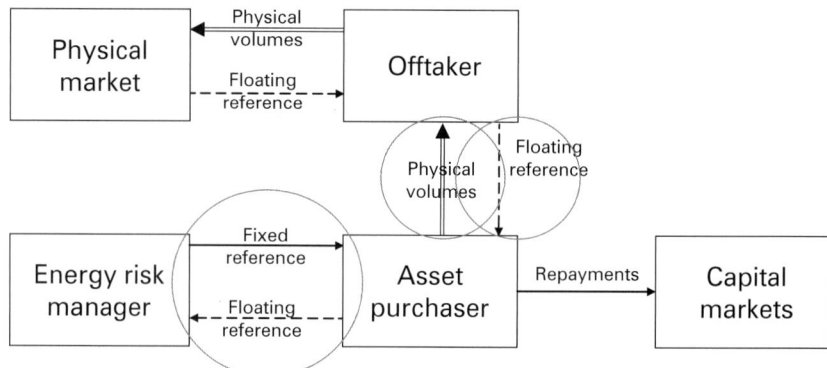

- Can the swap contract be structured to include some level of outages?
- If the physical flow stops for some unavoidable reason, will the asset purchaser be able to service the swap agreement, given that they'll not be receiving any floating payments from the market?
- Has the credit risk of the counterparty been tied satisfactorily to the technical data regarding the reliability of the asset?

Volumetric-Risk Questions (see Figure 183)

- What happens if the delivered volumes vary?
- Is there some element of take-or-pay built into the off-take agreement?
- At what point will variability attract penalties?
- Does the swap have any volumetric flexibility built in?
- Would building volumetric flexibility into the swap still allow the asset purchaser to service their loan repayments?

This simple look at just a few risks present in the risk matrix shows how important the mapping process is in physical and financial commodity transactions. In the next chapter, "Wider Risk Management Questions", we will see an assurance process based on the risk matrix that the author has found useful to ensure that mapping risk is properly mitigated.

Chapter Review and Look Ahead

This chapter has brought us to the end of our examination of energy derivatives *per se*, having introduced us to some extensions to the vanilla derivatives considered in previous chapters. Readers should now have a clear idea just how derivatives may be tailored to their specific market-risk exposures, and through reviewing the subjects of real options and hedge-based financing should now have a clearer idea of how derivatives may be employed in their physical energy operations.

This chapter has also completed the reader's introduction to risk management themes, and I hope that readers now feel equipped to understand just how derivatives can be used in the service of their company's risk management needs. The next chapter addresses some of the wider issues of risk alluded to in this chapter, and rounds out what is meant by risk.

Risk management themes encountered so far:

- locking in;
- tying costs to revenues;
- switching one price exposure for another;
- joint hedging of combined currency and commodity exposures;
- protecting against downside;
- delaying a locking in decision;
- sharing the pain using participation;
- sacrificing upside;
- contingent premium payment;
- buying down;
- selling up;
- volume flexibility;
- extendability;
- cancellability;
- embedding derivatives within physical agreements;
- cross-commodity protection;
- monetisation of embedded optionality; and
- hedge-based financing.

Technical Appendix: Getting the Most Out of Your Quants

Derivative-valuation techniques are based on some fairly sophisticated mathematics. If you intend to employ these techniques in your business in an attempt to quantify your risks and flexibilities you may end up hiring a quantitative analyst, or "quant". A good quant knows how to apply derivative valuation methods to your business in a way that is consistent with your company's ability to exploit these techniques. Some junior quants are drawn more by the mathematical interest of a technique than its applicability to your business, so be on your guard. If the quant can't explain what they are doing, and why it is relevant to you, in terms that you understand, then you've probably hired the wrong quant. This section tries to demystify what it is quants do for a living.

Generally speaking, the more sophisticated the option-valuation technique being employed, the more data are needed to train and drive the model, in a process known as *calibration and estimation*. Energy markets are not as liquid as their financial cousins, and fewer and less sophisticated exotic instruments tend to trade. With this lack of derivative-market liquidity it may be difficult, or even impossible, to imply the volatilities, correlations, jump parameters, transition probabilities and the like needed to drive more sophisticated models. A junior quant attracted to these sophisticated models for mathematical reasons may well end up producing a wonderful model, with large numbers of free parameters that your risk managers and accountants wouldn't have a clue how to choose. Only the most sophisticated of exotic-energy-option traders knows how to estimate and, where necessary, take a view on such parameters.

Option-valuation techniques fall into a number of main categories:

- analytic;
- semi-analytic or approximation techniques;
- simulation methods; and
- tree- or grid-based methods.

Almost all practical derivative pricing is conducted in the so-called *Black–Scholes–Merton framework*, which recognises that the value of a derivative is precisely what it costs a trader to replicate that position by dynamically hedging it in the market.

The classic Black–Scholes formula (on a spot price or futures contract) is a very special case of an option-pricing formula in that it has a *closed-form solution* – this just means it can be written down on paper, and evaluated exactly (see the section "Technical appendix: Black–Scholes option valuation" in the chapter "Fundamental Option Concepts" above). Most other derivatives require that some form of approximation technique be used in order to arrive at an answer.

Semi-analytic and *approximation techniques* tend to gather together different probability distributions (eg, all the different underlying price fixings that make up an Asian average), and approximate them with one or two simple distributions. This simplified, but approximate, model of the problem can then be put into a closed-form solution or other well-understood numerical algorithm to obtain an answer. Asian option, spread and basket option valuation techniques tend to fall into this category.

Simulation methods attempt to represent the full reality of the probability distributions, rather than simplifying them using approximation techniques. They obtain their valuations not by considering every possible combination of every possible sample from every possible distribution, but by taking a large number of representative samples across all these distributions, and inferring what the theoretical answer is from these samples. Monte Carlo simulation is so named because of the random nature of choosing these sampled values. Simulation methods tend to simulate prices forward in time, and they are especially useful where an option payoff depends upon the path that led up to it (ie, look-back options). Monte Carlo simulation is therefore used widely in the evaluation of those Asian and basket option problems for which no accurate approximation technique is available. The iterative nature of the problem solving means that simulation methods are often relatively slow to compute their answers.

Tree-based (and *grid-based*) *methods* slice the space of possible times and prices into little segments, and evaluate the derivative at each of these nodes. The valuation works by starting at the end of the tree, with the terminal payoff, and working backwards in time to see what the option value should be given these end states. Trees are most widely used where the value of an option is based on a decision either to exercise immediately or to hold for a further time period, as in the case of American options. Trees can be extended into so-called *forest techniques*, which consist of a number of trees, each representing a different physical state; these techniques are used in the evaluation of contingent optionality, as in many real-option problems, and allow the interdependency of exercise decisions to be encoded fully.

In choosing among the other candidate valuation methods it is important not to confuse the valuation method with the problem being solved – some problems can be solved with a number of different techniques, and the decision between methods is usually based on the trade-off between speed and accuracy. I have heard some real-option "practitioners" ponder whether a problem can be solved using Black–Scholes or whether Monte Carlo is needed – Black–Scholes is a framework based on fair-market valuation; Monte Carlo is a simulation method that can be (ab)used for everything from financial option valuation, through ill-thought-out real-option valuation to solving reliability problems in nuclear engineering!

Those who understand derivatives, of course, know that a classic Black–Scholes result can be obtained via analytic, tree, grid or Monte Carlo methods, and extended via smile modelling to encode non-lognormal underlyings too. Beware those who are not qualified to price even financial options who claim to be able to value real options!

Technical Appendix: Option Value Needn't Increase with Increasing Volatility

Consider a call spread option with payoff

$$\max(A - B - K, 0)$$

where the underlying prices are denoted A and B. If we make some simplifications[7] in our modelling (this isn't a quant guide after all) we may write the volatility of the spread as

$$\sigma^2_{\text{spread}} = \sigma^2_A + \sigma^2_B - 2\rho\sigma_A\sigma_B$$

where the volatility of risk factors A and B are written σ_A and σ_B respectively, and the correlation between them as ρ. We wish to consider how this spread volatility can change as one of the component volatilities is increased slightly.

Suppose the volatility of underlying A is increased by a small positive amount, to become

$$\sigma'_A = \sigma_A + \epsilon$$

Figure 184. Spread option premium as a function of asset 1 volatility

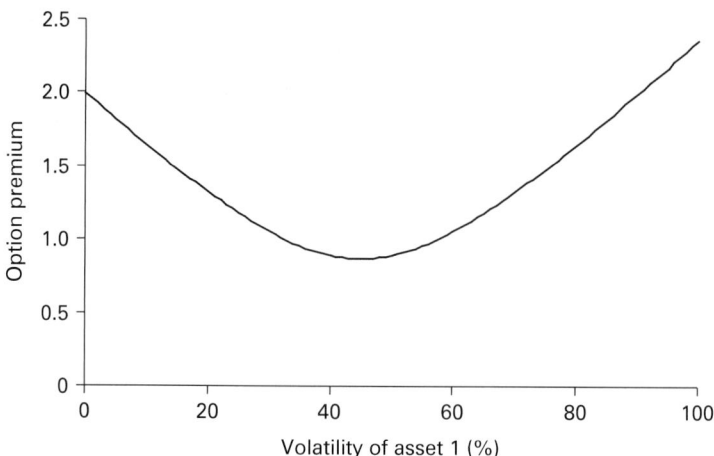

The spread volatility becomes

$$\begin{aligned}\sigma'^2_{\text{spread}} &= \sigma'^2_A + \sigma^2_B - 2\rho\sigma'_A\sigma_B \\ &= \sigma^2_A + 2\sigma_A\epsilon + \epsilon^2 + \sigma^2_B - 2\rho(\sigma_A + \epsilon)\sigma_B \\ &= \sigma^2_A + \sigma^2_B - 2\rho\sigma_A\sigma_B + 2\sigma_A\epsilon - 2\rho\epsilon\sigma_B + \epsilon^2 \\ &= \sigma^2_{\text{spread}} + 2\epsilon(\sigma_A - \rho\sigma_B), \text{ discarding the small term } \epsilon^2\end{aligned}$$

The new spread volatility will be smaller than the original value if

$$\sigma_A < \rho\sigma_B$$

even though the new spread volatility was formed by increasing the volatility of the first asset.

To see this in action, consider a zero-strike ATM call spread option with the volatility of asset 2 at 50.00% and the correlation between assets 1 and 2 at 90%. How does the premium vary with the volatility of asset 1? Following the argument above for asset 1 volatilities less than 90% of the asset 2 volatility of 50%, we expect the option premium to decrease. This is confirmed by examining Figure 184, which shows the option premium decreasing until the volatility of asset 1 reaches 45%.

Technical Appendix: Diagrammatic Notation

I created the diagrammatic notation in response to the need for non-technical management, structurers and quants to understand the subtleties of real-option valuation. The diagrammatic method allows its users to:

- express the optionality present in a deal;
- define how this optionality impacts value; and
- construct automatically the appropriate equations needed to price the deal.

With the synthesis of decision analysis and option valuation offered by the diagrammatic method, optimisation and tree-based derivative pricing emerge naturally as special cases of real-option valuation.

To learn the notation, one must be introduced to the symbols and *diagrammatic grammar* for assembling them, before studying some simple examples of *diagram arithmetic*. One then proceeds to examine DCF, decision trees and financial-option valuation using the diagrams. The process of framing real-option valuations using the notation must be covered next, and the *state spaces* commonly encountered in the energy sector and their diagrammatic representations must be learned. Grammatically consistent diagrams lead automatically to the appropriate pricing algorithms, meaning that quants can price directly from the very diagrams they were discussing with management.[8]

Let us return to the discussion in the box earlier ("Choice based on averages, or average of choices"), in which we looked at the difference between a choice based on averages and an average of choices. We will express this notion using the diagrammatic notation. To recap, the difference between the two approaches can be summed up symbolically thus:

◆ *Naïve or inflexible approach to valuation*:

$$\text{Value} = \max(\text{average outcome}, 0)$$

where the average outcome may be negative, and the decision to proceed is based purely on whether this average is greater than 0.

◆ *Option-style approach to valuation*:

$$\text{Value} = \text{average}(\max(\text{outcome}, 0))$$

where max(outcome, 0) can never be negative for each individual outcome, and thus the average of these choices can never be negative. This approach corresponds to flexible operation, allowing management to "carve off" the good outcomes only.

In the inflexible approach to valuation we have the real option diagram shown in Figure 185.

Figure 185. Real-option diagram for choice based on average

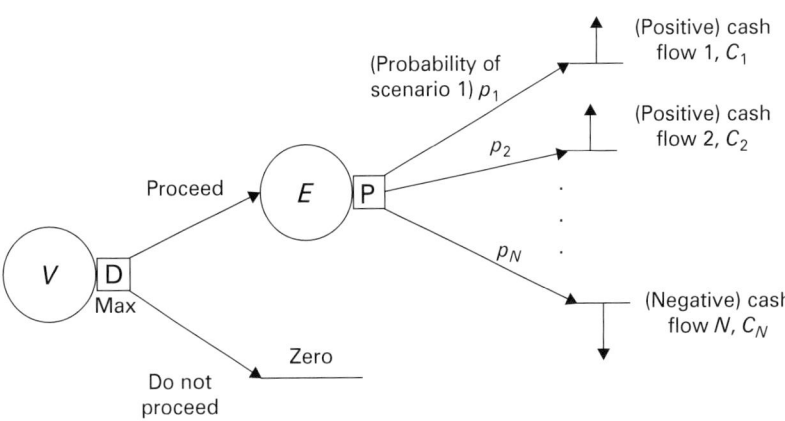

Figure 185 may be turned into a valuation by the following reasoning, reading the diagram from left to right, following the flow of time:

- The value of the project, V, is based on choosing whether to proceed or not. The decision to proceed gives an expected project value E, while abandoning leads to no cashflows. The formula reads:

$$V = \max(E, 0)$$

- The expected project value is computed by taking the probability-weighted sum of all outcomes for all scenarios:

$$E = p_1 C_1 + p_2 C_2 + \ldots + p_N C_N$$

This expectation may be positive or negative, according to the interplay between the scenarios and their probabilities.
- The final project valuation is therefore:

$$V = \max(p_1 C_1 + p_2 C_2 + \ldots + p_N C_N, 0)$$

Clearly the project will proceed only if the expectation of all outcomes is positive. This reasoning fails to account for the fact that one may have flexibility to choose what the cashflow should be in each scenario, if one can operate the project or asset flexibly.

In the option-style approach to valuation, the project value is based on the average of all decisions that may be made. The diagram is shown in Figure 186.

The project valuation in Figure 187, E, derives from taking the average of all future decisions:

$$E = p_1 V_1 + p_2 V_2 + \ldots + p_N V_N$$

Figure 186. Real-option diagram for average of choices

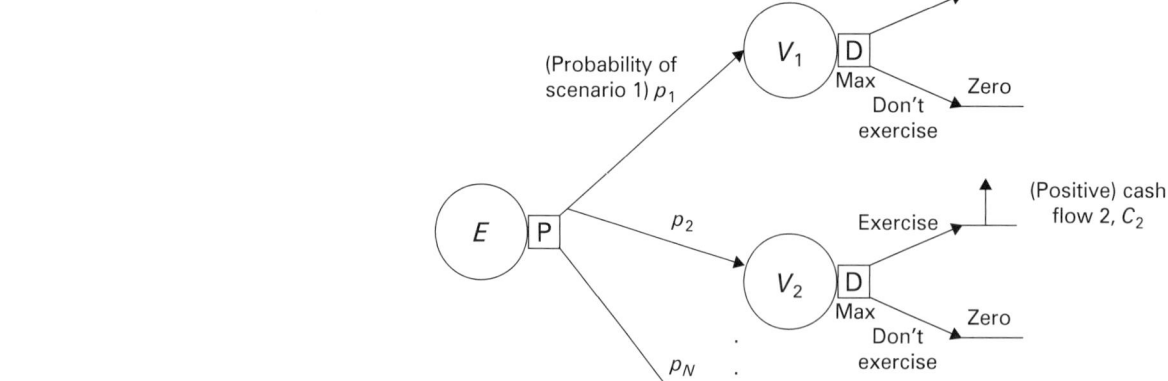

Further Topics in Derivatives Structuring

Each of these future decisions is based on the management's right to choose whether to operate or not in that mode; if it is economic to exercise the right to operate, then the positive cashflow is received, if not, nothing is received:

$$V_i = \max(C_i, 0)$$

The project valuation may therefore be positive, even if many of the outcomes are negative, since it is not necessary to be exposed to the unfavourable outcomes:

$$E = p_1\max(C_1, 0) + p_2\max(C_2, 0) + \ldots + p_N\max(C_N, 0)$$

This approach is the root of all option valuation techniques, whether traded or real options.

Those readers interested in seeing and perhaps learning more about the notation are referred to the specialist real-options book *Real Options in Energy Management* (see References).

Notes

1. An oil refiner is a *producer* of refining margins, and thus seeks protection using basket *puts*.
2. This assumes that the producer will be engaging in ruthless exercise, making the crude oil available in the month that hurts the refiner most.
3. Some practitioners perform *Monte Carlo simulation* to generate these price scenarios. Monte Carlo simulation is just another method for generating scenarios, through using statistical techniques to extract scenarios from (an often dreamed-up) distribution, rather just inventing the scenarios "by hand". I have seen many practitioners put their faith in Monte Carlo because it sounds sophisticated and therefore "must be right", and I have seen their equally unsophisticated managers impressed because the results look as if they are based on sound quantitative reasoning. Monte Carlo simulation is no excuse for ignorance, and I advocate the use of simple techniques and hard thinking rather than the converse.
4. And their linear and mixed-integer-optimisation cousins, for those familiar with operational research techniques.
5. And, I would insist, should be employed.
6. Simple examples of this have been seen already in American options, where an exercise decision removes all later exercise decisions (the unit of optionality has been "spent"), and in swing options.
7. This simplification assumes that the spread between two lognormal distributions is itself is lognormally distributed.
8. Real-option and derivatives practitioners experienced in the use of stochastic dynamic programming (SDP) will find little mathematical novelty in the notation, and its principal use is its powerful way of expressing the derivation and assumptions underlying the SDP formulation to non-technical management.

8 Wider Risk Management Questions

Assume nothing

Market Risk

For the purposes of this report we have considered *market risk* to encompass commodity, foreign exchange and interest rate risks, and have defined it as exposure to uncertainty in these traded markets.[1] In this guide we have looked at how market players may be exposed to these sources of market uncertainty, and have examined a wide range of derivatives instruments and structures which may be used to reduce these exposures.

At all points we have considered the cost *versus* the benefits of entering into a derivatives structure, where the cost is derived from the mark-to-market values, or premia, of the derivatives comprising the structure at the point of transaction. The process of marking to market, explained in the chapter "Market Value of Physical and Financial Commitments", answers the question: "Where does the market say we are today?" In a trading organisation it is the job of the middle office to establish the MTM value of all commitments, and to explain how daily movements in the MTM relate to recent changes in the market and portfolio composition.

We have seen that a portfolio's MTM changes continuously with the traded markets, and one day after entering a structure its mark-to-market value will have changed. Should a hedger wish to exit or *unwind* a derivatives structure it is unlikely it could be done without any financial impact.

Example: Oil Producer Unwinds Lock-in Hedge

In late October an oil producer had sold swaps on 1095000 barrels (3000 barrels per calendar day) of oil to lock in a firm price of 49.91 US$/bbl for the next calendar year. Technical issues have forced a revision to their production schedule, and in November they realise they now need to lock in only 2000 barrels per day; they must unwind their hedge for 1000 barrels per day of production.

Unwinding their hedge will involve buying 1000 barrels per day of swap from the market. Between October and November:

Figure 187. Unwinding swap position

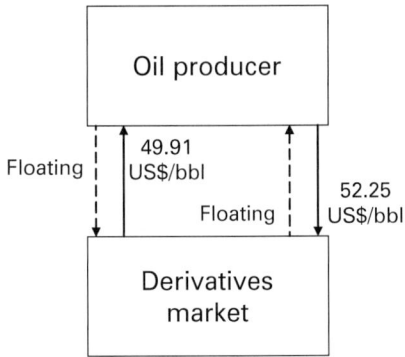

- the swap price for crude oil has moved;
- interest rates have moved; and
- the time to each monthly settlement of the swap has decreased.

In November the swap price for the next calendar year has risen to 52.25 US$/bbl, and the producer must buy 1000 barrels per day of this swap to cancel the 1000 barrels per day they had sold at 49.91.

The original selling, and subsequent cancellation, of the swap are shown in Figure 187.

The cost of unwinding this 1000 barrel per day position is 19071250 US$, since the market moved against the producer's swap contract during this time.

This, admittedly large, volume illustrates just how important it is to:

- Estimate one's volumes accurately to ensure that the physical and hedge positions are consistent.
- Follow the market, and understand the mark-to-market value of one's portfolio.

> What would the cost of unwinding the hedge be if the market had dropped?

If the market had dropped the producer would have *profited* from unwinding the hedge.

Techniques exist to help management assess the impact of future market movements on their portfolio: *value-at-risk* and *stress testing*. Value-at-risk, or *VaR*, is a single number which summarises, with a certain level of confidence, how adverse moves in the market could impact the portfolio in dollar terms. Stress testing is essentially scenario analysis designed to show how significant events could affect the portfolio, though without necessarily proposing a probability for such an event occurring. Value-at-risk models are generally based upon probabilistic scenarios of normal market conditions, while stress testing is most often concerned with extreme or rare scenarios for which it is difficult to assess probabilities.

In trading organisations the company's risk management group is responsible for computing and monitoring the VaR and stress test results, as well as putting limits on the portfolio's riskiness expressed in these terms. Since VaR has wider application than pure market risk we may qualify the term as we are using it here and call it *Market Value-at-Risk*, or *MVaR*. The uses and interpretations of value-at-risk in the energy industry deserve an entire guide in themselves, and so in the following sections I have presented a short overview of what the technique is, and why and how it can be used.

> MTM and market risk techniques
> **Marking to market** answers the question: where does the market say we are today?
> **Market risk techniques** address the question: how might market moves affect our portfolio?
> **Value-at-risk**: a single number measure which summarises, with a certain level of confidence, how adverse moves in the market could impact the portfolio in dollar terms, under normal market conditions.
> **Stress testing**: a method for assessing extreme adverse market moves on the portfolio in dollar terms.

Market Risk Concepts

Market Value-at-Risk can be defined formally as:

"The worst-case loss, in dollar terms, that a portfolio may suffer under normal market conditions, over a given period of time, with a given level of confidence."

Let us decompose this definition, and examine some of its components:

- MVaR is a *single number measure* of risk in dollar terms. A company's portfolio may have thousands of different exposures to dozens or even hundreds of different risk factors, but MVaR crystallises the risk down to just a single figure.
- The VaR is based upon a *pessimistic view* of future; MVaR isn't concerned with how well things might go, only how badly.
- The VaR uses some model of what constitutes *normal market behaviour*. Since the future cannot be known (or there wouldn't be a need for MVaR), this model must be based upon statistical assumptions for how the market will behave.
- The VaR is based upon what might happen to a *fixed portfolio* if it is held for a *given period of time*, whether that's one day, 10 days or longer. The model assumes that the *portfolio doesn't change* over this holding period.

As a forecasting technique value-at-risk needn't be extremely accurate. The simplifications and assumptions that go into deriving the single number measure mean that any claims to true *forecasting* accuracy probably get lost along the way. The main use of VaR is in allowing management to see the company's risk position, without unnecessary complications, at their level of concern, in an easy-to-digest form.

VaR and stress testing techniques produce a range of portfolio P&Ls over the holding period, where these P&Ls are due to possible future movements in the traded markets. The definition of P&L we've encountered so far in this guide states that P&L is based upon two days' portfolio MTMs, and in the chapter "Market Value of Physical and Financial Commitments" the P&L was understood to be between historical days' actual MTMs. In market risk techniques the future MTM is modelled in some way, the difference between that and the current day's known MTM is taken, and this P&L added to a set of possible future P&Ls.

For value-at-risk this set of P&Ls will have a set of corresponding probabilities for each of the scenarios, while for stress testing no such measurement of likelihood may be possible. In a VaR calculation the worst possible P&Ls are examined, and the P&L corresponding to the required level of confidence is reported.

Example: 10 Million US$ 99% 10-day MVaR

Suppose the MVaR for our portfolio, currently worth 10 million US$, is approximately 930 thousand US$ at the 99% 10-day level. This means that based upon our models we are 99% confident that over the next 10 trading days our portfolio will not lose more than 930000 US$ due to price movements in the traded markets.

While it is possible to lose more than 930000 US$, this is judged to have a likelihood of less than 1%.

> What happens to the VaR if a large new hedge is entered into before the end of the current day?

The VaR calculation is based upon possible changes to the MTM of a fixed portfolio. If a large new hedge position is entered into then the portfolio will change, and thus possible values of the future MTM will also change. In the chapter "Risk in Energy Markets" I defined hedging as trading activity "… intended to reduce the riskiness of a portfolio". If a hedge transaction has been entered, and the portfolio's riskiness has been reduced, then one would expect the VaR to decrease also.

The *holding period* for VaR is the period of time over which market evolution is being considered. Clearly the longer the holding period, the greater the range of new values market prices may assume, and the greater the potential for unfavourable P&Ls to occur. This behaviour arises because prices resemble *diffusion processes*, in which known prices today have distributions which "spread out" into the future in accordance with their volatilities and time elapsed. (Readers may wish to consult Figure 71 to Figure 75 in the chapter "Fundamental Option Concepts" above, which illustrate price diffusion.)

The confidence level for value-at-risk is the so-called *one-tailed confidence level* of a probability distribution, since it is concerned only with adverse outcomes. Consider the standard normal distribution in Figure 188. The graph illustrates the probability of a given outcome, with mean zero and standard deviation one. The symmetry of the normal distribution means that the probability of an outcome of less than zero is exactly one half. Expressed in language we wish to use in value-at-risk, we say the left-tailed confidence level of 50% corresponds to an outcome of 0 drawn from a standard normal distribution.

Figure 188. Standard normal distribution

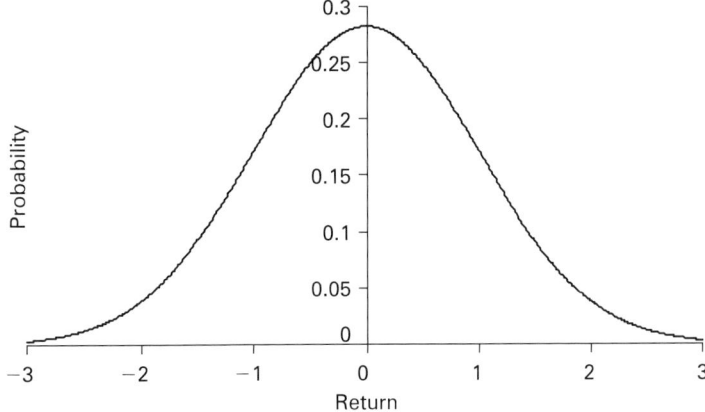

Figure 189. Left tail of normal distribution containing 5% of possible outcomes

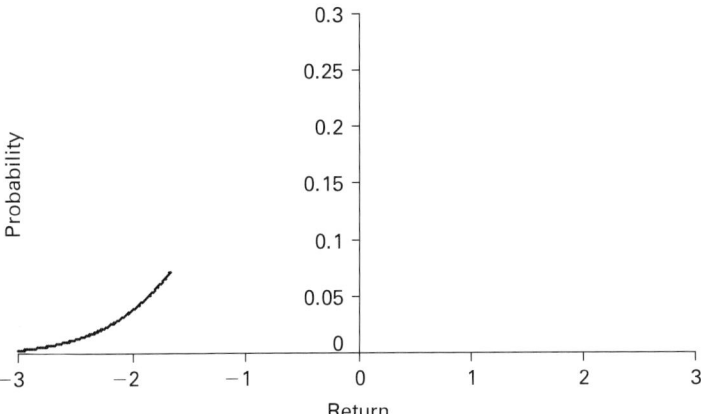

Using the same concepts we can now ask what outcome corresponds to a left-tailed confidence level of, say 95%. In other words, what return from the distribution are we 95% confident we will exceed? This return is illustrated in Figure 189.

Examination of statistical tables reveals that we are 95% confident we will exceed approximately -1.64 on sampling from a standard normal distribution.

All other things being equal, the value-at-risk of a portfolio increases for longer holding periods, or for higher levels of confidence. Various techniques have evolved for the measurement of market VaR as we shall see in the next section.

> Delta approximation to an option's value
> The delta of an option tells us, to first order, how sensitive is the option's value to changes in the underlying market. The delta can be used as the basis for a linear approximation to the option value, which is much used in market value-at-risk computation.
>
> Suppose we know the value of a call option where the underlying market price is 50, we know the delta, and we'd like to approximate the call option value where the market price is 51. While we could recompute the option's premium for this new value of the underlying, constant use of the Black–Scholes formula can be relatively slow
>
> (continued)

for a large portfolio. We use instead the delta to tell us in approximate terms what the new option premium is. Suppose the option premium when the underlying market is 50 is

$$prem(50) = 5.671012$$

the call option's delta at this point is

$$\Delta = 0.532325$$

and we want to compute the approximate premium where the market is 51. These two underlying values differ by 1, so we simply add 1 delta to the original premium:

$$prem(51) \approx prem(50) + 1 \times \Delta$$

Using this approximation we find the approximate value of the premium to be around 6.2033, compared with the exact value of 6.2157. Likewise if we wanted to compute the approximate option premium where the market is at 49.5, which is 0.5 less than the value at which the premium was computed, we simply subtract half a delta from the option premium at 50:

$$prem(49.5) \approx prem(50) - 0.5 \times \Delta$$

Continuing this process for all values of the underlying gives the delta approximation shown in Figure 190.

In the simpler delta-normal approaches to MVaR computation the delta of an option portfolio[2] is used in this way to map changes in the underlying values onto approximate changes in the portfolio value. Note that the larger is the market movement from the point on which the approximation is based (50 in this case), the less accurate is the approximation. There are several obvious problems:

- it approximates the curve only where it touches, by matching the gradient;
- for large market movements it is not a good approximation; and
- for large enough market movements it can even give negative option values! (This is clearly meaningless)

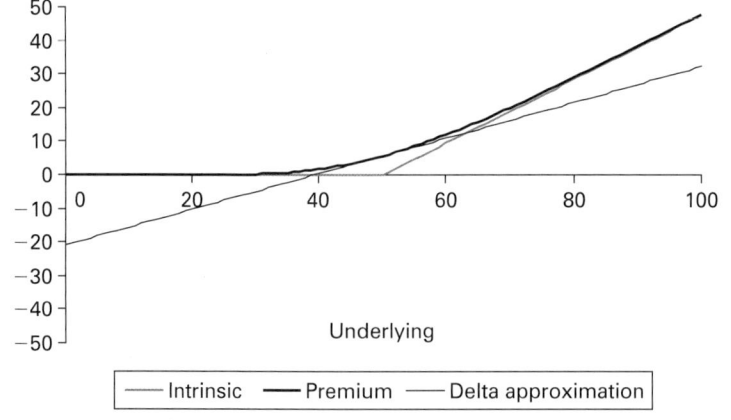

Figure 190. Delta approximation to option value

Many discussions of VaR also discuss stress testing, which is a useful complement to VaR. While MVaR is concerned with *normal* market evolution, which it is assumed can be modelled using probabilistic techniques, stress testing is basically a form of scenario analysis in which the impact of *large* or *significant* market movements is quantified. The scenarios taken are usually those perceived to be too rare to be properly represented, or not represented at all, by MVaR models.

In common with VaR, stress testing involves re-evaluating the portfolio MTM for these new market scenarios, computing the P&L from today's and each of these new P&Ls, perhaps reporting only the worst case P&L. What stress testing essentially does in this case is to consider a number of scenarios and to ask "which one hurts the most?" Clearly different scenarios will hurt at different times, and stress testing reveals how the portfolio would respond to historically extreme or unlikely events.

While historical events may be considered in stress testing by taking the appropriate historical market data, there are difficulties in inventing scenarios which have never occurred to be realistic and internally consistent. While it is relatively easy to consider extreme market price and volatility movements for crude oil, oil products, gas, and power markets in isolation, there are real challenges in integrating these individual market scenarios into one large scenario. For example:

- Should upward crude market movements only be paired up with sharp upward movements in product markets? While this may be believed to reflect "normal" market correlation behaviour, it doesn't necessarily represent a supply shock stress scenario.
- Likewise for power and gas markets.

If stress testing is intended to uncover what hurts a portfolio the most, then the scenarios cannot be created in isolation from consideration of the portfolio contents:

- pure production or consumption portfolios may be most sensitive to outright flat price movements along the forward curve;
- portfolios based upon calendar spread or storage positions may be most sensitive to the opening or closing of interseasonal spreads; and
- Transforming portfolios, such as those for oil refining or power generation, may be more sensitive to relative price movements between commodities than to movements in individual commodities.

Creation of coherent stress test scenarios is extremely challenging, but risk managers should never lose sight of the fundamental use of the technique: to inform management of what might happen under non-standard market movements. Provided the scenarios throw some light upon this issue, they have served their purpose. As a scenario technique one shouldn't demand too much predictive power from stress testing; its fundamental use, like VaR, is in steering portfolio managers away from too much concentration of their portfolio on risk factors that are subject to adverse movements.

Market VaR Techniques

We start by taking a quick look at the *delta-normal* approach to computing VaR, which is commonly used for linear portfolios, or for portfolios containing small numbers of options. The delta-normal technique derives its name from the fact that it uses only the delta-equivalent position for options (thus a unit of ATM call option would be represented by roughly half a unit of underlying), and that it models the market using normally distributed returns.

Example: 10-day 99% MVaR

Suppose we have a portfolio currently worth 10 million US$, and that we are interested in computing the 10-day 99% MVaR. Examination of historical underlying and portfolio returns data leads us to believe that:

- the distribution of underlying market returns is statistically approximately normal;
- the distribution of portfolio returns is also approximately normal;
- that the underlying returns feed linearly through to the portfolio returns; and
- that the returns distribution has an annualised standard deviation (ie, volatility) of 20%.

We will scale a standard normal distribution (one with a mean of zero, and standard deviation of one) by our volatility to obtain the portfolio VaR, and we need to use the pessimistic left-tailed behaviour of the normal distribution.

The properties of a standard normal distribution dictate that we are 99% confident that a sample from this distribution will yield a return greater than -2.33, that is

$$P(\text{sample} < -2.33) = 0.01$$

The holding period of 10 days must be used to scale the variance of returns for this VaR calculation, and the behaviour of price diffusions means that the variance increases linearly with time, or equivalently that standard deviations scale with the square root of time. Since volatility is the standard deviation of price returns we take the annualised volatility, 20%, and de-annualise it to 10 trading days, to find the 10-day volatility. This is achieved using

$$\text{10-day volatility} = \text{annualised volatility} \times \sqrt{\frac{10}{250}}$$

where we assume there are 250 trading days in a year for scaling purposes.

With these matters in hand we can compute the 10-day 99% MVaR of a 10 million US$ portfolio as:

$$\text{10-day 99\% VaR} = 10m \text{ US\$} \times 20\% \times \sqrt{\frac{10}{250}} \times -2.33$$

$$= -930539 \text{ US\$}$$

That is, we are 99% confident that over a 10-day period our portfolio will not lose more than 930539 US$.

> Covariance matrix of risk factors
>
> Correlation effects need to be considered in computing portfolio value-at-risk for multi-commodity portfolios, though the details won't be given here. The full set of data needed to drive multi-commodity VaR, even for these simplest delta-normal market risk models consists of:
>
> - a set of risk factors;
> - number of dollars invested in each of these risk factors;
> - volatilities of each risk factor; and
> - correlations between these risk factors.
>
> Correlations may be combined with the volatilities to form the covariances:
>
> $$\text{covariance}(A, B) = \text{correlation}(A, B) \times \sigma_A \times \sigma_B$$
>
> Here σ_A represents the volatility of risk factor A, and so on. The covariance of an asset with itself is just its variance, or its volatility squared, and the covariances when assembled into matrix form give the *covariance matrix* used as a basis for the VaR calculation. For this reasons the delta-normal approach to VaR calculation is sometimes known as the *Variance-Covariance*, or *VCV*, approach.

Increasing the confidence level of a VaR calculation increases the worst case loss scenario; the variation of VaR with increasing confidence level for the example shown above is demonstrated in Table 57.

In a similar fashion, varying the holding period feeds through to the worst-case loss P&L at the specified confidence level. In general terms the longer the holding period, the worst can be the loss due to market price evolution. Table 58 shows how the VaR for the previous example increases as the holding period increases.

Table 57. 10-day VaR for increasing confidence levels

Confidence level (%)	10-day VaR (US$)
50	0
60	−101339
70	−209760
80	−336648
90	−512621
95	−657941
99	−930539
99.90	−1236093
99.99	−1487607

Table 58. Variation of VaR with holding period

Holding period	99% VaR (US$)
1	−294262
2	−416150
3	−509677
10	−930539
30	−1611741
365	−5621874

Table 59. Increasing VaR with increasing volatility

Volatility (%)	10-day 99% VaR (US$)
0	0
10	−465270
20	−930539
30	−1395809
40	−1861078
50	−2326348
60	−2791617
70	−3256887
80	−3722157
90	−4187426
100	−4652696

Just as options "carve off" beneficial market movements to their holders, so VaR pays attention to adverse market movements and their impact on the portfolios. If the portfolio contains linear instruments that are equally exposed to up- and downside, then VaR will tend to increase as volatility increases; this is because with increasing volatility the tendency for a wider range of positive and adverse movements occurs, and a portfolio with linear exposures will be subject to both, as shown in Table 59.

The delta-normal approach to VaR calculation assumes that linear changes in the market feed through directly to affect the portfolio in the same linear fashion. Use of delta equivalent positions is unlikely to be acceptable for portfolios containing significant numbers of options, and so other value-at-risk techniques have evolved.

An energy trading portfolio may consist of a whole range of instruments, including:

- Exchange-traded futures and options
- OTC forwards and swaps
- OTC options
- Exotic options

The portfolio composition may constrain what VaR computation techniques may be employed, since significant numbers of nonlinear instruments may render use of the delta-normal approximation invalid.

The most obvious suggestion is to generate a set of market scenarios using some form of simulation, and to carry out a *full revaluation* of the entire portfolio under each scenario. The two principal methods for simulation of market scenarios are:

- **Monte Carlo simulation**, in which a model of the market is used to generate future scenarios.
- **Historical simulation**, in which actual historical returns data are applied to the current forward curves to produce a set of possible future price curves.

Despite the names of these techniques, Monte Carlo simulation also uses historical data, though only indirectly, in the estimation of volatilities and

Table 60. Monte Carlo and historical simulation methods

Technique	Advantages	Disadvantages
Monte Carlo simulation	Allows modelling based upon forward view of the market Uses well-understood principles also employed in derivatives pricing	Requires a model of the market, most often based upon normally distributed returns Cannot easily capture extreme events or fat tails
Historical simulation	Uses actual market data, so captures all extreme events and correlations	Lack of historical data may make use of this method impossible Short data sets may contain trending data Long data sets may contain irrelevant data

correlations for use in the model. Each technique has its advantages and disadvantages, and these are summed up in Table 60.

If a simulation technique is chosen then the simulation will produce a MTM for each of its simulated scenarios, which, on finding the difference between these simulated MTMs and the current MTM, can be used to produce a sorted set of P&Ls. Finding the desired worst-case scenario for VaR is a simple matter of picking from the bottom of the list; if a 5% VaR is required from 1000 scenarios then the 50th worst P&L is the desired number, since it has 95% of scenarios above it, each of which occurred one one-thousandth of the time.

Simulation methods with full revaluation can be extremely slow. Options valuation techniques can be quite computationally intensive, and even a single revaluation of a company's portfolio may take many minutes. Simulation techniques require that thousands of such portfolio valuations be carried out, and even for modest-sized portfolios of options this can put a strain on a company's computational resources. If an options portfolio consists mainly of vanilla options then it may be possible to farm the simulations out across a large number of computers to reduce the computational time. For portfolios consisting of computationally slow derivatives valuations even this method may not be practical.

Many Monte Carlo simulations use *reduced market models* or *principal components models* to simulate only some subset of a portfolio's risk factors, though enough to explain, say, 95% of all portfolio variations. If these methods are not able to yield acceptable computation times then some form of portfolio valuation approximation technique must be used.

> Delta-Gamma approximation to an option's value
> While the delta of an option tells us the first-order sensitivity of the option's value to changes in the underlying market, the gamma gives us the second-order sensitivity, allowing us to encode some aspect of the option payoff's curvature. Both deltas and gammas may be used to provide a better approximation of a portfolio's sensitivity to changes in the underlying market.
>
> (continued)

Suppose again (as on p. 197) that we know the value of a call option where the underlying market price is 50, we know the delta and gamma, and we'd like to approximate the call option value where the market price is 51. We use now both the delta and gamma to tell us in approximate terms what the new option premium is. If the option premium when the underlying market is 50 is

$$prem(50) = 5.671012$$

the call option's delta at this point is

$$\Delta = 0.532325$$

the gamma at 50 is

$$\Gamma = 0.25016$$

and as before we want to compute the approximate premium where the market is 51. These two underlying values differ by 1, so we simply add 1 delta to the original premium, and a new term consisting of half the gamma multiplied by the market change squared:

$$prem(51) \approx prem(50) + (\Delta \times 1) + \frac{1}{2} \times \Gamma \times (1)^2$$

The approximate value of the premium is now around 6.2158, compared with the exact value of 6.2157.

Again if we wanted to compute the approximate option premium where the market is at 49.5, which is 0.5 less than the value at which the premium was computed, we simply use:

$$prem(49.5) \approx prem(50) - 0.5 \times \Delta + \frac{1}{2} \times \Gamma \times (-0.5)^2$$

The delta-gamma approximation to the option value at 50 shown in Figure 191.

The delta-gamma approximation to an option's value tracks the curve of the payoff function for a much wider range of values, though it is still subject to the problem of allowing negative option values, and may even permit deep OTM options with more value that OTM options.

Figure 191. Delta-gamma approximation to option value

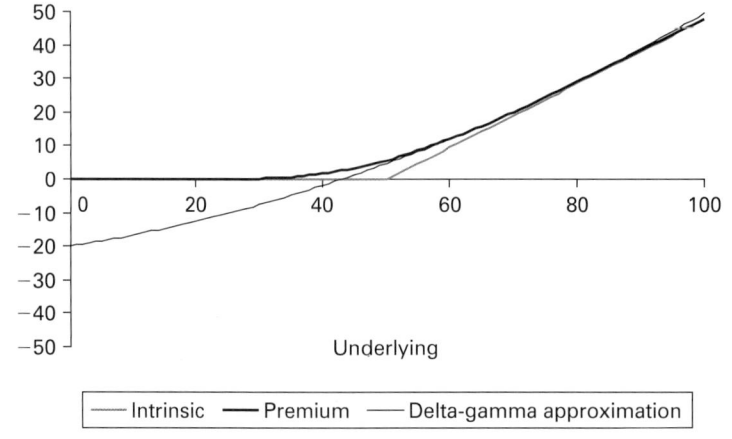

The *delta-gamma approach* to portfolio valuation uses the first and second order sensitivities of an option to the underlying risk factors to approximate the MTM for different simulated market scenarios. The delta-gamma approach may be used in conjunction with either Monte Carlo or historical simulation,[3] and is very widely used. Its main attraction is that it is computationally much faster to approximate an option's value using the delta-gamma approximation, which just involves a few additions and multiplications, than to run full-blown option valuation codes. Delta-gamma may also be used with reduced market models in Monte Carlo simulation to further improve execution time.

We may understand the range of value-at-risk techniques by the two steps needed to compute VaR:

1. **Generation of scenarios**: Popular techniques are analytical (used in delta-normal), full Monte Carlo simulation, principal components Monte Carlo simulation, historical simulation.
2. **Portfolio revaluation**: Popular techniques are analytical delta-normal, delta-gamma, full revaluation.

The delta-normal technique is an analytical method, and achieves its generation of scenarios and revaluation all in one analytical step; the other techniques all rely on separate simulation and revaluation for each scenario.

Simulation techniques have additional benefits insofar as they allow access to the scenarios beyond the scenario which led to the VaR number; these scenarios are often taken as forms of stress test in their own right. The P&Ls of all the scenarios in the tail beyond the VaR may also be averaged to find the *conditional tail loss*; this important measure of market risk answers the question: "Given that we exceed our VaR, how much do we expect to lose?"

Controlling Market Risk Exposures

In addition to providing valuable information about what may happen to one's portfolio over the holding period VaR and stress testing can also be used to control one's risk exposures. In the chapter "Market Value of Physical and Financial Commitments" above, a system of hierarchical position limits was introduced as a means of controlling a risk manager's activities. While position limits are useful for limiting *volumetric* exposure, they give no direct way of assessing what the market may do to harm a company's P&L in cash terms. Complementary to position limits, therefore, are *VaR limits*, which management may impose on the risk manager's hedging activities. If management institute a set of, say, 99% 1-day VaR limits then the risk managers must ensure that their 99% 1-day VaR is always within this number.

In common with position limits these VaR limits will often be constructed in a *limit hierarchy*, allowing different VaR limits for different portfolios, with the VaR limits higher up the hierarchy being smaller than the sum of those limits below them. This structure accounts for diversification effects at higher levels, while giving risk managers room to manoeuvre in their own area of expertise.

Value-at-risk provides a direct way of demonstrating the effect of hedging on the company's portfolio since portfolio variance is precisely what VaR depends upon. This enables management to quantify the impact of putting a new hedging programme in place in direct dollar terms; if one's VaR systems are sufficiently flexible then they can be used for "what-if" style analysis in designing these hedging programmes.

For management to have confidence in their VaR system the models must be subject to rigorous *back testing*, in which historical P&Ls are compared with historical VaR numbers. The P&Ls should fall outside the computed VaR numbers with the probability suggested by the tail of the probability distribution; thus, for one year of history, the P&L should fall outside the computed 99% 1-day VaR numbers 2 to 3 times on average. Back testing is necessary to ensure that the VaR computational models are properly calibrated; if not, the models need to be recalibrated. Not only is back testing an essential discipline to maintain management confidence in the models, but it may be required for regulatory purposes in trading institutions.

Stress test limits may also be used to constrain a company's hedging activity. Rarely can stress tests be interpreted in any consistent probabilistic sense, though stress test limits may be used by management to state: "If such an event were to occur again, we are prepared to be exposed at no more than this level." Stress test limits will naturally be much higher than VaR limits, consistent with the rare or extreme nature of the scenarios being modelled.

Beyond Market Risk: Physical Risk Management

In the previous chapter "Market Value of Physical and Financial Commitments" we considered the impact of physical *force majeure*, technical and volumetric events on real options and structured transactions. The lack of hedgeability of such risks prevents us from putting a fair market value on the risks, or of mitigating them in any trading fashion, but it doesn't stop us from quantifying the impact of such events on our portfolio.

Traditional market risk management techniques of the type considered so far in this chapter obtain their results by holding the portfolio position constant, and assessing the impact of changes of market scenario. Physical risk management works by allowing the position itself to change, since:

- *Force majeure* and technical risk events correspond to positions disappearing.
- *Volumetric risk* events correspond to volumes of positions being flexed.

The risk events may arise from reliability or performance problems of physical assets, extreme weather or other natural events, variations in ambient temperature affecting plant efficiency, and so on. I have written on physical risk management in Reference 10, and provide here only the briefest glimpses of this important topic since it lies largely outside the scope of this work, not being directly concerned with hedging *per se*.

The physical risk management techniques I present in Reference 10 break into the categories of physical stress testing and physical VaR techniques, where:

- **Physical stress testing** assesses the P&L of a major physical event on the portfolio. This may include moving the market in the case of the loss of a major pipeline, gas storage facility or interconnector. Physical stress testing is often the most appropriate way to assess the impact of *force majeure* events.
- **Technical VaR**, or **TVaR**, computes a distribution of P&Ls corresponding to the complete loss of physical assets in a diverse portfolio, where these failures are based upon engineering reliability models. Technical VaR in its simplest form doesn't consider movements of the market.
- **Volumetric VaR**, or **VVaR**, also computes a distribution of P&Ls, although this time corresponding to variations in the volumes of various positions. These variations may be due to the arrival of new customer demand information, arrival of more accurate weather forecasts, and so on. In common with technical VaR the basic version of volumetric VaR doesn't consider movements of the market.

Physical stress test limits and *physical VaR limits* may be defined as complementary to the more conventional MVaR limits, since they arise from a different source of risk to commodity, currency or interest rate market fluctuations. These limits must be obeyed by physical asset traders, and ensure that should the portfolio suffer some physical losses then it will not be overhedged, leading to the need to buy back potentially expensive hedges from the market.

Since portfolio deltas and gammas are additive, the probability distributions of positions arising from these physical models may also be used to build distributions of deltas and gammas. This may also be used as the basis of a technique for the option-style hedging of physical positions, by declaring limits that must be obeyed by the portfolio delta and gamma in the face of physical risk events at a specified level of confidence. These prevent the overhedging of the portfolio using option positions with their potentially unlimited downside.

The Risk Matrix Approach to Transaction Analysis

Introductory Notes

All new physical and derivatives transactions expose your company to a variety of risks which must be understood and managed correctly. Most written proposals for new business will contain a discussion of both the upsides of the activity, and potential risks. In many companies the discussions of the risks inherent in an activity can be fairly *ad hoc*, and so in this section I introduce readers to my *Risk Matrix Approach* to risk analysis.

In analysing and documenting new business some risk analyses ask individuals for no more than an informal assessment of the normal range of risks those individuals are concerned with; there is no guarantee that all risks can be captured, and no ability to capture those risks that don't currently fall within someone's current responsibilities. In response to this I created the Risk Matrix Approach to:

- provide a comprehensive list of risks and their definitions (the so-called "galaxy of risks");
- define the different measures needed to manage the risk exposure;

- ensure no risks "fall through the gaps" between different groups' responsibilities;
- allocate accountability for accepting the risk exposure into the company.

The Risk Matrix Approach can be used formally as part of a new business approvals procedure, or informally during normal business activity as a prompt for what needs to be done.

The Galaxy of Risks

The "galaxy of risks" is a term used to describe the full range of risks that a transaction may expose the company to (see Table 61 for a partial list used by the author in his current role). Being aware of this list in itself can improve one's approach to risk analysis.

Recognising which of the risks in Table 61 are present in a deal is the first step in a formal risk management process, but recognising a risk is present is quite different from knowing how to monitor and control it, and accepting the exposure on behalf of the company. Some risk events can be categorised under any one of a number of risks in the matrix in Table 61, and it is essential to be pragmatic. If ever you're having trouble deciding which risk to list an event under, ask yourself the following:

- What would a physical or financial expert categorise the risk as? Risk managers often have a highly formal view of the world, so think about what the non-risk-specialists would call it.
- Does it actually matter what you call it? Provided you've thought about it, analysed the situation, and intend to do something about it, you've done all that's required. Issues of nomenclature are less important than making sure you've not forgotten anything.

With practice members of your company will get accustomed to the style of risk analysis, and very quickly issues of nomenclature will fade away to be replaced by more substantive debates.

The Risk Management Process

As I've mentioned earlier in this report, risk management consists of a number of related activities; merely identifying that a risk exists is not sufficient when analysing a commercial prospect – it is necessary to decide if something needs to be done about it. The formal risk management process requires that we carry out the following steps:

1. Identify the risks the company may be exposed to.
2. Quantify those risks (that can be quantified) to aid the risk management process.
3. Set authority levels and/or risk limits that the risk exposure will be measured against, where possible.
4. Monitor the risk exposures against these limits, or monitoring for key events, and reporting these levels or events.
5. Police and control the risks should they exceed their exposure limits or trigger events take place.

Table 61. Galaxy of risks

Risk	Description	Notes
Accounting	Correct application of accounting principles to our business	Are we correctly applying mark-to-market accounting to commodity derivative business? Are we using mark-to-model inappropriately?
Compliance	The risk that our internal procedures, systems or actions may cause us to be in breach of regulations	
Counterparty concentration	Arises when a significant percentage of a portfolio is exposed to the same or highly correlated market counterparties, increasing the risk of losses caused by default events affecting these counterparties	
Country default	The risk that a country won't be able to honour its financial commitments. When a country defaults it can harm the performance of all other financial instruments in that country, as well as other countries with which it has relations	
Credit	Risk that a counterparty fails to honour its financial commitments under the terms of a contract	How effective is our credit analysis? How robust are our credit analysis procedures in the face of changing counterparty info (eg, watch lists)?
Currency	When investing in foreign countries one must consider the fact that currency exchange rates can change the price of the asset as well	
Curve construction, interpolation or extrapolation	Risk that the assumptions involved in construction, repair or extension of a market curve do not accord with the reality of the traded market	Includes matrices (eg, swaption volatility matrices, correlation matrices, etc.)
Force majeure	Risk of an unforeseen or rare event for which there is no contractual mitigation	It is essential to analyse which *force majeure* events can be passed along the chain of contractual arrangements, and which will leave one's company exposed
Funding liquidity	Risk that we are unable to meet (interim) payment requirements, eg, for margin calls	Even a pure back-to-back position, with zero market risk, can expose the company to funding liquidity risk if the settlement dates are different
Geographical	Risk that physical assets concentrated in the same geographical region could be impacted by natural events in that region	For example, offshore oil production assets concentrated in one zone lose production simultaneously. Form of technical or *force majeure* risk: may be mitigated with event insurance/weather derivatives
Index specification	Risk that a price index used as the basis of a financial contract stops being quoted, or changes the convention used for its quotations	Need to include clauses in contracts to account for index disappearing. Change to specification may require rehedging
Interest rate	Impact of interest rates upon your valuation or hedging	
Knowledge	Risk of having inferior market data or intelligence compared with your competitors	
Legal	Risk that arises when a transaction is found to be unenforceable in law	
Liquidity	The risk stemming from a lack of marketability that an investment cannot be bought or sold quickly enough to prevent or minimise a loss. Usually reflected in a wide bid-ask spread or large price movements	

Table 61. (continued)

Risk	Description	Notes
Litigation	The risk that the transaction will lead to a lawsuit exposing the company to legal costs, potential damages, management distraction and reputational risk	There is also reputational risk arising from possible from litigation, but that is listed as a separate risk
Mapping	Risk that a deal is decomposed into its constituent positions in a way that doesn't satisfactorily represent the risks present in the deal	
Market	Risk that market prices, volatilities or correlations move beyond the holder of a contract's expectations	Many of these risks are, in principle, hedgeable in sufficiently liquid markets. Attention must be paid to the meaning of market risk where there is no market in an underlying valuation parameter such as correlation
Modelling	Risk that pricing, hedging or other quantitative models misrepresent reality	Could be due to problems in specification, development, testing, calibration, user understanding
Operational	Risk of systems or processes failing to operate as required to support the business	Many different groups are required to assess and control operational risk
Political	Risk that a country's government will suddenly change its policies	
Position concentration	Arises when a significant percentage of a portfolio is exposed to the same or similar market factors or other risk factors, increasing the risk of losses caused by adverse market or economic events affecting these risk factors	
Proxy	Risk associated with unanticipated movements in relative prices of assets in a hedged position	Pay attention to the risk of correlated markets undergoing "defragmentation" due to transportation or transmission disruptions
Raw data	Risk that raw data may contain errors or omissions that make its subsequent use in modelling problematic	Need to consider omissions, typographical errors, validation, consistency
Regulatory	Risk that a change in market regulations will have an adverse impact on our business	
Reputational	Risk that involvement in an activity, or a *force majeure* event arising from an activity, adversely affects the wider community's view of your company	
Settlement	Also known as time lag risk. Risk that a settlement payment expected from a counterparty in a different time zone doesn't arrive after we've sent our own. Form of default risk	
Sovereign	Risk that a country imposes exchange rate controls, making it impossible for counterparties to honour their obligations	Country specific
Systems/procedural	Falls under operational risk	
Tax	Risk that a change in a country's tax regime will adversely affect a contract or position	
Technical	1. Risk that a physical asset's performance makes us unable to meet delivery obligations, or fully realise the apparent optionality inherent in the asset 2. Risk that a project will fall behind schedule due to unforeseen technical events	Informally technical risk is like "something has gone wrong". Technical risk is best modelled using a discrete distribution, like a binomial/Poisson distribution, in which the volume is zero or some "normal" level. Cannot be hedged, but can be dealt with through diversification or insurance. Technical risk does not exist for virtual assets

Table 61. (continued)

Risk	Description	Notes
Technology	Falls under operational risk	
Volumetric	Risk arising from changes in the volume of commodity supply or consumption	Informally volumetric risk may be thought of as flex in volumes during regular production/consumption. From a quant modelling perspective, volumetric risk is best modelled using a continuous probability distribution around some expected "normal" level. Volumetric risk may include errors in expert estimation of capacities, reserves, or other technical performance characteristics of an asset

In addition to these steps it is necessary to assign accountability for the acceptance of the risk on behalf of the company, and for running the risk management process. Without these formal steps and accountabilities there can be no assurance that a business activity is properly understood or controllable.

Philosophy of the Risk Matrix Approach

The philosophy underpinning the Risk Matrix Approach to risk analysis is simple:

> "If all risks are identified, understood, subject to monitoring and control, and accepted by the authorised signatories on behalf of the company, then there is no reason why an activity should not be engaged in."

This philosophy works because the galaxy of risks is so broad – not only does it require that signatories assess the usual range of market and credit risks, but explicit attention must be paid to mismatches of *force majeure* clauses through a chain of contracts, reputational and litigation risks, data quality risk, and of course operational risk.

In practice some risks may have no natural point of accountability; using the Risk Matrix Approach doesn't mean that you've created a problem, it means you always had that problem but perhaps weren't aware of it. The Approach means that management will be able to make an informed decision whether to authorise a deal in full knowledge of the gaps in the company's coverage. Since there can be no return without risk, there is no issue of waiting until all risks are fully mitigated – this is a sure way to stifle commercial activity. Pragmatism is key, and very rarely is a Risk Matrix completed in full before a deal is authorised.

What is the Process?

The Risk Matrix Approach to risk analysis involves:

1. Taking each risk in turn.
2. Identifying who is the person accountable for:
   a. Initial identification of the risk (an informal opinion, often the commercial deal lead or the structuring desk)

b. Quantification of the risk (where possible)
   c. Defining the risk limits (where appropriate)
   d. Monitoring the risk exposure against these limits, or reporting on trigger events
   e. Policing and controlling the risk exposures in the case of a limit breach or occurrence of a trigger event
   f. Accepting this risk exposure and its associated risk management process on behalf of the company
3. Asking the person accountable for each step of the process:
   a. Have you assessed and, where appropriate, quantified the risk?
   b. Do you have limits in place, or defined events (eg, change in regulations, physical events, etc.) against which the risk can be monitored?
   c. Do you have monitoring and reporting procedures in place to follow this risk throughout the lifetime of the deal?
   d. Do you have control and policing procedures in place to define what should occur in the event of a breach of these limits, or in the case of a trigger event which may include physical, regulatory, standards, etc.)?
   e. Do you accept ownership of this risk on behalf of the company?

Mapping Responsibilities and Following the Approach

The Risk Matrix Approach is a formalised method for the mapping of a deal onto its set of constituent risks. In the author's experience the structuring desk conducts this mapping exercise, including the requesting, collection and collation of feedback for reporting to management, and it may be necessary to hire dedicated resources to coordinate this risk assurance activity. By formalising the activities and assuming these responsibilities the structuring desk acts as the company's mitigation against mapping risk.

Practical points to note are:

1. Signatories may accept a risk without procedures being put in place; in this instance they are providing their personal assurance that the risk will be managed. This usually provokes some reflection about the company's approach to risk, and is ultimately a good thing, if a little painful at first.
2. Where no point of accountability can be identified for a given step of the process or for a given risk, then management will be made aware of this, and will need to make their own call on whether to accept this risk on behalf of the company.

As each authorised person responds to these questions it is possible to present in simple summary form how far through the process of gaining sign-off the deal has proceeded. The simple "yes/no/not applicable" nature of the questions above lends itself to a simple "traffic light" view of which risks are properly covered and to what extent.

Discussion of Some of the Risks

In this section some practical hints and tips in the use of the Risk Matrix Approach are discussed.

Wider Risk Management Questions

Accounting Risk

Accounting risk is defined as "correct application of accounting principles to our business." The finance department is ultimately responsible for the identification and assessment of this risk. Of course no limit setting is possible, but deals will need to be reviewed if accounting regulations change. There is thus an ongoing monitoring and control responsibility in case regulations change. The ownership of the risk clearly sits with the finance group.

Market Risks

Commodity, foreign exchange and interest rate risks are among the best understood risks on trading floors. While an informal identification of the risks may be carried out by the commercial deal lead, structuring desk or other front office representatives, the formal quantification, limit setting, monitoring and control responsibilities lie with the independent risk management group. VaR and stress testing are the standard tools used to control market risks.

Credit Risks

Credit default, country default and counterparty concentration risks all fall within the usual range of assessment and monitoring activity for the credit experts within the independent risk management group.

Force Majeure

Force majeure risk, defined as "risk of an unforeseen or rare event for which there is no contractual mitigation" is an excellent counterexample to the non-integrated approaches to risk assessment. Ensuring that *force majeure* events can be passed along a chain of contracts, leaving the company with no or limited exposure to the events, may be managed as follows:

- **Initial identification**: Deal lead and/or structuring desk and/or legal department may be consulted, but only the legal department can be the point of accountability.
- **Assessment/quantification**: Where a *force majeure* event occurs, and the company is exposed, it corresponds to a change of position in the trading book. This can be modelled using the physical risk management principles outlined briefly earlier in this chapter, and as such is part of the mapping and valuation exercise conducted by the structuring desk. Where *force majeure* is declared, and the company is exposed, it will be necessary to go to the market and enter into new positions to compensate for this change in position. The risk may, however, have be mitigated through good drafting of contractual terms, and as such should be assessed by the legal department. The structuring desk and legal department should therefore work together to arrive at a common view of the level of this risk, and what can be done to mitigate against it. Formal assessment lies with the lawyers.
- **Limit setting**: The company's management need to express their appetite for exposure to *force majeure* events by declaring the level of market risk they are prepared to bear in entering compensating market positions. These limits may be expressed as dollar numbers in the same way as credit limits, though they are not correlated to the strength of the counterparty's balance sheet in any way. There is no natural place for *force majeure* limit setting in most companies, though the credit part of the independent risk management group is often the most appropriate home.

- **Monitoring and control**: Where *force majeure* events occur they resemble credit events. The physical traders are most likely to be aware of the *force majeure* event first, and should flag it appropriately, though traders are not the appropriate people to monitor, report and control such risks. Credit risk managers are often the most appropriate people to assume these procedural responsibilities.
- **Risk acceptance**: Once again, credit risk tends to be the appropriate department to accept the exposure on behalf of the company.

Curve Construction and Data Risks

Curve construction, interpolation or extrapolation risk is defined as the "risk that the assumptions involved in construction, repair or extension of a market curve do not accord with the reality of the traded market". This is closely associated with whether a position is marked to market, or marked to model, and as such we would expect it to sit in the domain of the financial department's responsibilities. Given the technical nature of the risk, the finance department may wish to seek the independent risk management group's input, much as they would for modelling risk.

Raw data risk is defined as the "risk that raw data may contain errors or omissions that make its subsequent use in modelling problematic", and involves consideration of omissions, typographical errors, validation, and consistency. Since our main concern in the use of raw data is its use in formal P&L, we would again expect it to sit in the domain of the finance department's responsibilities. Given the technical nature of the risk the finance department may wish to seek risk management's input, much as they do for modelling risk.

Reputational Risk

Reputational risk is not formally quantifiable (though scenario analysis may be possible), and its assessment, monitoring, control and accountability need to sit with management.

Rolling Out the Approach in Your Company

The Risk Matrix Approach is a framework for assessing new business – it is intended to tighten the way in which one approaches new business by asking definite questions across a range of well-defined risks, and expected committed answers and assignment of definite accountabilities. The intention of the Approach is not to slow down new business by insisting this approach is pursued for every business prospect, no matter how small or improbable. The commercial sense of deal leads and management is necessary in deciding when to invoke the full Risk Matrix approach.

The range of accountabilities, interpretations of the risks, and so on, usually evolves through time, and it is not possible to be too prescriptive when first rolling out an Approach of this nature. When you first start using the approach there may be some discomfort with:

- the range of risks that apparently have no owner in your company;
- the level of rigour being demanded in assessing and following these risks;
- the principle of assigning an individual signatory to each risk.

though transparency and honesty in recognising these limitations will help management decide when and if to plug any gaps.

Notes

1. Markets also exist in credit risk, and it may be possible to enter into a credit derivative to offset one's exposure to counterparty default. Credit derivatives are outside the scope of this guide, and credit risk is therefore not considered to be a market risk here.
2. Recall that deltas are additive, and that the delta of an option portfolio is the sum of the deltas of each constituent option.
3. A widely held, and erroneous, belief is that Monte Carlo and historical simulation are valuation techniques – they are not. They are scenario generation techniques, and can be used with a variety of portfolio revaluation methods.

Conclusion

Teach the deserving

This Executive Report has attempted to introduce the world of energy market hedging and risk management in an easily digestible form for non-specialist management. The guide is intended to fill a gap in the literature for a publication about derivatives that is not aimed at traders, and a book about energy that is not aimed at quants. The survey has taken in a wide variety of material, starting from a discussion of risk, moving through the notion of marking to market, before examining linear instruments, vanilla options, option packages, exotic options, real options, VaR and stress testing, and formal risk mapping.

Space constraints mean that much has been omitted, but I hope that the reader's interest has been piqued enough to learn more. I would like to emphasise again that in energy hedging what really matters are not the instruments themselves, but the themes these instruments may be used to address. The risk management themes encountered in this guide were:

- Locking in
- Tying costs to revenues
- Switching one price exposure for another
- Joint hedging of combined currency and commodity exposures
- Protecting against downside
- Delaying a locking-in decision
- Sharing the pain using participation
- Sacrificing upside
- Contingent premium payment
- Buying down
- Selling up
- Volume flexibility
- Extendability
- Cancellability
- Embedding derivatives within physical agreements
- Cross-commodity protection

♦ Monetisation of embedded optionality
♦ Hedge-based financing

Following the last chapter, "Wider Risk Management Questions", we might also add some other, wider, risk management themes to this list, including:

♦ Assessing portfolio variation forward in time due to market fluctuations.
♦ Assessing portfolio variation forward in time due to physical risk.
♦ Transparency in risk and assurance.
♦ Rigour in conducting the mapping of physical and derivatives transactions into contractual, derivative and process terms.

I hope that the principles laid out in this guide, and the various forms of diagram such as contractual timeline diagrams, payoff and P&L diagrams, block diagrams and real option diagrams aid the reader and their staff in their efforts to understand and manage their energy risk.

References

Respect your guide

Preamble

Unfortunately for the majority of people, quants seem to be better served than non-technical people in the literature of energy derivatives and risk management. I have attempted to distil down the essential parts of many of these quantitative references for readers in this guide, though in doing so I have barely done justice to much of the deep and insightful work carried out by practitioners over the past couple of decades.

General and Finance

The quotations at the head of each chapter are taken from:
1. Shaolin System Nam-Pai-Chuan, the Precepts and Tenets of the System, copyright Christopher Lai Khee Choong. I am grateful to *Sifu* Lai for his permission in reproducing them in this book.

The first book I recommend to anyone trying to get to grips with derivatives and risk management is John Hull's:
2. John C. Hull, 2005, "Options, Futures and Other Derivatives" (6e), Prentice Hall, London.
    This book comes with some excellent, free, option pricing software, and is always near-at-hand whenever I'm working. The book is quite quantitative in parts, but is worth persevering with for the definitive insights it offers.

An excellent, thought-provoking book on the nature of market risk, from a seasoned professional trader and academic is:
3. Nassim Taleb, 2001, "Fooled by Randomness", Random House, London.

Readers trying to get to grips with options from a trading and valuation perspective should see:
4. Kevin B. Connolly, 1997, "Buying and Selling Volatility", John Wiley and Sons, London.
5. Sheldon Natenberg, 1994, "Option Volatility and Pricing", Irwin Professional, New York.

Energy Derivatives

There are relatively few non-technical books devoted to commodity derivatives and hedging, although worthy of note is:

6. George Kleinman, 2000, "Commodity Futures and Options: A step-by-step guide to successful trading", Financial Times, Prentice Hall, London.

   This book is devoted primarily to trading strategies, though its level and style of coverage is consistent with that of this book.

The NYMEX website contains a number of excellent documents introducing energy hedging from an exchange-traded futures and options perspective:

7. A Guide to Energy Hedging, www.nymex.com
8. Crack Spread Handbook, www.nymex.com
9. Risk Management with Natural Gas Futures and Options, www.nymex.com

A broad, highly important and up-to-date reference is:

10. Vincent Kaminski, 2004, "Managing Energy Price Risk", 3rd Edition, Risk Books, London, which contains many articles of interest. In particular this author has the final chapter "Valuation and Risk Management of Physical Assets", which expands upon the physical risk management concepts laid out in the chapter "Wider Risk Management Questions" above.

The following books are quite quantitative in nature, but are listed here since they are devoted to commodity derivatives:

11. Les Clewlow and Chris Strickland, 2000, "Energy Derivatives: Pricing and risk management", Lacima Publications, London.
12. Alexander Eydeland and Krzysztof Wolyniec, 2003, "Energy and Power Risk Management: New developments in Modeling", Pricing and Hedging, John Wiley and Sons, London.
13. Helyette Geman, 2005, "Commodities and Commodity Derivatives: Modelling and Pricing for Agriculturals, Metals and Energy", John Wiley and Sons, London.

Real Options

The field of real options has boomed since the 1990s, and much of what has been written hasn't stood the test of time (check out anything you can find justifying the overblown valuations of tech companies during the late 1990s internet boom). Some excellent references are:

14. Lenos Trigeorgis, 1996, "Real Options: Managerial Flexibility and Strategy in Resource Allocation", The MIT Press, Boston.
15. Avinash K. Dixit and Robert S. Pindyck, 1999, "Investment Under Uncertainty", Princeton University Press, New Jersey.
16. Lenos Trigeorgis (ed.), 1999, "Real Options and Business Strategy: Applications to Decision Making", Risk Books, London.

A specialist volume on real options in the energy industry is:

17. Ehud I. Ronn (ed.), 2002, "Real Options in Energy Management: Using Options Methodology to Enhance Capital Budgeting Decisions", Risk Books, London.

    This book contains the definitive written account of my diagrammatic approach to real options in the third chapter.

Risk Management

The starting point for anyone trying to learn about value-at-risk is Jorion's classic:

18. Philippe Jorion, 2000, "Value at Risk", McGraw-Hill, New York.

The GloriaMundi website contains an ever-growing list of superb review and technical materials, and I encourage all readers to have a dig around at:

19. www.gloriamundi.org

The Value-at-Risk technique was developed by JP Morgan in the early 1990s, and their spin-off company RiskMetrics has set much of the standard for market value-at-risk techniques. Several documents are available at:

20. www.riskmetrics.com

An excellent, though mathematical, reference on the statistical modelling of markets is Carol Alexander's:

21. Carol Alexander, 2001, "Market Models: A Guide to Financial Data Analysis", John Wiley and Sons, New York.

Quantitative Derivative Finance

Those readers brave enough to tackle quantitative derivative modelling have a wide variety of books to choose from (or delegate the reading of to their quants). In increasing order of mathematical difficulty I would recommend:

22. Martin W. Baxter and Andrew J. O. Rennie, 1996, "Financial Calculus: An Introduction to Derivative Pricing", Cambridge University Press, Cambridge.
23. Salih N. Neftci, 2003, "An Introduction to the Mathematics of Financial Derivatives", Academic Press, London.
24. Peter James, 2003, "Option Theory", John Wiley and Sons, New York.
25. B. Oksendal, 2003, "Stochastic Differential Equations: An introduction with applications", Springer-Verlag, London.
26. I. Karatzas and S. E. Shreve, 1991, "Brownian Motion and Stochastic Calculus", Springer-Verlag, London.

Two quantitative books on the reality of hedging derivatives positions from a trading perspective are:

27. Riccardo Rebonato, 1999, "Volatility and Correlation: The perfect hedger and the fox", John Wiley and Sons, New York.
28. Nassim Taleb, 1997, "Dynamic Hedging: Managing vanilla and exotic options", John Wiley and Sons, New York.

Two books on the computational implementation of derivatives models (though not specifically energy models) are:

29. Espen Gaarder Haug, 1997, "Complete Guide to Option Pricing Formulas", McGraw-Hill, London.
30. Les Clewlow and Chris Strickland, 1998, "Implementing Derivatives Models", John Wiley and Sons, New York.

Index

A
ABCDAir Mark-to-Market 21, 24
ABCDAir Q1
  jet fuel consumption 18
  jet fuel supply 18
  jet fuel volumes and market data 22, 25
Accounting risk, definition 213
AllyProdCo example
  gas and aluminium floating leg payments 61
  gas and aluminium market prices 61
  gas price exposure replaced with aluminium price exposure 61
American option timeline 107
American swaptions 171
American-style 88, 109
Anual risk-free interest rate 27
Arbitrage 8–9, 19, 22, 58, 96
Asian American options 109, 171
Asian basket call options 158
Asian calendar multi-spread options 161
Asian digital
  call option payoff 163
  put option payoff 163
Asian option contractual timeline 101, 111
Asian price average 99
Asian quanto options 168–169
Asian-style swaps 66
Asset, commercial or industrial optimisation 8
Asymmetric or non-linear derivative instruments 73
ATM Asian call option 99
At-the-money (ATM) 22, 83, 88
Average Price Option contracts 98
Average priced options 43, 88

B
Barrier options 172
Basic option transaction 76
Basis or proxy risk 41
Basket option
  payoffs 158
  transaction block diagram 157
Basket swaps 50, 68, 156
Bear call spread construction 119
Bear call spread package 119, 120
Bear put spread construction 120
Bermudan options 109
Bid price 19
bid-offer or bid-ask spread 19, 27
Black-Scholes
  formula 96–97, 116, 186, 197
  implied volatility 97
  machinery 95
  Merton framework 186
  model 96–98
  option premiums 103
Block diagrams, disadvantages of 48
Brent crude oil 40, 43, 55, 57, 81–82, 91, 97, 168
Brokered markets 42
Bull call spread
  block diagram 118
  construction 119
  P&L before expiry 118
  package 119
  payoff at expiry diagram 118
Bull put spread Package 120

C
CAC40 7
Call option
  dependence on strike price 113
  with US$50 strike price 75, 77
Call swaption quotations 112

Capped-price physical (CPP) contract 102, 150
"claw-back zone" 142
"climbing up the vol curve" 95
Closing price 20
Coal mining company (CoalMineCo) 59
  floating-for-floating swap 59
Collar instrument 125
Commodity forward prices 20
Commodity market 2–4, 12–13, 16, 27, 36–37, 39, 62, 182
Commodity position 17–19
Commodity-indexed interest-rate swaps 68
Commodity-market questions 182
Company's commodity position 17
Compound options 171
Computation of compounded interest, formula used for 28
"cone of possibilities" 89, 174, 176
Consumer collar
  payoff diagram 126
  transaction 126
Consumer extendable swap 147
Consumer three-way option diagram 131
Contango 20–21
"contingent optionality" 108–109, 177, 187
Contingent premium structure 130, 166–167
Contractual timeline
  diagrams 4, 23, 27, 218
  for European option 77
  for physical natural gas forward contract 24
Correlation matrices 170, 209
Covariance matrix 201
Crack spreads 50, 68, 175

223

Cross-commodity 'arbitrage'
    trading example 9
Crude oil collar quotations 128
Crude oil grades 10
Currency-market questions 183
Curve construction, definition 214

D
Daily P&L 26–27
Delivery period 24
Delta approximation 197
Delta-normal approach 201–202
Delta-normal technique 205
Diffusion processes 196
Digital call option, delta and gamma of 168
Discounted cashflow (DCF) 21, 172

E
Energy futures contracts 39
Energy risk manager (ERM) 62
Energy trading
    portfolio 202
    types of 8, 115
Enhanced collar 128
European and American options,
    categorising 108–109
Euro FPP 65
European-style options 74
Example of
    (3,1,3) Swap 67
    (9,0,1) Swap 66
    10 million US$ 99% 10-day MvaR 196
    arbitrage 9
    asian option payoffs 98
    asset disposal with market-contingent rebate 164
    call option 74
    cargo load date slippage 160
    coal mining company fuel purchases 59
    consumer phased three-way 141
    contingent premium structure using digital options 166
    CPP gasoline supply 102
    crude oil producer seeks price protection with a collar 128
    crude oil producer three-way 132
    crude producer hedge using european put options 81
    european airline, fixed-for-floating quanto swap 62
    european call option as consumer hedge 80
    fixed-price physical (FPP) contract 56
    futures contract expiries and nearby contracts 43
    gas consumer participating collar 138
    gas supply contract with embedded lock-in optionality 152
    gasoline consumer collar 126
    gasoline reseller hedge 47
    implied volatility calculations 93
    implied volatility for different strike prices 97
    natural gas consumer 129, 144, 147
    natural gas consumer extendable swap 147
    natural gas consumer with volumetric flexibility 144
    natural gas swaption 111
    oil producer floorPP 105
    oil producer put with phased upside participation 140
    oil producer sells up a swap using cancellation optionality 148
    oil producer unwinds lock-in hedge 193
    oil producer ZCC physical offtake 150
    oil refiner seeks downside protection 157
    option value dependence on volatility 91
    power consumer bought-down swap 133
    price diffusion 89
    price paths 84
    producer put with upside sharing 136
    producer requires flex down hedge 146
    refined products purchasing 48
    refiner crude purchasing consumer hedge 135
    refinery 3-2-1 basket swap 52
    refinery upgrade investment decision 175
    swap proxy risk due to lot size and volumetric effects 51
    ten-day 99% MVaR 200
Exotic options 155, 171, 202, 217
Extendable swap time line 148

F
Fair market value 73, 96
"fear factor" 94
financial block diagrams 31
Financial and Commodity Markets 7, 175
Financial theory 15
Fixed-for-floating swaps 45, 58, 60, 68
Fixed-price physicals (FPPs) 150
Flex-up swap
    package 145
    P&L diagram 145
Floating leg 45–47, 54, 59, 61, 68
Floating-for-floating swaps 59–60, 68
Floored-price physical
    (FloorPP) 104, 150
    structuring 107
Force majere event 38
Force majeure, definition 57, 213
Foreign-exchange (FX) rate 13
Forest techniques 187
Forward contract
    block diagram 44
    definition 43, 71
    P&L diagram 45
    timeline 44
Forward curve 20–21, 54, 95, 175–176, 199
FPP example 57
"free lunch" 76, 113

FTSE100 7
Futures contract block diagram 41
Futures contracts 39, 41, 43–44, 67, 70, 74, 108, 123
Futures markets, disadvantages 43
Futures P&L diagram 41

G
"galaxy of risks" 207–209, 211
Gas consumer three-way structure 130
Gas forward market 9
Gasoline collar quotations 127

H
Hedge-linked loan financing
    buyer and seller 180
    offtaker signs firm agreement to lift physical 180
    summary 181
Hedging
    activity 1, 8, 27, 206
    basic principle 41
    effect of a swap contract 55
    instruments 1, 31, 41
Historical simulation 202–203, 205
Historical volatility 89, 93

I
Impacts option values 88
Implied volatility 89, 93–95, 97–98, 116
Indexation or Asian-style swaps 66, 68
Interest-rate risk questions 183
In-the-money (ITM) 22, 83, 88
Intrinsic value 85–89, 92, 176
IPE 19, 39–40, 43, 54, 59

J
Jet Fuel Physical Position 17

L
Location arbitrage, trading example 9
Long call option P&L diagram 78
long forward contract 43, 70–71
Long put option P&L diagram 78
Longer-term hedges 15
Look-back or path-dependent option 98

M
Managed-price physical (MPP) contracts 102, 150
Mapping risk 57, 184, 210, 212
Market price quotations 19
Market Value-at-Risk, definition 195
Marketers, definition 3
Mark-to-market (MTM) value 17, 25
Mark-to-Market Quantities 21
Maximum function, definition 76
Monte Carlo simulation 174, 186, 202, 205

N
Natural gas consumer call swaption 112
NBP natural gas 55, 138, 168
Net present value (NPV) 21, 172
North Sea oil producer 41
NYMEX heating oil 98, 168

O

Oil or gas storage owners 176
Oil producer flex down exposure 146
One-tailed confidence level 196
Option
   basic concepts of 73
   contracts 70, 73–74, 109
   delta 95, 162, 167, 198, 204
   exercise 88
   gamma 162
   intrinsic value 85–87
   package nomenclature 139
   premium sensitivity to volatility 92
   time value 85
Option-style approach 174, 189–190
OTC cousin 43
OTC forwards and swaps 202
OTC options 202
OTC swap markets 50
OTC-traded markets 19
OTM Asian call option 99
Out-of-the-money (OTM) 22, 83, 88
over-the-counter (OTC)
   bilateral 42
   markets 11

P

P&L
   diagrams 31, 35, 77–78, 100, 115, 141, 218
   table for put option with 78
   table for the call option 77
   tables 31, 35
Payoff
   diagrams 4, 55, 74, 77, 132, 163, 165
   table for call option 75
   table for put option 75
   for Asian options 98
Peak-power generation 176
Physical consumer fixed-price
   block diagram 33
   P&L diagarm 34
Physical consumer floating-price
   block diagram 33
   P&L diagram 33
Physical delivery, fact of 7
Physical energy market 1
Physical producer fixed price
   block diagram 32

P&L diagram 33
P&L table 32
Physical producer floating reference
   block diagram 31
   P&L diagram 32
   P&L table 32
Physical transformer
   definition 34
   floating-index block diagarm 35
   P&L diagram 35
   P&L table 35
Platts and Argus survey 98
Platts index 46
Platts Med gasoil reference 48
Prepayment swaps 68
Present value (PV) 29
Price diffusion 89–90, 196
Pricing period, definition 46
Principal components models 203
Producer collar
   block diagram 127
   payoff diagram 127
Profit-and-loss (P&L) figure 25
Proxy swaps 68
Proxy-risk questions 183
Put option contracts 74
Put-call parity
   diagram 122
   payoff table 123

Q

Quantitative analysts 3
Quanto Asian basket options 170
Quanto basket digital options 172
Quanto options 167
Quanto swap 61
Quarters cascade 21

R

"real option" 10, 177
Reduced market models 203, 205
Refined Products Company (RefPCo) 48
RefPCo hedged cashflows 50
Risk, definition 11
Risk Management Process 2, 5, 15, 208, 211–212
Risk Management Programme, designing 14–15, 38

Risk Matrix Approach 207–208, 211–212, 214

S

Semi-analytic and approximation techniques 186
Short call option P&L diagram 79
Short put option P&L diagram 79
Short-term hedges 14
Simulation methods 186–187, 203
Slippage swap
   payoff table 161
   synthesis 161
   transaction 160
Standard normal distribution 116, 196–197, 200
Swap contract payoff diagram 54
Swap-call block diagram 122
Swaption timeline 111
Swing options 109, 147, 171

T

Technical failure event 37–38
Technical VaR, (TvaR) computes 207
Term structure of volatility (TSOV) 95
Time-value sensitivity 92
Tree-based (and grid-based) methods 187

U

UK natural gas forward curve 21
UK NBP natural gas 168
Unwinding swap position 194
US Department of Energy 19

V

Value-at-risk (VAR)
   analysis 26
   main use of 195
Vanilla call option delta 124, 125
VaR limits 205
Variance-Covariance (VCV) approach 201

W

WidgeCorp's decision analysis 173

Z

zero-premium structures 143, 155